WORKSHOP TECHNOLOGY
PART I
AN INTRODUCTORY COURSE

WORKSHOP TECHNOLOGY

PART I
AN INTRODUCTORY COURSE

BY

W. A. J. CHAPMAN
Ph.D., M.Sc. (Eng.), M.I.Mech.E., M.I.P.E.

PRINCIPAL, HATFIELD COLLEGE OF TECHNOLOGY, HERTFORDSHIRE

LONDON
EDWARD ARNOLD (PUBLISHERS) LTD.

© W. A. J. Chapman 1962

First Published	.	.	.	.	*1943*
Reprinted	.	*1944 (twice), 1945, 1947, 1950, 1952*			
		1953, 1954			
Second Edition	.	.	.	.	*1955*
Reprinted	.	.	.	*1956, 1957, 1958*	
Third Edition	.	.	.	.	*1959*
Reprinted	.	.	.	.	*1960*
Fourth Edition	.	.	.	.	*1962*
Reprinted	.	.	.	.	*1963*
Reprinted	.	.	.	*1964, 1965*	
Reprinted	.	.	.	.	*1968*

SBN 7131 3032 6

Other Books by DR. CHAPMAN

Problems in Workshop Calculations (Intermediate)
viii + 148 pages. Crown 8vo. with 210 diagrams and 450 examples.

Applied Workshop Calculations
viii + 247 pages. Crown 8vo. with 295 diagrams and 250 examples.

Senior Workshop Calculations
viii + 432 pages. Crown 8vo. with 324 diagrams and 550 examples.

Printed in Great Britain by
Butler & Tanner Ltd., Frome and London

PREFACE TO FIRST EDITION

The scheme of the present work was in my mind, and partly on paper, before the present catastrophe overtook us, and, with many other works of peaceful construction, was shelved. The trend of events, however, indicate that its publication should be of value to the war effort, so that I have persevered in completing this first portion.

My chief regret is that I was not qualified to write it fifteen years ago. At that time the status of our artisan workers was being allowed to fall relative to other members of the community. The artisan professions were neglected by educationalists, by writers and by public thought, a state of affairs which led to a dearth of suitably qualified prospective workers. What this policy has cost us cannot be assessed, but it is now obvious that it almost brought us to disaster.

That the artisan is worthy of a reasonable social position can be testified by those who have lived and worked with him. That the work he does calls for high skill and training should be evident from jobs such as that of turning the pair of rolls shown at Figs. 39 and 41, an operation demanding a level of performance comparable with that in many so-called professions.

I have written for the men who do such work and for those who aspire to it. It is difficult to compromise between academic theory and everyday practice, but it is hoped that the fundamental principles underlying workshop processes have been clearly explained and that the reader will be able to understand more easily the processes described and to perform them in the workshop. The work covered in this volume is approximately that of the first two years of a senior part-time course in Technical Colleges and includes most of the material necessary for the City and Guilds Intermediate Examination in Machine Shop Engineering. It should also be useful to students for the preliminary work in Workshop Technology leading to the Higher National Certificate in Production Engineering.

In the preparation of the diagrams a great deal of help has been given by the kindness of various firms and institutions. Their names are appended to the illustrations concerned and I should like to offer them my sincere thanks. Finally, I feel that the Publishers in producing this book at such a price, and amid such difficulties, have performed a task worthy of commendation.

W. A. J. C.

Oakengates 1943

PREFACE TO THIRD EDITION

Our critical shortage of trained scientific and engineering manpower has been proved by events since the previous preface was written, and extensive plans have been made for the expansion of technical education. However efficient we may become in producing highly qualified academic technologists, we shall not get far unless they, themselves, possess practical appreciation and are backed by teams of enlightened technicians and craftsmen. The workshop is fundamental in the education and equipment of all engineers, and this book should in the future, as in the past, serve both the academic and the practical student. It should be useful for the new City and Guilds course No. 193—Mechanical Engineering Craft Practice—since it covers most of Part I and portions of Part II, and with *Workshop Technology*, Part 2, complete coverage is given.

From the reputation the book has earned, I have confidence in the future service it can render, a service which should be improved by the revisions of a new edition. To all its friends, known and unknown, I extend my thanks for the goodwill they have expressed.

Hatfield 1958   W. A. J. C.

PREFACE TO FOURTH EDITION

It has been suggested to me that the book would be improved and its value increased by the inclusion of some work on the shaping machine. This appears to be good advice and I have therefore taken advantage of an opportunity to add a new chapter on the subject. I hope this will prove to be as readable and as informative as so many friends claim for the remainder of the book. The additional chapter results in a new edition ; there are no changes in the remaining material and those who have the previous edition can obtain the new chapter separately.

Since the third edition was published there have been noteworthy developments in technical education for those aspiring to become craftsmen or technicians, and for whom this book was written. The Government White Paper " Better Opportunities in Technical Education," published in January 1961, has set off a train of new measures and new courses. A new General Course in Engineering will prepare for and regulate entrance to a new Ordinary National Course and to a new City and Guilds course for Mechanical Engineering Technicians, which will replace the present course in Machine Shop Engineering.

In its revised form the book will give complete coverage for " Workshop Processes and Materials " in the General Course in Engineering and for most of " Workshop Processes and Practice " in the City and Guilds No. 293 Mechanical Engineering Technicians Part I. With *Workshop Technology*, Part 2, adequate coverage is given for Part I and for much of Part II of the course. Its proved value in National Certificate courses should be enhanced by the additional coverage introduced by the additional chapter.

Now that we, as a nation, have at last decided to recognise the value of the craftsman, and to educate him accordingly (see Preface to First Edition), it is to be hoped that in the future his contribution will be accorded the dignity and status befitting those whose pride is in a job well done. It is my hope that this book, with its associate volumes, will continue to serve such a cause.

Hatfield 1961   W. A. J. C.

CONTENTS

vii

CONTENTS

CHAPTER 1

INTRODUCTION—MATERIALS—IRON AND STEEL

The wealth of a community is measured by the variety and quality of the articles it possesses for its use and consumption. All the material things we possess are made from substances which in the first place are won from the earth, or from Nature. Our prosperity depends upon our ability to convert these raw materials into useful articles of consumption, and to distribute these articles equitably amongst the various members of our community.

The production of our engineering workshops forms an important part of our general industrial scheme since a large proportion of our industries are of an engineering nature. Moreover, other industries such as clothing, food, etc., depend to a large extent upon the help of workshop mechanics for making and maintaining the machinery they use. Our ability, therefore, to maintain a high standard of skill in our engineering workshops is an important factor in our general scheme of wellbeing, and the reader may be sure that the efforts he makes to acquire efficiency in workshop technique will re-act to the benefit of the community. From his own individualistic standpoint the fact of his being a master of his trade will add to his independence, increase his status and income, and ultimately enable him to enjoy a larger share of the commodities he is helping to make.

The knowledge that a skilled workshop engineer must possess takes many years of observant experience to acquire. The reader should note the term " observant " experience, because unless he enters the workshops prepared to give thought and enquiry to every piece of work he will never acquire the sense and skill which go to make the thorough craftsman. One person may spend years in doing a certain job and learn less from his experience than another, who after a few weeks of studious application, has mastered the technique and is ready to advance further.

The amount of " book " knowledge necessary to become a skilled craftsman is not great, and the reader need not be despondent of his chances if he is not very good at mathematics or English. What he must have, however, is an interest in mechanical things, and the ability to give patient application to a job until it is satisfactorily completed. An impatient worker, unable to concentrate his attention to the completion of what may be a rather tedious job, is unlikely to make a first-class artisan. The would-be workshop engineer should have a keen realisation of his responsibilities both towards his work and to his fellows. He should be capable of doing a fair day of good work without the need of constant supervision and should be scrupulously honest. The reader will find, that if he adopts as his guiding principle the idea of giving service, without bothering overmuch about what profit he will get out of it, he will usually find that the financial and other rewards will follow also without his needing to worry about them.

Many of the aspects of workshop technique can only be acquired by experience, by teaching on the spot and by contacts with experienced craftsmen.   There is much, however, which may be learned by reading, and the object of these two books is to provide the student with a preliminary insight into his work.   He should endeavour to keep his knowledge up-to-date by reading technical journals, and it is hoped that the time he so spends may help him to bring a critical and scientific viewpoint to bear upon his work.   Probably, when he has passed through the first stages of his experience, he will feel like studying more advanced books, and he can be assured that by his reading and experience, he will find the workings of Nature to be as profoundly evident in the workshop as in any other branch of natural science.

Materials

Since the object of all manufacturing is to start with a raw material, and to add work to it until it is at some finished, or semi-finished state, it seems logical that we should commence by taking some note of the materials we use.   The materials chiefly used in the shops are metals, and these are divided into those which come from iron and those which do not.   The iron group which includes all irons and steels are called *ferrous* metals (ferrum = iron), whilst the others are specified as *non-ferrous*.

Iron and Steel

There is scarcely a single aspect of our daily lives in which iron does not play an important part.   Our food, our means of transport, the buildings we use, our fireside and its comforts—iron is necessary for them all.   The magnetic property of iron alone, by making possible the electrical age in which we live, has conferred incalculable benefits on humanity.

Pure Iron

Pure iron is a soft metal having a crystalline structure.   A representation of its microstructure is shown in Fig. 1.   This diagram, together with others, which will be seen later, has been drawn to represent a photomicrograph, a method used extensively for the examination and study of metals.   To obtain a photomicrograph a small piece of the metal is filed to a flat surface, and the surface is gradually brought to a high finish by successive polishings.   The polished surface is then treated with dilute acid which etches the constituents and their boundaries, enabling them to be distinguished when seen through a microscope.   By placing a camera at the microscope eyepiece, a photograph of the microstructure may be obtained.   The microscope reveals the structure to an enlarged scale, and the magnification is usually stated underneath the photograph (e.g. × 200 as shown in Fig. 1).

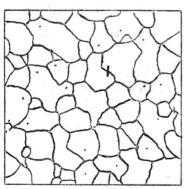

Fig. 1.—Microstructure of Pure Iron × 200.

It will be noticed that the structure of pure iron looks like a map with fields separated by hedges. The shapes looking like the fields are the crystals, and the lines like hedges are where they join together. It may help us to visualise the structure of the metal if we imagine it as similar to bricks and mortar ; the crystals being the bricks and their boundaries the mortar. A section through such a structure would appear somewhat similar to our photograph. If the reader measures the average size of the crystals on Fig. 1 and divides by the magnification factor, he will find that the crystal size of the specimen is about $\frac{2}{1000}$ in. The size of the crystals in iron and steel depends upon the treatment the metal has received, and in the steel used in the workshop the crystals may vary from $\frac{1}{1000}$ in. to $\frac{8}{1000}$ in. These micrographs represent a portion of metal structure about as large as a pin point.

Pig Iron

In its pure state, iron has very few practical uses, and if we tried to machine it we should find it so soft that it would tear badly and give a poor finish. Moreover, to obtain pure iron is a difficult process, because during smelting it is not easy to rid the metal entirely of certain elements for which it possesses a great affinity. We may regard iron in its pure state, therefore, as a metal mainly of theoretical interest, but one which may comprise 99% of a certain steel we may be using. That remaining 1% of other substances, however, makes a great difference !

A diagram showing the chief ferrous materials and their production is shown at Fig. 3, and as we proceed we will discuss the processes mentioned. From the diagram it will be seen that the starting point in the commercial preparation of iron and steel is the smelting of ore to give pig iron. The chief ores of iron are the oxides and the carbonates. The most important oxides are red hæmatite, black magnetite and brown ores. The carbonates are represented by spathic ores, clayband ores and blackband ores. When it is taken from the mine the ore is mixed with earthy impurities, and before smelting it is separated from these as far as possible.

The furnace used for smelting and reducing the ore to metallic pig iron is a tall structure called a Blast Furnace. This furnace

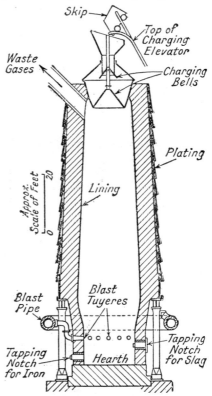

FIG. 2.—Section through Blast Furnace.

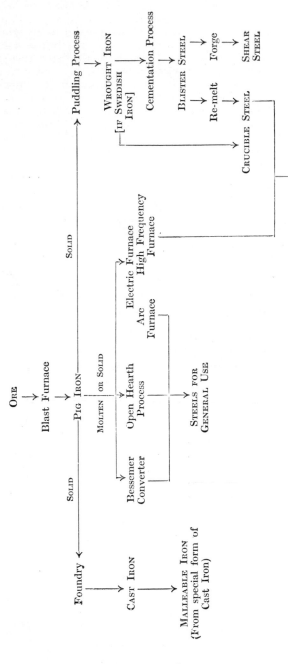

Fig. 3.—Diagram showing Production of the Materials in the Iron and Steel Group.
(*The production of tool steel from the Cementation process is now mainly of historical interest only.*)

4

operates continuously and is charged at the top through the bell which serves as a seal. In addition to the ore, the furnace is charged with suitable quantities of coke and limestone. The coke provides fuel for maintaining the heat necessary to carry on the reducing action and at the same time some of the carbon (as carbon monoxide) from the coke combines with the iron oxides, reducing them to iron. The limestone serves as a flux and combines with the non-metallic portions of the ore to form a molten slag. Hot air is blown into the lower portion of the furnace via the tuyères, and as the action proceeds, the molten iron and slag fall to the bottom of the furnace, the slag floating on top of the iron.

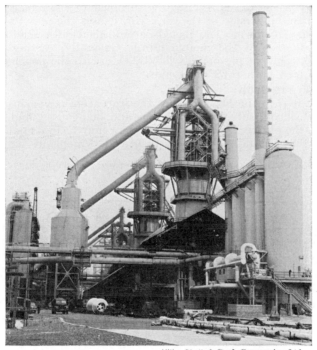

[*The United Steel Companies Ltd.*

FIG. 4.—General view of Blast Furnace Plant.

From time to time the slag is tapped off from the hole shown, and the molten iron from the hearth. Diagrams showing a blast-furnace section and a general view of an installation are shown at Figs. 2 and 4.

According to the type of plant the molten iron may be used in one or more of the following ways :

(*a*) Cast in pig beds.

(*b*) Cast in pig-casting machine.

(*c*) Transferred in hot metal ladles direct to an adjacent steelmaking process. This applies to composite iron and steel plants (Fig. 14).

Pig beds are sand moulds in the form of a grid prepared in the ground alongside the furnace, and the bars (pigs) cast in this way are about

3 ft. 6 in. long with a D-shaped cross-section measuring approximately
4 in. each way.

The modern method of casting pig iron which has largely superseded
the older pig-bed method is to employ a pig-casting machine. This
consists of a series of hematite iron or steel moulds, each about
22 in. × 8 in. × 3½ in., fixed to an endless chain conveyor, the assembly
being mounted on a suitable construction arranged on a slight slope.
Molten iron from the blast furnace is conveyed in a ladle and poured
into a channel feeding the moulds as they emerge from the underside
of their travel at the foot of the slope of the conveyor. The moulds
charged with iron move up the slope, the metal cooling off on the way
up, and when the top is reached the turnover of the moulds, as they
reverse to the underside of the conveyor, causes the pigs to discharge
into a wagon below. (The moulds are washed with lime or tar to
prevent adhesion of the molten iron.) Generally, casting machines
have two strands of pig moulds side by side with the pouring channel
forked to feed both rows of moulds.

Nature of Pig Iron

Whilst it is in the blast furnace the iron absorbs varying amounts
of carbon, silicon, sulphur, phosphorus and manganese, and these are
present in the pig iron. The carbon present may be in its natural state
as *graphite* and is normally finely dispersed throughout the metal in

Matrix of
Pearlite

Flakes of
Graphite

(a)   (b)

FIG. 5.—Structure of Cast Iron.

(a) Normally cooled with flaked graphite.   (b) Spheroidal graphite (see p. 12).

the form of small flakes (Fig. 5 (a)), or it may be in the form of iron
carbide, a chemical combination of carbon and iron called *cementite*.

Generally some of the carbon is free and some combined, the proportion of each depending mainly upon (a) the rate at which the iron
cools down from its molten state and (b) upon the amount of silicon
present in the iron. Slow cooling allows the carbon time to separate
out and there is more free graphite. Quick cooling (called chilling) does
not allow so much graphite to form, and a larger proportion of the

carbon is in the combined form. When cooling is normal the fracture of iron has a greyish-black crystalline appearance and the graphilitic carbon may be easily discerned (Fig. 6 (a)). The fracture of quickly cooled iron is whiter, showing that there is less free carbon, and when all, or nearly all, the carbon is combined the metal is called white iron (Fig. 6 (b)).

[The British Cast Iron Research Association.

(a) Grey iron.   (b) White iron.

FIG. 6.—Fractures of Pig Iron.

The pigs, even with high silicon content, produced by machine casting generally have a white fracture since cooling is fairly rapid and the moulds are often cooled in a water bosh on the conveyor to speed the process. Cementite is a very hard substance, so that the greater the amount of combined carbon the harder will be the iron. Cast iron is essentially an iron-carbon alloy modified by the presence of silicon, phosphorus, sulphur and manganese in varying amounts (see page 12).

TABLE 1. APPROXIMATE ANALYSIS OF PIG IRONS

Constituent.		No. 1 Iron.	No. 3 Iron.	White Iron.
Iron	%	92	92·5	94·2
Graphitic carbon . .	%	3·5	3	Nil
Combined carbon. .	%	0·20	0·5	3·1
Silicon . . .	%	2·8	2·5	1·0
Sulphur . . .	%	0·05	0·05	0·3
Phosphorus . . .	%	0·8	0·75	0·9
Manganese . . .	%	0·65	0·70	0·5

Cast Iron

The pig iron as tapped from the blast furnace is the crude form of raw material from which are prepared the various grades of iron and steel which we use. It is not suitable for making castings without some degree of refining, and this takes place in the foundry cupola. This is a small form of blast furnace, and a diagram of its essential details is shown at Fig. 7. The size of the cupola varies according to the nature of the work which has to be done ; the diameters vary from 3 ft. to 7 ft., with a height of from four to five times the diameter. A 3-ft. diameter cupola 12 ft. high will melt about 2 tons of iron per hour.

Charging Door

Blast Pipe

Charging Platform

Receiver

Channel for Tapping-off Metal

[*The Institute of British Foundrymen.*

FIG. 7.—Sectional View of Cupola and Hot Metal Receiver.

Generally cupolas are not worked continuously as are blast furnaces, but are run only for such periods as may be required. To start the cupola a coke fire is first lit at the bottom and when this is established charging commences by adding alternate layers of coke and pig iron together with a little limestone. The pig iron is broken into pieces about a foot long before being fed in, and is generally mixed with an agreed proportion of iron and steel scrap, the proportion depending upon the desired quality of the melt. For example, adding low carbon scrap will reduce the percentage of carbon in the melt. An hour or two after charging, and when the charge has burnt up, the blast is gradually increased and the cupola closed up. The iron melts and sinks to the bottom of the furnace, and when sufficient has accumulated it is tapped into a ladle, or directly into the moulds. A receiver is attached to some cupolas into which the metal is directed when it falls down (see Fig. 7).

The amount of coke consumed is not large, as in the cupola the iron has only to be melted, there being no chemical changes to be produced

Fɪɢ. 8.—Casting not supported under Point of Clamping.

as in the blast furnace. The amount of coke necessary varies from 1 to 2½ cwt. per ton of iron melted. The limestone is added to combine with the sand on the surface of the pig iron, and with the ash from the coke, to form a liquid slag which floats on top of the molten iron. This slag is tapped off separately. About 7 to 10 lb. of limestone is necessary for each ton of iron melted.

Properties and Uses of Cast Iron. Grey iron is a very useful metal in engineering construction. The main advantages in favour of its use are as follows : (a) its cheapness, (b) its low melting temperature [1150–1200° C.] and fluidity when in the molten condition, and (c) it is easily machined. A further good property of cast iron is that the free graphite in its structure seems to act as a lubricant, and when large machine slides are made of it a very free-working action is obtained. The reader may demonstrate this for himself by comparing the relative easiness with which scribing blocks with steel, and cast-iron bases may be slid about on a cast-iron surface plate. He will find that the movement of the cast-iron base is sweeter and it does not drag as much as the steel one.

The fluidity of iron when in the molten condition enables it to be used widely for making castings of parts having intricate shapes such as the bodies of machines and other components. These are cast with metal from the cupola, in moulds prepared in sand, the moulds being made from wooden patterns. The process will be described in more detail in a later chapter.

The fracture of grey cast iron shows a crystalline or granular structure and a strong light will give a glistening effect due to reflection on the free graphite particles. The presence of this free graphite is also shown when filing or machining cast iron as it makes our hands black. Cast iron is brittle and may easily be broken if a heavy enough hammer is used. Small thin castings should not be dropped, because of the risk of their being cracked or fractured. In the same way, if clamps or vise jaws are pressed too hard against unsupported sections of a casting, fracture may occur (Fig. 8).

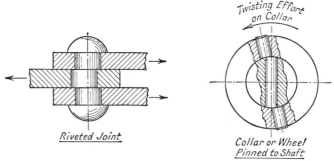

FIG. 9.—Examples of Failures due to Shearing.

The strength of iron is much greater in compression than in tension. It is usual to express the strength of a metal as the number of lb. or ton required to fracture a section of the metal 1 sq. in. in area. This load is called the Ultimate Strength of the material and it may be tensile (tension), compressive, or shear. (Shear is when fracture is caused by forces which compel failure to occur across a plane parallel to the forces, Fig. 9.) The ultimate tensile strength of cast iron varies between 8 and 20 ton per square inch and depends on the composition of the iron. * In compression, iron will withstand about 40 to 50 ton per square inch before fracturing, whilst in shear its strength is approximately 10 to 15 ton per square inch. Because cast iron is brittle and weak in tension it cannot be used where these deficiencies would be detrimental. Bolts and machine parts which are liable to tension, and which often require to have fine screw threads on them, could not be made of cast iron, because of its unreliability in tension, and because the cast iron would rapidly break and crumble away at the threads. Shafts which have to withstand bending loads cannot be made of brittle metal and therefore grey cast iron cannot be used for them.

* See " Alloy Cast Irons " p. 12 giving recent developments in spheroidal iron.

Parts subjected to such conditions of service are made of steel which can be hardened ; grey cast iron cannot be hardened. There are many applications in engineering and machine tool practice, however, where an intricate shape is required, and where large tensile loads have not to be carried. Examples are the beds, slides and bases of machine tools, the bodies of electrical machines, the cylinders and beds of engines and so on. For constructions of such types grey cast iron is an ideal material, because it can be cast to the general shape required, and machined only on such faces as are required to fit with mating components. The hard outer skin of such castings gives a good appearance when cleaned of sand and painted, and is hard wearing against knocks or other damage.

Composition of Cast Iron. We have seen in our discussion of pig iron that the carbon may be in the free graphitic state or may be chemically combined as cementite. Also that cementite is hard and is caused by quick cooling, whilst slow cooling gives graphitic carbon and soft, easily machined castings. Quick cooling is generally called " chilling " and the iron so produced is " chilled iron." All castings are chilled at their outer skin by contact of the molten iron with the cool sand in the mould, but on most castings this hardness only penetrates about $\frac{1}{32}$ in. in depth, and if we put on enough cut to get beneath the skin we can machine it off without damage to the tool. Most readers have probably experienced what happens if they try to machine

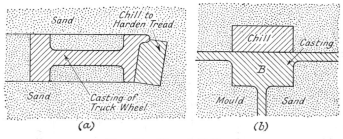

FIG. 10.—Use of Chills.

or file the skin of a casting without getting beneath the hard crust ; if they have not, they should try it.

Sometimes a casting is chilled intentionally and sometimes becomes chilled accidentally to a considerable depth. Intentional chilling is carried out by putting inserts of iron or steel (chills) into the mould, so that when the molten metal comes into contact with the chill its heat is rapidly conducted away and the formation of combined carbon is promoted. Chills are used on any faces of a casting which are required to be hard for the purpose of withstanding heavy wear and friction (Fig. 10a). Of course, chilling complicates the problem of machining, as ordinary tools will not stand up to their work and either specially hard tools or grinding must be employed In some cases chilling is employed to accelerate the cooling of a part of a casting and so avoid some portions cooling before others and thus giving rise to strains. In Fig. 10b, the thin portions of the casting would normally

cool before that at B and set up internal strains due to uneven contraction.   If a chill is placed as shown the rate of cooling is equalised
and the risk of distortion or cracking is minimised.   Castings which
have very thin sections of material cool quickly in the mould and are
always liable to become chilled, and hence difficult to machine.   To
minimise this and promote the formation of graphite, an iron high in
silicon content is often used.

We observed earlier that as well as carbon, cast iron generally
contains small amounts of silicon, phosphorus, sulphur and manganese.
It will be well for us to have some idea of the effect of these elements
on the iron.

Silicon promotes the formation of free graphite and by so doing
acts as a softener and gives an iron which is easily machinable.   It
has a high affinity for oxygen and thus helps to produce sound castings
free from blowholes.   The silicon content of the average cast iron
varies up to about 3%.

Phosphorus, although not always wanted, gets into the iron as an
impurity in the blast furnace and is very difficult to remove.   In cast
iron phosphorus makes for great fluidity and is used for castings which
must be made to intricate and delicate shapes (e.g. thin switch boxes
with cast lettering, etc.).   Cast iron may contain up to $1\frac{1}{2}\%$ phosphorus.

Sulphur and Manganese.   These two elements have the same general
effect, viz. a tendency to harden the iron.   Too much sulphur promotes
unsound castings, and the sulphur content is generally kept as low as
possible (0·1%).   The amount of manganese present varies up to
about $1\frac{1}{2}\%$, depending upon the type and use of the casting.

The following table shows the composition of cast irons for various
uses :

TABLE 2.   CONSTITUTION OF VARIOUS CAST IRONS

Type.	Iron.	Total Carbon.	Silicon.	Manganese.	Sulphur.	Phosphorus.
Light section machinery . .	93·65	3·2	2·2	0·5	0·1	0·35
Hydraulic cylinder .	94·45	3·2	0·9	1·0	0·1	0·35
Lorry cylinder . .	93·46	3·3	2·1	0·9	0·09	0·15
Switch boxes . .	91·6	3·5	2·8	0·8	0·1	1·2

Alloy Cast-Irons

To overcome certain inherent deficiencies in ordinary cast iron and
to give qualities more suitable for special purposes, whilst retaining the
important casting advantage of this metal, a large number of alloy cast
irons have been developed.   Two recent examples are acicular and
spheroidal cast irons.   Acicular iron has nickel and molybdenum in its
composition and is being used for cast crankshafts.   In spheroidal iron
the graphite content is converted from a flaky to a spheroidal form
(see Fig. 5b) by the alloying of a small amount of magnesium or cerium,
this change in the graphite form raising the tensile strength to about
40/50 tons per square inch, and producing a tough metal which can be
twisted and bent.

Wrought Iron

Wrought iron was probably the first form of iron with which man was acquainted, and long ago, all the articles made from it would be shaped by the blacksmith, who was an important artisan. It is now one of a large selection of ferrous products, and of all the common types of iron and steel, wrought iron is the nearest approach to pure iron. The chemical analysis of the metal may show as much as 99·9% of iron. Even when strongly heated, wrought iron does not melt, but only becomes pasty, and in this form it may be forged to any shape, and separate parts joined by hand welding.

Puddling Process. The chief point in the manufacture of wrought iron is the oxidation of nearly all the carbon and other elements from pig iron, and in this country the process is carried out in a puddling furnace. This is a coal-fired reverberatory furnace as shown in Fig. 11. The term reverberatory is applied to furnaces of this type because the charge is not in actual contact with the fire, but receives its heat by reflection from the shaped furnace roof.

In the process the furnace hearth is lined with iron oxide and grey pig iron and millscale (oxide) are fed on to it. The metal soon softens and melts, and as melting proceeds, the puddler, working with a long rake through the puddling door, hastens melting by drawing lumps of unmelted metal to the centre. When melting is complete the impurities

Fig. 11.—Puddling Furnace.

form a slag with some of the oxides present, and this slag floats on top of the bath, but from time to time the slag is stirred into the melt and more millscale is added. The addition of this oxide to the slag, already rich in oxide and being continuously stirred into the melt, brings about the oxidation of the carbon and the other elements originally present in the pig iron. Carbon monoxide bubbles from the mass of molten iron and burns at its surface, the mass for a time having the appearance of boiling, and at this stage some of the slag rises up and flows out from the slag notch. As the carbon becomes oxidised away, the bubbling subsides and the iron becomes stiffer and pasty in form. The temperature of the furnace is now raised to its highest possible point, the charge, meanwhile, being continuously puddled until at last it becomes a quiescent mass of pasty iron intermixed with slag. This is now taken from the furnace in the form of balls (or blooms) weighing about 1 cwt., which, whilst white hot, are hammered to squeeze out a portion of the slag and then rolled into rough bars which rolls the remainder of the slag into long fibres. The rough bars are subsequently re-heated to a white, welding heat, and a number are bundled together and re-rolled, which welds the layers together and further elongates the slag.

The presence of slag gives the fracture of wrought iron a fibrous appearance and it is by this characteristic that it may easily be distinguished. When it is filed or machined to a surface parallel to the direction of rolling, the slag may be seen as long lines running along the surface. It is rather soft and tends to tear under such processes as screw-cutting.

Wrought iron is easily forged and welded at the forge. It is ductile (see p. 25), and easily bends when cold, in fact a medium-sized bar should withstand being doubled upon itself without the outer side cracking at the bend. The iron has the property of being able to

Fig. 12.—Microstructure of Wrought Iron (in direction of rolling). × 100.

withstand sudden and excessive shock loads without permanent injury, for which reason it is used for chains, crane hooks, railway couplings, etc. The fibrous nature of its composition gives visible warning on the surface of an impending fracture before complete breakdown takes place and arrangements can be made to replace the damaged part. Were the same conditions imposed on any other metal it would probably show no signs until it fractured suddenly across its whole section.

Wrought iron has an ultimate tensile strength of about 23 tons per square inch, and the approximate chemical composition of a Staffordshire wrought iron is as follows :

Element.	Carbon.	Silicon.	Sulphur.	Phosphorus.	Manganese.	Slag.	Iron.
% Present	0·02	0·12	0·018	0·22	0·02	0·07 to 1	Remainder

The microstructure of wrought iron is shown at Fig. 12, in which the slag may be seen clearly.

Malleable Cast Iron

A malleable metal is one which may easily be caused to spread and flatten under pressure or hammering. Lead is the best example of a malleable metal we have in the workshop, and the reader may soon prove for himself that this metal is easily beaten out and flattened.

The application of the term " malleable " to castings of that type is rather a misnomer because they are not very malleable when compared with the usual standards of malleability. When compared with grey iron castings, however, which are fairly brittle, malleable castings do possess a degree of toughness, and this is probably why they have been so named.

For many purposes it is necessary to produce small, thin parts having a reasonable degree of strength such as would not be obtained in a grey iron casting which, as we have seen, is brittle and would break under rough usage. Such parts could be built up or forged from steel, but it is much cheaper to produce castings, and the process of converting castings to the tougher form of " malleable iron " has been evolved to meet the need for such products.

We have seen that the structure of cast iron contains flakes of graphite dispersed throughout it, and it is the breaking up of its continuity by these rather large flakes of weak material that makes the iron brittle. If the carbon were all removed there would be left wrought iron, a ductile material which bends easily. Obviously, we could not subject finished castings to a process similar to that used for the manufacture of wrought iron, but if we can produce a structure in which the carbon, instead of being flaky, or in the combined form, is dispersed as tiny specks, it would not have such a weakening effect, and our casting should not break when dropped. This, in general, is what takes place in the process of making malleable castings. First, castings are made from an iron having all of its carbon in the combined form. Two methods are then used for malleabilising the castings : the Whiteheart, used in England, and the Blackheart, more common in America and for large castings in this country. The names refer to the colour of the fracture given by castings produced by each method.

In the Whiteheart process the castings, composed of cast iron with most of its carbon in the combined state, are packed in iron or steel boxes and surrounded with a mixture of used and new hæmatite ore. The boxes are heated to a temperature of 900–950° C. and maintained at that temperature for several days, during which time part of the carbon is oxidised out of the castings, and the remainder is dispersed in small specks throughout the structure. In thin sections the structure might be almost pure iron, but in thicker sections the outside approaches to nearly pure iron and the centre has the dispersed specks of carbon. The heating period is followed by a very slow cooling which occupies several more days and the result is a casting which is tough and which will stand hard treatment without fracture. The tensile strength of malleable castings is about 25 ton per square inch.

Steel

The essential difference between cast iron and steel is in the amount of carbon contained in the constituency of the metal. Pure iron, as we have seen, is a soft metal having a structure made up of iron crystals or grains. In metallurgy, pure iron is called *ferrite*.

If now we make up a series of alloys of iron and carbon, with the carbon content increasing to about $1\frac{1}{2}\%$, we shall have a series of steels, the metal becoming harder and tougher as the carbon content increases. Up to a content of about $1\frac{1}{2}\%$, all the carbon is present in chemical combination with the iron, and none of it exists in its free graphitic state. If, however, we go on increasing the carbon above $1\frac{1}{2}\%$ a stage soon arrives when no more can be contained in the combined state and any excess must be present as free graphite. It is at this stage that the metal merges into the group termed cast irons, and we may go on increasing the carbon content up to about $4\frac{1}{2}\%$ whilst producing a range of cast irons.

Steel, then, is fundamentally an alloy of iron and carbon, with the carbon content varying up to $1\frac{1}{2}\%$, whilst cast iron is an alloy of these two elements with the carbon content ranging from about 2% to $4\frac{1}{2}\%$. For a material to be classed as steel there must be no free graphite in its composition ; immediately free graphite occurs it passes into the category of cast iron. It is true that other elements are present in small quantities, and are put there to confer certain desired properties on the metal, but the carbon is by far the most important modifying element and, if he can appreciate this, the reader may study the effect of other elements later.

The plain steels are usually classified according to their carbon content, the commonest of the range being *mild steel* with a carbon content ranging from about 0.15% to 0.3%. When the carbon content is less than 0.15% (say 0.07 to 0.15) the steel is classed as a *dead mild steel*. *Medium carbon steels* include the range with the carbon content varying from 0.3% to 0.8%, whilst steels with a carbon content between 0.8% and 1.5% are classified as *high carbon steels*.

Applications of Steels. The following is an indication of the carbon content of steels for various purposes :

TABLE 3. APPLICATIONS OF CARBON STEELS

Carbon %.	Uses.
Dead mild 0·1 to 0·125 .	Wire rod, thin sheets, solid drawn tubes, etc.
Mild 0·15 to 0·3 . .	Boiler plates, bridge work, structural sections, drop forgings, general workshop purposes.
Medium carbon ⎰0·3 to 0·5 . .	Axles, drop forgings, high tensile tubes and wire, agricultural tools.
⎱0·5 to 0·7 . .	Springs, locomotive tyres, large forging dies, wire ropes, hammers and snaps for riveters.
High carbon ⎧0·7 to 0·9 . .	Springs, small forging dies, shear blades, cold setts, wood chisels.
⎨0·9 to 1·1 . .	Cold chisels, press dies, punches, screwing dies, woodworking tools, axes, picks.
⎩1·1 to 1·4 . .	Razors, hand files, drills, gauges, metal-cutting tools.

As we shall see in a later chapter, the high carbon steels may be hardened by heating and quenching in water or oil. The low carbon steels, also, may be hardened on the surface by a process called case-hardening.

High carbon steels having a carbon content somewhat over 1% are often called " Cast Steels," or " Carbon Tool Steels."

The Manufacture of Steel. The wide range of uses to which steel is applied and its consequent high consumption causes the supply of it to be an important problem. The consistency of its quality, also, is a factor upon which the success of our workshop production depends. The low and medium carbon steels are much more widely used than the high carbon and tool steels, these latter being used mainly for tools and for specialised work calling for high quality and performance. These considerations have caused a separation to be made between the methods employed in steel manufacture. We will deal with the low and medium carbon group first.

The Open Hearth Process. Most of the steel made in this country is produced by the Siemens Open Hearth Process, so named after Siemens, its originator.

The furnace employed is shown in section at Fig. 13 and furnace sizes range from those taking melts of 5 tons to 200 tons. In the larger sizes manipulative problems cause some difficulties, and the big

[*Proceedings of the Iron and Steel Institute.*

FIG. 13.—An Open-hearth Furnace.

furnaces are often made of the tilting type. Probably the most useful range for fixed furnaces is that between the 50- and 100-ton sizes.

In the operation of the furnace the hearth is first prepared and well heated until its temperature is about 1500° C. The charge generally consists of a mixture of selected pig iron and scrap in proportions varying according to the class of steel required. The ratio of pig iron to scrap may vary from 1 to 4, to 4 to 1, a good average being 3 of pig iron to 2 of scrap.

The pig iron is generally fed on to the hearth first, followed by the scrap, whilst in the larger furnaces charging is done at intervals to avoid too much cooling down of the furnace. The larger furnaces (over 30 tons) are generally charged by mechanical chargers, which pick up boxes containing the previously weighed-out charge, push them into the furnace and tip them. When the steel-making plant adjoins the blast furnaces the iron for charging is conveyed by ladle in its molten state, direct from the blast furnace (see Fig. 14).

The fuel for the furnace, which is producer gas generated by a plant which forms part of the equipment, may be fed on to the hearth either through chamber GC_1 and port GP_1, or it may be made to travel by way of chamber GC_2, and port GP_2. Similarly, the air, which forms a combustible mixture when meeting the gas over the hearth, may be fed either through chamber AC_1 and port AP_1, or by chamber AC_2 and port AP_2. The air and gas directions are controlled by the valves V, and the chambers are built up with chequered brickwork like a honeycomb. These heating chambers, through which the air and gas are fed, are a characteristic of the open-hearth furnace, and it was their development by William Siemens which brought about the success of this method of steelmaking. It was found that intense heat was necessary to bring about the chemical reactions in the charge, and the air and gas heating chambers assist in obtaining this heat as follows : when the valve is in the position shown, the air and gas pass through the left-hand chambers, the flames and hot gases from the furnace being forced into the chimney stack by way of the right-hand chambers. The passage of the very hot waste gases heats up the honeycomb brickwork in the right-hand chambers, so that when the left-hand chambers have given up their heat to the incoming gas and air, the valves are moved over, causing the incoming products of combustion to enter through the newly heated right-hand chamber, and turning the furnace flames through the left-hand side. By changing the valves over at suitable intervals the incoming charges of gas and air are caused to pass through a network of very hot bricks which preheats them sufficiently to give the high temperature necessary when they burn at the hearth, and at the same time the hot waste gases are heating the opposite chambers ready for the next change-over   The brickwork in the chambers is chequered like a honeycomb to provide a large area against which the gases must scrub during their passage. The chambers are generally called Regenerators, and the alternative change-over system, the Regenerative System. An impression of the effectiveness of the system, and of the prevailing temperatures in the furnace, may be obtained from the facts that when the incoming air leaves the heating chamber it is at approximately 1250° C. (white heat),

FIG. 14.—Cross-section through Open-hearth Plant.

[*Proceedings of the Iron and Steel Institute.*

and that the temperature of combustion above the hearth is about 1800° C.

When the charging of the furnace is completed, the gas is put on and the melting completed as quickly as possible. This takes about 3 hours, by which time part of the carbon, and most of the silicon and manganese from the charge will have been removed by oxidation. Then follows the " boil," during which iron ore is added to help in oxidising away as much of the carbon as is necessary, and during this period the carbon content slowly falls, samples of metal being taken from time to time. When the bath is nearing the requisite carbon content the top slag is allowed to thicken so as to slow up the action, and the furnace is prepared for tapping. Just before tapping, or during the time that the metal is running into the ladle, a deoxidiser is added to the steel to remove air and ensure soundness in the finished steel. Such deoxidisers may be ferro-silicon, ferro-manganese and aluminium. The tapped metal is run into a ladle and cast into ingot moulds to give slightly tapering and generally rectangular ingots 5 ft. to 5 ft. 6 in. long of weights varying from 1 to 3 tons. After as short a time as possible, the ingots are stripped from the moulds and whilst still red hot, taken to the rolling mill for reduction into bars, or whatever other sections are being rolled. Should it not be convenient to roll them at once, the red-hot ingots can be re-heated, or stored in an underground furnace (soaking pit) until later. The complete cycle of operations for an open-hearth melt occupies from 6 to 12 hours. Fig. 14 indicates the scale of a steel melting unit.

The Bessemer Process. The discovery of producing steel in large quantities in a Converter by Henry Bessemer in 1856, was one of the epoch-making events in our industrial development, and led to tremendous strides in engineering construction. In this country, however, due to certain advantages in cost and control, the Bessemer method has been almost completely superseded by the Open Hearth process, but the Bessemer is still being employed in America and on the Continent.

The Bessemer converter is shown in its various positions at Fig. 15 and is constructed of an outer steel shell with ganister or basic lining, depending on whether the steel being made is acid or basic. The process starts by pouring molten pig iron into the converter until the level is just below the blast holes, when a blast of air at 20 to 25 lb. per square inch pressure is turned on. The converter is rotated into its upright position and that part of the reaction called the " blow " begins. This is divided into three stages : (a) the preliminary, (b) the boil, and (c) the finishing. These are all clearly indicated by variations in the smoke and flame issuing from the mouth of the converter, and the efficiency of the " blower " in charge of operations is the ability with which he can interpret them.

During the preliminary stage of the blow almost the whole of the silicon and manganese are oxidised from the charge and brown fumes accompanied by sparks and a short flame issue from the converter mouth. The size and luminosity of this flame gradually increase until after about 5 minutes from the beginning of the blow the " boil " commences. This stage is indicated by the ejection of molten particles of slag, and is accompanied by violent agitation of the contents of the converter caused by the escaping carbon monoxide gas which is formed by the chemical reaction of the air blast with the carbon in the melt. At this stage the blower estimates the heat of the charge and adds scrap or ferro-silicon according to whether it is too hot or too cold. When the carbon is almost completely oxidised away the boil is completed, the flame subsides and eventually drops altogether. The whole

FIG. 15.—Bessemer Converter.

blow, which has taken about 20 minutes, is now completed and the converter is rotated to the horizontal position. Its contents consist of an almost carbonless iron, containing small percentages of silicon, sulphur and phosphorus. For most purposes the carbon content of this metal would be too low, and, as it would be impossible to stop the blow so as to leave a definite amount of carbon present, the requisite amount of carbon is now added in the form of spiegeleisen or ferromanganese, which are varieties of pig iron rich in manganese. The charge is now ready for casting into ingots ready for the rolling mill.

The Crucible Process. The two processes of steel making just described supply the main output of plain commercial steels. For certain purposes, however, such as tools, gauges, etc., smaller quantities of very high-class steel are required, and this is often produced by the crucible process. This process was invented in 1740 by Benjamin Huntsman, a Sheffield watchmaker, who could not obtain a suitable steel for making his watch- and clock-springs.

A crucible melting shop consists of a series of melting holes arranged round one or more sides, the holes being lined with firebricks and having their tops level with the floor of the melting shop. Each hole takes two crucibles, and ashpit and flue arrangements are made as at Fig. 16, which shows a section through one hole. The crucibles are hand-made

from fireclay, and are shaped in cast-iron moulds with a wooden core
shaped to form the inside of the crucible.   Each pot holds about 50 lb.
of metal and is generally used for 3 melts before being discarded.

At the commencement of the process two pots with covers are
put in the hole on stands or bricks and the coke fire made up.   When
the pots are white hot the charge is put in through a charger shaped
like a funnel, the lid is adjusted and the melting hole is filled with coke.
The charge consists of cut pieces of Swedish iron and blister bars followed by pig iron and any alloying elements that may be required.
(Blister bars are bars of carbon steel made by heating pure iron in the
presence of charcoal, which converts the pure iron into a carbon steel
called " blister steel.")

After the charging the process consists of two stages—melting

FIG. 16.—Section through a Melting Hole for Crucible Steel Making.

and killing.   Two replenishments of the fire, which lasts about an hour,
are usually sufficient to melt the contents of the pot, which will then
have the appearance of a thick simmering liquid with the slag floating
on the top.   If an attempt were made to cast this into the ingot mould
the gases in it would cause the metal to boil over the top of the mould
and the ingot would be full of blowholes.   The metal, therefore, must
be " killed " to rid it of these occluded gases.   The last or " killing
fire " is made up and a small amount of manganese or aluminium
added to the contents of the pot.   This brings about chemical reactions
in the metal and results in the boiling off of the gases.   Finally the
crucible is pulled out of the hole with special tongs, and after the surface of the metal has been cleared of slag it is " teemed " or poured
into the previously prepared ingot mould.

Electric Steel

The methods used in the crucible process have changed very little
since Huntsman originated them.   Within recent years the melting of
steel by electric furnaces has developed rapidly, and although the

crucible method yields a fine product, electric melting possesses advantages which indicate that this method is the one of the future for the preparation of high-class steels.

There are two types of electric furnace in common use : the arc type and the high frequency furnace. In the *electric arc furnace* the heat required is generated by electric arcs struck between carbon electrodes and the metal bath. The impurities are oxidised from the charge by melting it underneath a covering of selected slag which absorbs the oxidised impurities and may then be run off by tilting the furnace. A diagram of an arc type furnace is shown in Fig. 17.

FIG. 17.—Diagram of the Heroult Electric Arc Rocking Furnace.

This type of furnace is used for making alloy steels such as stainless, high-speed steel, etc., and handles melts ranging up to 15 tons.

The *high frequency furnace* owes its principle of operation to the fact that when a piece of steel is held in a coil of wire in which an alternating electric current is flowing, the alternating magnetic field produced by the current induces an electric current in the steel. These currents are called eddy currents, and if they are powerful enough, their passage will cause the steel to be heated up.

The details of a high frequency furnace are shown in Fig. 18. A is the crucible for containing the metal and is made of a suitable refractory material. B is the inductor coil which carries the alternating current and which is insulated and water-cooled. The outer ring, C, is made of special magnetic iron laminations and shields the casing from getting too hot as well as serving as a magnetic shield to increase the magnetic flux in the coil. D is the outer sheet steel casing. An auxiliary to the plant is the electrical apparatus necessary to produce the high frequency current in coil B, the frequencies in use varying from 500 to 2000 cycles per second.

In the operation of this furnace the charge is introduced, together with the correct proportions of any alloying elements necessary and other materials as may be required to oxidise and flux the impurities from the melt. As the charge is brought to the molten condition the currents flowing in it cause a certain amount of agitation to take place

[*Birlec Ltd.*

Fig. 18.—High Frequency Coreless Induction Furnace
(Tilting Pattern, 3 cwt. capacity).

which serves to promote efficient mixing of the constituents. When the refining and mixing are complete the metal is poured into ingot moulds by tilting the furnace on the pivots at lip axis level.

High frequency melting usually deals with charges up to 10 cwt. and is used for high purity steels such as are necessary for tool and die steels, ball-bearing steels, etc.

A great advantage of the electric furnace is the absence of gas, fumes and impurities such as are present in fuel-fed furnaces, and which may introduce impurities into the melt, or oxidise a required constituent out of it. Whatever is put into an electric furnace may be relied upon to stay there, and if a well-fitting top is kept on the crucible, little oxidation can take place. For certain special purposes vacuum melted steels are now coming into vogue.

CHAPTER 2

THE PROPERTIES AND TREATMENT OF IRON AND STEEL

Mechanical Properties of Metals

Although we have mentioned certain properties already, it will be useful to study here the usual mechanical properties of metals. Later, when discussing treatment, we shall show how great is the influence of treatment on certain properties.

Brittleness is the property of breaking without much permanent distortion. It may be due to brittleness of the grain boundaries or of the crystals themselves. Cast iron is brittle because its structure is split up by flakes of graphite, which is a brittle material. Brittleness is often referred to as shortness. *Hot-*, or *red-shortness* in steel, is when it is brittle in the red-hot state. It is caused by too much sulphur which is present as iron sulphide and forms a brittle membrane surrounding the steel crystals. *Cold-shortness* means that a metal is brittle when cold. In steel cold-shortness is produced when the phosphorus content is too high.

Ductility. A metal is ductile when it may be drawn out in tension without rupture. Wire drawing depends upon ductility for its successful operation. A ductile metal must be both strong and plastic, e.g. lead wire is difficult to draw because the strength of lead is low.

Elasticity. The elasticity of a metal is its power of returning to its original shape after deformation by force. A material may be stretched, compressed, or its volume changed by pressure on all sides (e.g. immersion in a liquid). Many materials behave to some extent like powerful elastic, and, within limits, will recover their shape when the load on them is removed. The *elastic limit* is the limit of the elasticity of a material, and is expressed in pounds or tons per square inch of area. For example, if the elastic limit of a material were 15 ton per square inch, then, with a bar of the material 1 sq. in. in area, the material would return to its original length from a load of 15 tons (or $7\frac{1}{2}$ tons if $\frac{1}{2}$ sq. in.). If this intensity of loading were exceeded the bar would take on a permanent stretch, often called *permanent set.*

Elongation. When a material is pulled in a testing machine for the purpose of finding its tensile strength, stretch takes place before the bar fractures. The elongation is the amount of this stretch and is generally expressed as a percentage of the original length. For example, if a test length of 2 in. stretched to $2\frac{3}{4}$ in. before fracturing, the elongation would be

$$\frac{2\frac{3}{4} - 2}{2} \times 100 = \frac{\frac{3}{4}}{2} \times 100 = 37\frac{1}{2}\%.$$

A good elongation indicates a ductile material.

25

Hardness. The hardness of a metal is a measure of its ability to withstand scratching, wear and abrasion, indentation by harder bodies, marking by a file, etc. The machinability and ability to cut are also hardness properties important in the workshop. A rough, but often reliable test for the hardness of a hardened tool, is to see if the edge of a fine file will touch it. The *Brinell hardness* of a metal is found by pressing a ball on to the surface of the metal, the hardness number being found by dividing the load on the ball by the surface area of the impression. For testing steel, the ball is 10 mm. diameter and the load 3000 kilos. Brinell machines are usually supplied with a chart which gives the hardness number when the diameter of the ball impression is known.

Malleability. This is the property of permanently extending in all directions without rupture by pressing, hammering, rolling, etc. It requires that the metal shall be plastic but is not so dependent on strength, e.g. lead is a very malleable metal.

Plasticity. This is a rather similar property to malleability, and involves permanent deformation without rupture. It is the extreme opposite to elasticity, as may be shown by comparing the behaviour of a piece of elastic rubber and a piece of plasticine under a straining force. Plasticity is necessary for forging, and metals may be rendered plastic by heating them, e.g. steel is plastic when at a bright red heat.

Strength. The strength of a metal is its ability to resist the application of force without rupture. In service a material may have to withstand tension, compression, or shear forces. The strength of a material is measured by loading it in a testing machine. The *ultimate strength* is the load necessary to fracture 1 sq. in. of cross-section of the metal. The *tenacity* is the ultimate strength in tension. Ultimate strength and tenacity are always expressed in pounds or tons per square inch.

Toughness is the amount of energy a material can absorb before it fractures. A measure of the toughness of a metal may be obtained by nicking it, placing it in a vise and striking the end with a hammer. Certain woods are very tough and it is for this reason that hickory is a good material for sledge-hammer shafts.

Constitution of Steel

Reverting back to our discussion of iron and steel, it will be advantageous for us now to examine more closely the constitution of the plain steels. The mechanical properties, which are of importance to us, are so closely connected with the structure, and the structure with the treatment, that we shall gain a more thorough insight to the subject if we have a clear conception of the nature of the metal.

The microstructure of pure iron (Fig. 1) showed the clear crystals of iron (ferrite) with their grain boundaries. This metal is very soft and ductile with an ultimate tensile strength of about 19 ton per square inch. As soon as carbon is added to this iron a great change occurs in its structure and properties, and Fig. 19 shows the microstructure of a mild steel containing 0·25%–0·3% carbon. The white constituent is the ferrite, whilst the dark patches represent that part of the structure which contains the carbon. It must be remembered that these dark patches are not actual carbon but contain it in a chemi-

Pearlite (Black Areas)

Ferrite Crystals

FIG. 19.—Microstructure of Mild Steel (0·25–0·3% carbon × 100).

cally combined form. A chemical combination of two elements can be formed in which the final result is totally unlike either of the elements of which the combination is composed. Thus, hydrogen and oxygen combine in a certain proportion to form water (H_2O), carbon and oxygen may form carbon monoxide (CO), or carbon dioxide (CO_2), and so on. Now iron and carbon unite to form iron carbide (cementite) and they do so in the proportion by weight of 1 of carbon to 14 of iron. Iron carbide has the chemical formula Fe_3C and is a very hard, white and brittle substance, so that the more of it the steel contains the harder will it be.

If, now, we magnify further one of the dark portions of Fig. 19, it will show us that the dark, carbon-bearing constituent is in reality a substance built up of alternate light and dark plates, as shown at Fig. 20. These layers are alternately ferrite (iron) and cementite, and

FIG. 20.—Structure of Pearlite × 1,000 Approx.

FIG. 21.—Microstructure of High Carbon Steel.

(Black areas of pearlite surrounded by a membrane of cementite.)

allowing for the great magnification it will be seen how thin the plates are. This substance is called *pearlite* and is made up of 87% ferrite and 13% cementite. We have, then, that 100 parts of pearlite contain 13 parts of cementite, and since cementite consists of 1 part of carbon to 14 parts of ferrite (i.e. 1 of carbon to 15 of cementite), the 13 parts of cementite in 100 of pearlite will contain $\frac{13}{15}$ of carbon $= 0.87$, or about 0·9. Thus, pearlite contains approximately 0·9% of carbon, and the 0·25% C steel shown at Fig. 19 contains $\dfrac{0.25}{0.9} = 28\%$ of pearlite and 72% of ferrite. Pearlite is a strong metal and may be cut reasonably well with cutting tools. It has an ultimate strength of about 50 ton per square inch.

As we increase the carbon content of steel, the proportion of pearlite increases also, until when the steel contains 0·9% of carbon, its structure consists entirely of pearlite. If the carbon content is increased further still there will be some cementite left over and this will appear in the

Fig. 22.—Relation between Carbon Content, Structure, Strength, Hardness and Ductility for Steel.

[Rollason, *Metallurgy for Engineers.*

structure as a free constituent in the same way as free ferrite appears in the low carbon steels. This is shown in Fig. 21, which shows the microstructure of a 1·4% steel. Now, since ferrite is soft and not very strong, and cementite is hard and brittle but also without much strength, as the carbon (and the pearlite) is increased, the steel will get harder and stronger up to the point when it contains 0·9% of carbon. Beyond this, the cementite is increasing, but not the pearlite, so that its hardness will increase but its strength will decrease. This is illustrated in Fig. 22, which illustrates the effect of the carbon content on structure, strength, hardness and ductility.

The Behaviour of Steel when Heated

With the foregoing discussion fresh in our minds we will examine the changes which take place when steel is heated. These are of great importance, as they explain the reasons for, and effects of, heat treatments given to the metal, a subject upon which there is often much confusion.

If a piece of steel (say about 0·3% carbon) is put into a furnace, and gradually heated at a uniform rate, and the temperature of the steel observed at equal intervals of time, its temperature will at first rise uniformly, as would be expected. When, however, the temperature reaches 700° C. (a dull red heat) it will, for a time, remain stationary, and then rise at a somewhat slower rate until it reaches about 800° C. (a good red heat). After this, if the heating can be maintained, the temperature will continue to rise at approximately its initial rate.

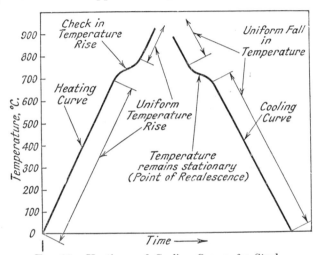

FIG. 23.—Heating and Cooling Curves for Steel.

Let us now assume that the piece of steel is heated to 900° C. in the furnace, then removed and observed in a darkened room. At 900° C. it will be a bright reddish yellow colour, and as soon as it is taken from the furnace it will begin to cool and lose its brilliancy. The cooling will proceed normally until the temperature has dropped to about the point where it received its first check when it was being heated, and here, if it is observed carefully, it will be seen that the cooling down has stopped. Not only will a check in the cooling down be observed at this point, but the steel will probably be seen to take on an extra glow as though heat had been imparted to it. After this, the rate of cooling will proceed normally until the metal is cold.

The heating up and cooling down may be represented on a graph of temperature-time. Fig. 23 shows the approximate form of such a graph.

Now when the steel was being supplied with heat at a constant rate in the furnace, had its structure remained in a stable and unchanged condition, its temperature would have shown a steady rise, and would not have remained stationary at 700° C. Similarly, the slowing down, and actual evolution of heat at the same point on cooling, indicates that at this temperature a structural change takes place in the metal which absorbs heat when the steel is being heated and gives up heat when cooling. It has definitely been established that a structural change does take place at this point, and because the steel glows when cooling, it has been called the *Point of Recalescence*. We have seen that the structure of steel, less than 0·9% carbon, is made up of areas of ferrite (iron), surrounding areas of pearlite, which is a substance made up of plates of ferrite and cementite. When steel is heated, this structure remains stable until a temperature of about 700° C. is reached, when the carbon in the pearlite commences to dissolve in the iron. (The reader may wonder how this can be when the whole structure is solid, but we may have a *solid solution* of carbon in iron just as we may have a liquid solution of salt in water.) This change of state continues, until the whole structure of the metal consists

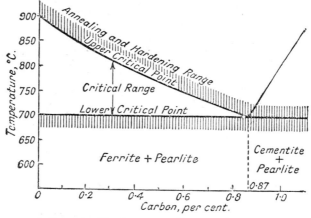

Fig. 24.—Heat-treatment Ranges of Steels.

of a solid solution of carbon in iron which is called *austenite*, and it was whilst this structure was building up that the steel in the furnace slowed up in its temperature rise, heat being absorbed to bring about the change. When the austenite is completely formed the temperature rise continues as at first. On cooling the reverse takes place, and at 700° C. the austenite changes back to pearlite again. This phenomenon is very important in the study of steel. The temperature points at which the change starts and ends are called the *critical points*, and the range including them the *critical range*. The temperature at which the change starts (lower critical point) is the same for all steels and is about 700° C., but the finishing point of the transformation (the upper critical point) varies according to the steel carbon content. This is illustrated in Fig. 24, from which it will be seen that for a steel containing 0·87% carbon (wholly pearlite), there is only one critical point, the whole transformation taking place at that temperature. Fig. 25 shows the change which occurs to the microstructure of the steel when the carbon goes into solution. Fig. 25 (*a*) shows the normal structure of ferrite and pearlite and (*b*) shows the austenite at the end of the change. Austenite is a solid solution of carbon in iron, and all ordinary steels above the critical range are in this condition. Naturally, the amount of carbon in solution will depend upon how much is present in the steel (as we may have weak or strong salt solutions). Austenite can hold up to $1\frac{3}{4}\%$ of carbon, which is more than the amount ever found in steel. Other changes, as well as the formation of a solid solution of the carbon, occur to steel during the critical range : (1) Austenite is a non-magnetic material, so that when it forms, the steel loses its magnetic quality, a change which is useful to us for determining the upper point of the critical range. (2) When being heated, a considerable contraction occurs at the critical range, and when cooling there is a corresponding instantaneous expansion. (3) The metal becomes extremely plastic at this point.

(*a*) Normal Structure of Ferrite and Pearlite.

(*b*) Austenite. Structure of the Steel when the Carbon has gone into Solution.

FIG. 25.—Showing Change in the Structure of Steel when heated to the Critical Range.

To sum up : when steel is heated, no structural change takes place until the lower critical point is reached. At this point, the carbon in the steel commences to form a solid solution with the iron, and this change takes place through the critical range. The transformation is completed at the upper critical point and at temperatures above this the steel consists of a solid solution of carbon in iron called austenite, which is a hard, non-magnetic substance. When the steel is allowed to cool down normally, on passing through the critical range, the austenite is transformed back to pearlite, accompanied by ferrite in steels less than 0.9% C., and by cementite in steels above 0.9% C.

Heat-treatment of Steel

For the proper heat-treatment of steel, some form of furnace is necessary together with an instrument for measuring the temperature inside the furnace. In the past a great amount of heat-treatment, particularly of tools, was done in the blacksmith's fire, and even to-day this method is still used in some places. At its best, however, this method of heating is not reliable, as for all except small tools the heating is not uniform, and, what is more important, the estimation of the correct temperature depends upon the skill and experience of the black-smith. If the steel is made too hot it becomes burnt, and if the critical range is not attained the changes which are sought for in the treatment do not take place.

Furnaces are made in many shapes, sizes and varieties. The methods of heating are usually by coal, oil, gas, or electricity, and furnaces may be obtained in capacities ranging from small ones with a chamber measuring about 6 in. wide × 4 in. high × 8 in. deep, suitable for small tools, up to huge structures dozens of feet long for heat-treating large bars and forgings.

Salt Bath Furnaces. For some purposes, particularly for the treatment of tools and special steels, furnaces are used which have a

(a)   (b)   (c)   (d)

[*The Industrial Gas Information Bureau.*

FIG. 26.—Corner of a Heat-treatment Shop.

bath of molten salt as their method of heating. For example, sodium cyanide fuses and becomes molten at about 600° C., and in its molten state may be heated up to about 900° C. If, therefore, we wish to heat certain articles to temperatures between these limits an excellent method of doing it is to immerse them in a bath of molten cyanide until they have reached its temperature. Whilst they are immersed in the liquid salt they are protected from the air and therefore do not oxidise and scale, and furthermore, they are being uniformly heated from all sides. Furnaces of this type are called salt-bath furnaces. The use of these furnaces involves taking certain precautions against the fumes given off, and care should be taken when quenching articles which may have a covering of molten salt because of the spitting which is liable to take place. To guard against this second risk, operators usually wear gloves and goggles.

A corner of an heat-treatment shop is shown at Fig. 26. The furnaces being (*a*) and (*b*) gas fired oven (or muffle) furnaces, (*c*) small tempering furnace with separate metal container and (*d*) gas heated salt bath furnace (shown with doors closed).

Furnace Temperatures. An important auxiliary to a furnace is some method of measuring its temperature, because the successful heat treatment of steel depends on close adherence to the correct temperature. There are many methods used for this, a simple one being to put in the furnace some substance which melts at the temperature it is desired to verify. The substances used for this are moulded in the form of cones from mixtures of Kaolin, lime, feldspar, magnesia, quartz and boric acid, with their melting temperatures arranged in steps from 600° C. to 2000° C. When a furnace temperature is required, several of these cones, covering a range of melting temperatures within which the temperature of the furnace is judged to lie, are put in and observed. The temperature is then judged from which cones collapse, and which remain unaffected by the heat of

Fig. 27.—Seger Cones after being in Furnace.

the furnace. For example, to verify a temperature judged to be 810°–820° C., cones having melting points of 790°, 815° and 835° might be put in, the temperature then being estimated from their condition after sufficient time had elapsed for them to be affected. These cones are called *Seger Cones* or *Sentinels* and Fig. 27 shows how they appear after a test.

Pyrometers. For modern heat-treatment furnaces the above method of measuring temperature is not very convenient because it is lengthy in operation and does not give a continuous reading of the temperature, as is often necessary. A more scientific and reliable method of measuring furnace temperatures is by an instrument called a *pyrometer*. There are various forms of pyrometers and two types in common use are : (1) The Thermo-Electric Pyrometer, (2) the Optical Pyrometer. The first type makes use of the principle that when two dissimilar wires are joined to form a complete electric circuit, and the two junctions maintained at different temperatures, an electric current flows in the circuit, the magnitude of the current depending upon the metals used, and the temperature difference of the junctions. The *hot junction*, which is placed in the furnace, is often made up of wires of platinum, and an alloy of platinum and rhodium welded together and is called a *thermocouple*. Leads from these wires are carried to a sensitive galvanometer which generally constitutes the cold junction, and which indicates the current flowing in the circuit due to the difference of temperature between the two junctions. The galvanometer is so calibrated, that instead of indicating electrical units, it reads in degrees of temperature. A diagram of this pyrometer is shown at Fig. 28 (*a*).

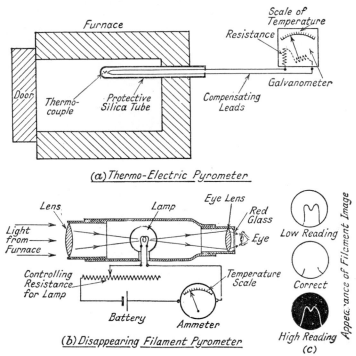

FIG. 28.—Methods of Measuring Furnace Temperatures.

The *optical pyrometer* compares the intensity of light being emitted from the furnace with that from some standard source. In the disappearing filament pyrometer the glow of a standard filament lamp is varied until it matches the light from the furnace and disappears when viewed through the telescope. The instrument, which is shown diagrammatically at Fig. 28 (*b*), is set up in front of the furnace and the light from the furnace is viewed through the eyepiece. The current through the lamp is varied by a resistance, and when a colour match is obtained the lamp filament disappears from sight, the lamp current required to cause this being indicated on an ammeter. This instrument may be calibrated so that it reads in degrees of temperature, instead of in units of electric current. The appearance of the filament, as seen through the telescope, is shown alongside the diagram Fig. 28 (*c*).

Heat Colours. The luminous colours corresponding to different furnace and metal temperatures are as follows :

Colour.	Temperature. °F.	°C.	Process for which suitable.
Black red (viewed in dull light or darkness) . .	800	426 ⎫	Toughening carbon tool steel after quenching. Tempering high-speed steel.
	900	482 ⎪	
	1000	538 ⎬	
Very dark red . . .	1100	593 ⎭	
	1200	648	
Dark red . . .	1300	704	
	1400	760	⎫ Hardening and annealing carbon tool steel.
Cherry red . . .	1500	815 ⎫⎬	
Light cherry red . .	1600	871 ⎭	
	1700	926 ⎬	Hardening alloy tool steel.
Orange red . . .	1800	981 ⎪	
	1900	1036 ⎭	
Yellow	2000	1093	
	2100	1149	
	2200	1204	
Yellow white . . .	2300	1259 ⎫	Hardening high-speed steel.
	2400	1315 ⎬	
White	2500	1371	Welding.

Reasons for Heat treatment. Metal is heat-treated to give it certain desired properties. Some of the properties which may be required and the treatments necessary are as follows :

To soften the metal—*Annealing.*

To harden it to resist wear, or to enable it to cut other metals—*Hardening.*

To remove some of the extreme brittleness caused by hardening—*Tempering.*

To refine the structure after it has been distorted by hammering or working when in the cold state—*Normalising.*

In addition there are various other treatments such as toughening the metal to better withstand shock, toughening soft steel so that it machines without tearing, treating special steels to increase their strength and so on.

Annealing

The purposes of annealing are (1) to soften the steel so that it may be more easily machined, (2) to relieve internal stresses which may have been caused by working the metal or by unequal contraction in casting. The process involves (*a*) heating slowly to the required temperature, (*b*) holding at that temperature for long enough to enable the internal changes to take place, (*c*) cooling slowly. We have seen that above the critical range steel consists of austenite. This is true whatever may have been the structural condition of the steel before heating. Furthermore, when austenite is cooled normally through the critical range, it changes to pearlite, mixed with ferrite or cementite, depending on the carbon content of the steel. This change occurs only if the cooling is slow. The true transformation to pearlite, therefore, is dependent on having true austenite to start with, and then allowing sufficient time for the metal to cool through the critical range for the

soft pearlite to form. The temperature for annealing must be 30°
to 50° above the higher critical point for steels up to 0·9% carbon,
and about the same amount above the lower critical point for high
carbon and tool steel * (above 0·9% C.). The reader may obtain these
from the graph (Fig. 24), and they are approximately as follows:

Carbon Content %.	Annealing Temperature ° C.
less than 0·12 (Dead mild)	875–925
0·12 to 0·25 (Mild)	840–970
0·3 to 0·5	815–840
0·5 to 0·9	780–810
0·9 to 1·3 (Tool steels)	760–780

The time taken by the metal to reach the temperature of the furnace,
and the period for which it should be " soaked " at the annealing
temperature vary according to the shape and dimensions of the article,
but the process should not be hurried.† The best method of cooling
is to turn off the furnace and leave the work inside, allowing the whole
to cool slowly together. If this is not possible the metal should be
taken out and buried in a non-conducting material such as sand, lime
or ashes.

Normalising

The object of normalising is to refine the structure of steel and
remove strains which may have been caused by cold working. When
steel is cold worked (hammered, rolled, bent, etc., in the cold condition) the crystal structure is distorted, and the metal may be brittle
and unreliable. Also, when steel is kept heated for a considerable
period well above the higher critical point (as may often be necessary
for prolonged forging), a growth in the grain size takes place, and
when cool the metal may have lost its toughness. If the steel is slowly
heated to its annealing temperature, the structure is in the most refined
state, and normalising consists of cooling it in air from this point.

Hardening and Tempering of Carbon Steels

We now know that the critical range is the interval between two
temperatures the lower of which is about 700° C., and that when steel
cools normally through this range, it is transformed from austenite to
pearlite, plus a free constituent. If we can by some means lower the
temperature of the transformation of austenite so that instead of taking
place at 700° it takes place at about 300°, it will not decompose into
pearlite, but will be transformed into a constituent called *martensite*.
We can lower this temperature of transformation by cooling the metal
suddenly, so that the change does not have time to take place at the
normal point, but is forced to occur at some lower temperature. The
sudden cooling is usually made to take place by quenching the steel

---

* The reader may wonder, in view of the foregoing remarks, why tool steel
should not be heated above the upper critical point for annealing. It is found
that this may result in an unsatisfactory structure and cause cracking when the
tools are hardened. Heating is therefore stopped when all the carbon in the pearlite
has gone into solution but not all the free cementite.

† If metal is placed in a furnace at (say) 800° C., at least 20 min. per inch of
thickness should be allowed for the heating-up period.

in water or some other liquid, and the efficiency with which the quenching occurs determines how much of the austenite is transformed to martensite, and the hardness of the steel.

The exact constituency of martensite is not clearly known but it serves our purpose to know that it is a very hard substance capable of resisting extreme wear and of cutting other metals. It has a needle-like structure as shown in Fig. 29. It should be clear that martensite cannot be formed (and the steel hardened) by quenching until the steel is in the austenitic condition, i.e. above the lower critical temperature, the carbon then being in solution. For this reason, the term *hardening carbon* has been given to the form of the carbon when the steel is above the lower critical temperature, and *cement carbon* when below this point (i.e. in the pearlite). When the carbon is in the cement (softening) form, the steel cannot be hardened by quenching.

FIG. 29.—Representing the Needle-like Structure of Martensite in Quenched Carbon Steel. The White Background is Austenite × 1000 approx.

Before passing on to the practical consideration of hardening and tempering it will be necessary to qualify our remarks somewhat for low carbon steels.

When steel contains less than 0·3% carbon, and this includes all the mild steels, the solution of carbon in iron which forms the austenite is naturally a much weaker solution, and contains more iron than for the higher carbon steels. When steel of this class is quenched, some of this extra iron is set free in the structure and this, together with the fact that the smaller amount of carbon results in a smaller amount of martensite, makes it impossible to harden mild steel in the manner just described. A mild steel will certainly be somewhat harder and of a more uniform texture as a result of quenching, but it will not be hard in the generally accepted meaning.

TABLE 4.   HARDNESS OF QUENCHED STEEL

Carbon % .	.	0·1	0·3	0·5	0·7	0·9	1·2
Brinell hardness	.	150	450	650	700	680	690

Tempering

Martensite, being an extremely hard and brittle substance, renders a dead hard tool made of it liable to cracking and chipping. The steel is therefore heated up again to a temperature below the lower critical temperature which causes a partial transformation of the martensite back to pearlite again, thereby taking away some of the hardness, but making the steel tougher.

The temperature at which tempering should be carried out depends upon the purpose for which the article or tool is to be used, and the table below gives the temperatures for some of the usual applications of high carbon steel.

When the article has been brought to the tempering temperature it may be quenched or allowed to cool off naturally. The temperature for this operation is often judged by the colour of the oxide film which appears on a freshly polished surface of the article, and these colours are given in Table 5. The reader should experiment with a few pieces of steel in order to familiarise himself with the order in which the colours appear.

TABLE 5. TEMPERING TEMPERATURES

Tool or Article.	Temperature ° C.	Temper Colour.
Turning tools	230	Pale straw.
Drills and milling cutters . . .	240	Dark straw.
Taps and shear blades	250	Brown.
Punches, reamers, twist drills, rivet snaps	260	Brownish purple.
Press tools, axes	270	Purple.
Cold chisels, setts for steel . . .	280	Dark purple.
Springs	300	Blue.
For toughening generally without undue hardness	450–600	

To sum up : carbon steels may be hardened by quenching from the annealing temperature (page 36), when they may be too brittle for their purpose. To toughen them they must be tempered by re-heating to a suitable temperature.

Quenching

We have seen that to transform the austenite to martensite efficiently, the cooling must be so rapid that the temperature of transformation is lowered from about 750° C. to 300° C. This involves very rapid cooling and brings troubles with distortion and cracking. There are two factors which tend to cause the metal to warp and crack :

(1) When metal is cooled it undergoes a general contraction which is not uniform, but occurs first at the outside surfaces, and in the thin sections of the article.

(2) When steel cools through the critical range an *expansion* takes place.

Now, if we could arrange to cool the metal so that its *whole volume* could be suddenly cooled at the same instant, we should not experience much trouble with volume changes, but unfortunately this is not possible. Let us examine what happens : after carefully heating the steel to the annealing temperature we quickly take it from the furnace and plunge it into water. The outer portion of the metal being in contact with the water is immediately cooled and undergoes its critical range expansion, followed by its cooling contraction, becoming a hard, rigid skin of metal. The inner portion of metal, however, has not yet felt the quenching effect and is still red hot. An instant later, the quenching effect is transferred to this portion which, as it passes through the critical range, must expand. It can easily be imagined what is likely to happen to the hard and brittle outer layer of cold metal when this inner core undergoes its critical expansion : it is a matter of very good fortune if it does not crack, and most of us must have had that mortifying experience.

The general contraction which takes place may be to some extent allowed for by the direction in which we quench the tool. For example, if a long tool such as a tap is quenched on its side, the whole length of one side meets the cold water at once and contracts. This sudden shortening of one side causes the tap to warp, and we must remember, that to try and straighten it afterwards will most surely break it. If the tap is plunged vertically into the water, the warping effect is greatly minimised. The reader should study every job he has to harden and endeavour to quench it in such a manner that warping effects are minimised as much as possible. When an article has been quenched it should be moved about in the water to expedite the cooling as much as possible.

After what has been said regarding the slower cooling down of the inner metal of large and thick jobs, it can be imagined that the section of such an article will not be of the same hardness throughout, and the very centre may almost have had time to transform to the pearlitic condition. This may not be a disadvantage as a rather softer core to a tool helps to give it strength and we are not likely to require to use the metal near the very centre for cutting. When extreme hardness can be sacrificed in favour of extra toughness, oil may be used for cooling instead of water, with less risk of cracking during quenching. As the specific heat of oil is less than that of water its cooling effect is less and the quenching effect is not so intense. This means that less martensite will be formed, and the tool will be softer and tougher.

It is often not necessary to harden the whole of a tool, but only that portion which is required to do the cutting and only the part required hard should be heated and quenched. This leaves us with a hard cutting portion merging on to a tough shank or body. Tools such as chisels, punches, drifts, etc., must on no account be hard where they are struck with the hammer or the metal will chip and may fly into the face or hands.

The heat required for tempering is generally obtained by placing the article on to a piece of plate which has been heated to redness. The portion of the tool to be tempered having been previously polished with emery cloth is carefully watched, and as soon as the correct tempering colour appears it may be cooled off. Round articles such as taps may be held inside a piece of red-hot tubing so that they are uniformly heated from all sides.*

For some tools such as chisels, punches, etc., time (and heat) may be saved by hardening and tempering in the same operation. The tool should be heated up to the hardening temperature for about half its length and then the cutting end quenched for a length of 1–2 inches. When it is quite certain that quenching is complete the tool should be removed from the water and the cutting edge quickly polished with

---

* When large quantities of work have to be tempered, an efficient way of heating is by immersion in a bath of molten metal or salt. A useful range of temperatures is provided by the tin-lead alloys which are molten between 183° C. (37% lead) and 327° C. (100% lead).

emery cloth.   The heat from the unquenched portion will soon travel, by conduction, to the end, and the tempering colours will show up. When the required colour appears the whole tool should be quenched. This method gives a good effect as the tool consists of the hardened and tempered cutting edge, with the metal gradually and uniformly decreasing in hardness towards the soft shank.

The Working of Steel

Practically the whole of the energy of the workshop engineer is aimed towards some aspect of changing the shape of metal and we shall now discuss the general question of hot and cold working. *Cold working* means the subjecting of metal to forces which cause it to undergo plastic deformation when it is below the lower critical temperature (pearlite condition).   *Hot working* is the same thing when the metal is above the lower critical temperature.   The processes included are forging, bending, rolling, drawing out, hammering, etc., and it will be realised that since cast iron is brittle and does not lend itself to any form of plastic flow, it is excluded from the following remarks which refer to wrought iron and steel, and in a general way to the non-ferrous metals which can be worked.

Cold Working.   It may at first seem strange why working steel at 600° C., which is a dull red heat, should be included in the category of cold work.   When it is remembered, however, that the pearlitic structure remains unchanged up to the lower critical (just over 700° C.), it will be realised that the effect, on the pearlite, of plastic working, will be the same at any temperature below this.

Cold working distorts the crystal structure of metal and renders it harder and more brittle.   Unless, however, the metal has been worked so much that it cracks, its structure may be brought back to its original state by annealing.   Whatever distortion may be in the structure of the

(a) Normal Structure of a Mild Steel (0·17% C.).   (b) Same Steel after a considerable reduction in Wire Drawing.

FIG. 30.—Effect of Cold Drawing on the Structure of Metal.

steel below the critical range, when it is brought to the upper critical temperature it re-crystallises into austenite and then, if cooled normally, transforms back to pearlite bearing little trace of the original ill-treatment.   The reader may imagine that when a metal has been bent and straightened again, or given a certain amount of permanent stretch, or has received some other such treatment, it has lost its " nature " and is rendered worthless. This is not the case, as provided the metal has not cracked the treatment will only have made it a little harder, stronger, and more brittle, and it may be brought back to its original condition by annealing or normalising. If, of course, the treatment has made the metal so brittle that it has cracked, then we may say it has lost its " nature " or any other word we like to use, for the only cure is the scrap-heap and re-melting. As we shall discuss later, cold working occurs when metal is cold rolled, drawn into wire, drawn into cups, cold headed, bent cold, etc. The distortion to the structure of a mild steel caused by being drawn into wire is shown at Fig. 30.

Hot Working. This consists of changing the shape of steel when its temperature is above the upper critical and is used in hot rolling, forging, upsetting, etc. Hot work refines the structure of steel by smashing up large grain formations and closing up any cavities which may be present. The shaping of hot, plastic steel may be by blows such as from a hammer or drop stamp, or the metal may be caused to flow by a slower and more even movement as by the pressure of a

Fig. 31.—Effect of upsetting End of Shaft.

hydraulic press. The hammering processes tend to give more thorough effects than the pressing, which is more in the nature of kneading. Where the thickness of metal is large the effects of hammering may not penetrate right through, and the surface metal will be better worked than that below. If forging is carried out with the strength requirements of the finished article in mind, a much improved and more reliable product may be obtained. This is because steel to some degree exhibits directional qualities in its grains, and by suitable forging, the flow of the metal may be so controlled that the direction of the grain adds strength. Fig. 31 is of a gear, solid with a shaft. At (a) is shown how the grain would run if the whole were turned from a solid bar, whilst at (b) the grain glow caused by forging up the end of a bar is shown. The metal in gear teeth cut on the gear at (b) will be more

FIG. 32.—Direction of Grain in a Forged Crankshaft.

durable than at (*a*). Fig. 32 shows the grain direction in a forged crankshaft, where again it can be seen that the directional qualities of the grain add toughness to the webs, and where they join the round parts of the shaft.

Finishing Temperature.—The temperature at which the hammering of a forging is left off has an important influence on the properties of the forging. When steel is heated to, and soaked at, a temperature considerably above its upper critical point, its grain size increases, and if cooled from this point its structure may be weak and without toughness. When a considerable amount of forging has to be done the metal must be made hot or it will cool too quickly and time will be wasted by continual re-heating. Whilst the metal is being hammered the grain growth is compensated for by the refining effect of the hammering, but if the hammering is discontinued at a high temperature, grain growth will occur as the forging cools. On the other hand, if the metal is hammered when it is below 700° C. it will be cold worked and may be given small hair cracks. The best time to leave off hammering is when the steel is just above the upper critical temperature and it will then have the best possible structure when it is cold. If there is any doubt, the forging should be normalised after it is finished. Fig. 33 shows at

(*a*) As Cooled from a High Forging Temperature.

(*b*) Refined Structure of the same Steel after Normalising.

FIG. 33.—Showing the Effect of Normalising in Refining Coarse-green Structures.

(*a*) the structure of a forging cooled from a temperature considerably above the upper critical point, whilst at (*b*) is the same steel after normalising.

Overheated Steel. Sometimes, by accident, steel is heated to a very high temperature—almost melting. This causes the structure to be rendered brittle, and is brought about by a film of oxide getting into the grain boundaries. When in this state the metal is often referred to as " burnt " and nothing except re-melting will bring it back to a usable condition.

Toughening Mild Steel. When the ferrite in the microstructure of mild steel, instead of being well dispersed amongst the pearlite is collected together in large patches, the steel gives unsatisfactory

results in machining and the surface tears, especially for such operations as screw-cutting. By quenching this steel from the critical
range it is often possible to improve matters. The quenching breaks
up the segregations of ferrite and confers enough additional toughness
to avoid the tendency to tear.

Case-hardening. Case-hardening is a method of hardening the
surface of mild steel to a depth varying up to about $\frac{1}{16}$ in. We have
seen that heating and quenching has no appreciable effect on low carbon
steel, but if we can convert the surface of mild steel into a high carbon
steel we may harden it by heating and quenching in the usual way.
This is what actually takes place in case-hardening and the operation
is divided into two main parts : (1) converting the outer skin (case)
to a high carbon steel (carburising) and (2) hardening this case and
refining the core. To increase the carbon content of the case, the
steel is packed in cast-iron or steel boxes together with a substance
rich in carbon such as charcoal granules, hoof clippings, bone dust, etc.,
and the boxes are charged into a furnace at about 900° C.–950° C.
At this temperature the carbon infuses into the surface of the metal,
converting it to a high carbon steel, and the depth to which this takes
place depends upon the time of treatment, but generally 3 or 4 hours
are sufficient. At the end of this time the box is allowed to cool slowly
and when removed the steel parts consist of a soft mild steel core with
a case of high carbon steel.
Due to the prolonged heating
at a high temperature the
grain structure of the core will
be relatively coarse, so that as
well as hardening the case, a
treatment will be necessary to
refine and toughen the core.
The core may first be refined
by heating to about 900° C.
and quenching in oil, after
which the case is hardened
by heating to about 770° C.
and quenched in water. This
leaves an article having a
soft, tough core and a glass-
hard case which should have
its brittleness relieved by

[*W. T. Flather Ltd.*

Fig. 34.—Fracture of a case-hardened
bar showing the hard " case " and tough
" core."

tempering at about 200° C. or over, depending on the final hardness
required. Fig. 34 shows the fracture of a case-hardened shaft.

On some jobs it is necessary for certain portions to be left in the
soft condition. For example, if a thread is hardened it will chip in
service owing to its brittleness. There are two ways of leaving any
portion of a case-hardened part soft : (1) by preventing infusion of
carbon, (2) by cutting away the high carbon steel case before it is
quenched. In the first method the part to be left soft is covered with
clay, or copper plated. This retains it in the low carbon condition by
preventing infusion of carbon. In the second method extra metal is
left on the portions that must be left soft. After carburising this is

machined off, which exposes the mild steel underneath and when quenching takes place this is left unhardened.

Case-hardening is applied to parts such as spindles, pins and similar components which require to be tough but hard, and wear-resisting on the surface. The steel used should be of low carbon content (0·08 to 0·25%). Some tools, such as hand-reamers, which are only subjected to light working conditions, may be made satisfactorily from case-hardened steel.

Superficial Hardening. For the rapid surface hardening of small parts such as screws, clamps, washers, etc., a form of surface hardening may be used. This uses cyanide, or prussiate of potassium, and may be carried out either by placing the article in the fused salt, holding it at the quenching temperature for a few minutes and then quenching out, or by sprinkling the red-hot article with the powdered salt, heating up again and quenching. This method is often spoken of as case-hardening, but is not a true case-hardening process.

Tests for Iron and Steel

It is sometimes necessary to make sample tests on the metal being used. The test may be to differentiate one metal from another, to test the hardness or toughness of a metal and so on. Whilst the reader may not have access to elaborate testing machines and metallurgical apparatus he can, with the workshop tools at his disposal, gain a useful insight into many of the properties of metals. With the help of a simple lens he can follow the course of hardening cracks and use the information to help him to do better next time. The colour and quantity of the sparks given off by grinding various steels will tell him about the steels. The appearance of a fracture will give an indication as to whether he is forging at too high a temperature and getting grain growth and so on.

The reader should purposely submit steel to certain treatments, e.g. hammering hot, hammering cold with and without normalising, prolonged heating, severe overstraining (of a wire), quenching different ways and in various liquids and so on. After such experiments he should put the metal to test and examination in order to study the effect of what he has done, and compare it with a normal sample of the same steel. In this way he will develop an instinct which, in later life, will serve him in good stead. We may learn a great deal from books and very soon forget what we have learned, but the knowledge we gain by doing things is rarely, if ever, forgotten.

The following tests may all be carried out with the appliances and tools in the workshop. At (a) are given tests for properties. These will not give actual numerical results, but will be useful for comparing the degree of each property possessed by different metals. The distinguishing tests under (b) will help the reader to recognise the various grades of iron and steel. Distinguishing tests for high-speed steel have also been given. This is a special alloy steel used for making cutting tools, and its properties and treatment will be discussed later.

TABLE 6.

(a) *Tests for Properties*

Hardness. (*a*) *Unhardened Metals.* Use some form of pressure (e.g. vise or arbor press) to force a $\frac{3}{8}$-in. ball on to the polished surface of the metal. Exert the same pressure each time and compare the diameters of the impressions made.

(*b*) *Hardened Metals.* Try to file the metal with the edge of a small, fine file. Grind smooth, and scratch with a needle point. Use scratch test to try for hardening at the *centre* of a piece of quenched steel (after previously nicking and breaking the bar).

Strength. Take bars about $\frac{1}{2}$ in.–$\frac{3}{4}$ in. diameter and 3 ft. long and support at each end. Load centre with weights, and compare sag at centre. Or, clamp one end of 2-ft. bar in vise and load the other end. Strong metals give least deflection. Keep loading within the elastic limit of the material (i.e. no permanent set when load removed).

Toughness. Saw a $\frac{1}{2}$-in. bar about $\frac{1}{8}$ through, hold in vise and hit with 2-lb. hammer until severed. Force, and number of blows necessary is an indication of toughness. Test on quenched carbon steels which have had varying degrees of temper up to 600° C.

Brittleness. Brittle metals break easily under the above test for toughness.

Ductility

(1) Take a piece of the material $\frac{1}{4}$ in.–$\frac{3}{8}$ in. diameter, hold it in the vise with about 2 in. protruding. Bend the end backwards and forwards and count the number of times it may be bent before it fractures. A ductile material will stand a greater number of bends than one which is not ductile.

(2) Take a bar or strip and double it over on itself like a hairpin. Examine the outside of the bend for cracks, and if the material is ductile it should be free from them.

(3) By some means, pull wires of the material until they fracture. Compare the lengths under tension before and after fracture. Wires which have stretched the most before fracture are the most ductile.

Malleability. Hammer a round bar until it has been flattened. Examine the edges of the flattened portion for cracks. Materials which are most easily flattened, and which show least signs of cracking are the most ductile. This test also gives a measure of the *plasticity* of a material.

TABLE 6. WORKSHOP TESTS FOR IRON AND STEEL

(b) *Distinguishing Tests*

Nature of Test.	Cast Iron.	Wrought Iron.	Mild Steel.	Medium Carbon Steel.	Cast Steel.	High Speed Steel.
Appearance of bar	Grey and sandy. Shows line of casting.	Red and scaly.	Smooth finish. Bluish sheen.	Bluish black sheen. Smooth.	Bright black. Very smooth. Sharp corners on square bars.	Not as smooth as cast steel. Oftenpainted.
File with rough file.	Skin very hard. Black powder from filed metal. Resistance low.	File drags and tends to clog. Whitish filings. Slag visible	Not as much drag as W.I. White finish and filings.	Increasing difficulty in making file bite into metal. Surface becomes more glazed as carbon increases.		Not as hard as cast steel.
Turn in lathe	Cuts easily. Black crumbly chips. Black powder when surface wiped.	White curly turnings. Poor finish. Slag lines visible.	Turns easily. White curly turnings.	Increasing hardness under tool. Turnings break into short pieces and may be brown or blue. Rather glazed finish.		Turns fairly easily. Long chips. Distinctive smell from scale.
Hammer at full red heat	Crumbles under hammer.	Flattens very easily.	Flattens fairly easily.	Increasing resistance to flattening as carbon increases.		Cons'derable resistance to flattening.

TABLE 6 (*continued*)

Nature of Test.	Cast Iron.	Wrought Iron.	Mild Steel.	Medium Carbon Steel.	Cast Steel.	High Speed Steel.
Quench from full red	No appreciable change. May crack.	No appreciable change.	May harden slightly but not much.	Hard when tested with file.	Hard when tested with file.	Moderately hard.
Grind on emery wheel	Small stream of dull red sparks with an occasional bright burst.	Lighter sparks than C.I. and greater quantity.	Stream of long white sparks.	As carbon content increases spark stream becomes more bushy with secondary "bursts."		Dull red sparks rather like C.I.
Drop a ½–¾ in. dia. bar, 1 ft. long, on to ground.	Very dull sound.	Dull, but metallic sound.	Medium metallic sound.	Higher note than mild steel.	High, ringing sound.	Lower ring, more like mild steel.
Saw about ⅓ through a ½-in. bar, 1 in. from end. Hold in vice and break off with 2-lb. hammer	Snaps easily.	Bends well over.	Bends over, then breaks.	Bends a little before breaking.	Good resistance to blow. Then breaks off.	
Examine fracture of last test	Large crystals. Bright specks of free carbon.	Earthy, fibrous fracture.	Medium crystalline fracture.	Finer fracture than mild steel.	Very fine crystalline fracture.	Fine, velvety fracture.

47

CHAPTER 3

MATERIALS (*cont.*). NON-FERROUS METALS AND ALLOYS USED IN THE WORKSHOP — ALLOY STEELS — " RARE " METALS—CERAMIC TOOLS—PREPARATION OF METALS

Although iron and steel are the most common and important of the materials with which we have to deal, there are other metals used in the workshop about which it will be necessary for us to have some knowledge. The chief pure metals in the non-ferrous group with which the reader will have to deal are aluminium, copper, lead, tin and zinc. These may be mixed to give *alloys*, many of which are of great importance. The reader, if he likes, may regard the above metals in the light of primary colours which may be mixed in different proportions to give a wide range of varying shades.

Aluminium

Aluminium is a white metal produced by electrical processes from the oxide (alumina), which is prepared from a clayey mineral called bauxite. Bauxite is found in large quantities in various parts of the world and the successful extraction of the metal depends upon the supply of large amounts of cheap electricity. Owing to its light weight aluminium is used largely for aircraft and automobile components where the saving of weight is an advantage. The specific gravity of aluminium is about 2·68 as compared with 7·8 for steel. In its pure state the metal would be too weak and soft for most purposes, but when mixed with small amounts of other alloys it becomes hard and rigid. Aluminium is very ductile and malleable. It can be rolled into leaf $\frac{1}{1000}$ in. thick and drawn into wire $\frac{4}{1000}$ in. diameter. It can be given a high finish by burnishing and polishing. Aluminium melts easily and may be formed into parts by casting. In its natural state (about 99% pure), it has a tensile strength varying from 6 to 10 tons per square inch depending upon the amount of mechanical treatment it has received. Its good electrical conductivity is an important property and aluminium is used for overhead cables on the Grid system pylons. To give the strength necessary to carry the large spans, the cables are made of aluminium with a thin core of high tensile steel wire. The high resistance of aluminium to corrosion makes it a useful metal for cooking pans. It owes this resistance to a thin film of oxide which covers its surface and protects it. Aluminium foil is used for wrapping chocolates and cigarettes and for sealing milk bottles, whilst the powdered metal is used as the base for aluminium paint. Weight for weight aluminium is only exceeded in tensile strength by the best cast steel.

Aluminium Alloys. It is when alloyed with small amounts of other metals that aluminium finds its widest uses. The addition of small quantities of other elements converts this soft, weak metal into hard, strong metals with a wide range of applications. For the

48

casting of crank cases and for general engineering use, aluminium is alloyed with small amounts of copper and zinc. The alloy containing $12\frac{1}{2}$ to $14\frac{1}{2}\%$ of zinc with $2\frac{1}{2}$ to 3% of copper (B.S.S. No. 1490) * has a minimum tensile strength of 11 tons per square inch and is used for castings. For use in bar form B.S.S. No. 918 specifies an alloy containing 2–4% copper, 4–8% zinc and not more than 1% of iron and silicon. These last two metals are nearly always present in aluminium as impurities. For castings which must be tough to withstand shocks and severe stresses, an aluminium-copper alloy is used containing 12% of copper. An important series of casting and forging alloys having high strength have recently been developed for use in aeroplane construction. These contain copper, nickel, magnesium and zinc together with small amounts of other substances. One example of such alloys is as follows : zinc 5%, magnesium 3%, copper 2·2%, nickel up to 1%, aluminium the remainder. To bring this alloy to its maximum strength and hardness it must be heat-treated, and when this has been carried out an ultimate tensile strength of 33 tons per square inch may be obtained. Another alloy containing copper, nickel and magnesium, and which may be cast or wrought is known as Y-alloy. The wrought alloys are specified in B.S.S. Nos. 414 and 478 and contain $3\frac{1}{2}$–$4\frac{1}{2}\%$ copper, 1·8–2·3% nickel and 1·2–1·7% magnesium. This alloy has the characteristic of retaining a good strength at high temperatures and for this reason is used for engine pistons. It is also used largely in the form of sheet and strip, and after proper heat treatment may be brought to a minimum tensile strength of 23 tons per square inch.

An important and interesting wrought alloy is known as *Duralumin*. This is composed of copper $3\frac{1}{2}$–$4\frac{1}{2}\%$, manganese 0·4–0·7%, magnesium 0·4–0·7%, aluminium the remainder. It is used widely in the wrought condition for forgings, stampings, bars, sheets, tubes and rivets. Duralumin has the property of *age-hardening*, and at room temperature its hardness increases rapidly for the first day, and then slowly up to a maximum value after 4 or 5 days. When it is aged it is too hard for work to be done on it, and it must be annealed. This is effected by heating to about 375° C. and cooling in air, water or oil. After annealing, the metal must be worked within the time that its age-hardening will have rendered it too hard for further work, or re-annealing will become necessary. When in the heat-treated and aged condition duralumin may have a tensile strength up to 25 tons per square inch.

Copper

Copper is easily distinguished from all other metals on account of its red colour. The fracture of cast copper is granular, but when forged or rolled it is slightly fibrous. The chief ore of copper is the pyrites, which contains on the average 32% of copper. Extraction may be by the dry or wet process, the former being the most common, carried out in a reverberatory or blast furnace preceded by various stages of ore refinement and followed by various metal refining pro-

* British Standards Institution Specification.

cesses. In the wet process the ore is treated with acids and the metal afterwards precipitated. Electrolytic copper is a pure form obtained by electrolysis from impure lumps of smelted copper.

The metal is malleable and ductile, and because of its high electrical conductivity it is used extensively for wire and cable, and all parts of electrical apparatus which must conduct the current. Copper also is a good conductor of heat and is highly resistant to corrosion by liquids. For this reason it is used for locomotive fireboxes, water heating apparatus, water pipes and vessels in brewery and chemical plants. For its high heat conduction it is used for soldering iron bits.

Copper may be cast, forged, rolled and drawn into wire. Rolling and drawing harden it, but it may be softened again by heating to 320° C. The mechanical properties of copper depend upon its condition. Castings may have a tensile strength of 10–11 tons per square inch, which may be increased to 14 or 15 by working (hammering or rolling). The strength of hard-drawn copper wire may be as high as 25–30 tons per square inch.

Aluminium Bronze. Copper alloys with aluminium to give aluminium bronze and the chief alloys are those containing 6% and 10% of aluminium respectively. These alloys have good strength and working properties and the 6% aluminium alloy has a fine gold colour, being used for imitation jewellery and decorative purposes.

The 10% aluminium alloy, which often contains 5% nickel and 5% iron, is interesting because it can be hardened like high carbon steel. In its softest condition the alloy has a maximum strength of about 25 tons per square inch, but if it is quenched from 900° C. it is hardened and its strength rises to about 50 tons per square inch. After hardening it may be tempered in the same way as steel. Alloys of copper with tin and zinc are important and will be discussed on pp. 53 and 54.

Lead

Lead is the heaviest of the common metals, having a specific gravity of about 11·3 as compared with 7·8 for steel. It has a bluish-grey colour and a dull, metallic lustre, but this is lost on exposure to the air, the surface becoming a dull grey. Lead is very soft and may easily be cut with a knife. It is plastic and malleable, being easily forced cold into mould shapes and rolled into thin sheets.

The chief ore of lead is the sulphide, called " gelena," and smelting may be carried out in reverberatory or vertical furnaces. As gelena nearly always contains some silver, the extraction of lead is generally accompanied by the reclamation of silver has a by-product. One of the principal properties of lead is its freedom from any effect due to the action of water and acids, and because of this it is used for water-pipes, roof covering, the sheathing of electric cables and for containers in chemical plants. It has a low melting point (330° C.), and when sheets have to be joined, they may be butted together and the metal fused (burned) with a blowpipe. Two large industrial users of lead are the electrical and paint industries. It is used for the plates of lead-acid electrical accumulators, and its oxides are used largely as the base for lead paint. When added in small quantities to steel and brass, lead improves their machining properties, and the reader may have heard of " Ledloy " steel and leaded brass in this connection.

Lead alloys with tin to form *solders*, and with other metals to make *bearing white metals*. These alloys will be discussed later.

Tin

Tin is obtained from tinstone, an oxide, which after a preliminary roasting in a reverberatory furnace to give a refined tin oxide is reduced to crude tin in a similar furnace. The crude tin is further refined to remove various impurities.

In appearance the metal has an almost silvery whiteness with a slightly yellowish tinge and its structure is crystalline. Tin is harder than lead and at ordinary temperatures may be beaten and rolled into tinfoil. It is ductile but not very strong. Tin melts at 232° C. but at 200° C. it is so brittle that it may be hammered into powder. A characteristic of this metal is the crinkling sound made when a bar of it is bent. This sound is called " tin cry " and is easily heard if a thin bar is held close to the ear and bent. It is caused by the crystalline deformation taking place, and is a useful method of judging the quality of solder, as solder rich in tin gives a louder " cry " than when not much tin is present.

The greatest use we have for tin in its ordinary state is for coating thin steel sheets (tinplate). It is also used for tinning copper wire before the latter is made into cables.

Alloys of Tin

Tin is used to a great extent for alloying with other metals and as a result, many useful alloys are obtained.

Tin-Lead Alloys. The tin-lead alloys constitute the soft solders, and those of chief interest to the reader are shown in the table below. In addition to tin and lead, a little antimony is recommended in some cases. A full list of the solders is given in B.S.S. No. 219.

TABLE 7.   SOFT SOLDERS

Purpose for which Solder is used.	Tin. %	Lead. %	Antimony. %	Melting Range. ° C.	Remarks.
Plumber's wiped joints	30	69	1	180–250	Prolonged pasty stage when melting or solidifying.
Tinsmith's general work and hand soldering	45	52·5	2·5	180–210	Solidifies fairly rapidly.
Tinsmith's and Coppersmith's fine work. Hand soldering	50	47·5	2.5		
Steel tube joints and work requiring low melting point	65	35	—	180	Solidifies quickly. No pasty stage.

The proportion of tin in a solder may be estimated by appearance, by judging the " tin cry " or by watching the time the solder remains in a pasty stage during solidification. Lead-rich solders have the dull bluish colour of that metal whilst those rich in tin show a white surface with a slight yellow tinge. Alloys with more than 25% of lead will mark paper. The long pasty stage associated with the solidifying of the lead-rich solders enables the plumber to make his " wiped " joint.

Bearing Metals. It has been found by experience that to give an efficient bearing combination the following conditions are necessary : (1) That the shaft and bearing be dissimilar in their natures with the bearing softer than the shaft. (2) That the most efficient bearing metal is one consisting of small pieces of a comparatively hard metal embedded in the softer body of another metal. In general, a metal consisting of one uniform constituent does not serve well as a bearing. The " white " metals all contain tin alloyed with various other metals,

Fig. 35. — Microstructure of Tin with 10% Antimony and 3% copper. Showing Hard Cubes × 80.

of which antimony is always present. A micrograph of an alloy containing tin with 10% antimony and 3% copper is shown at Fig. 35, and the hard cube-shaped copper-tin constituent set in the soft body of the general metal can be clearly seen. It is thought that in practice the soft constituent wears away slightly and the shaft is carried on these " high spots," the lower level of the remainder of the bearing helping to maintain the film of oil necessary for efficient lubrication. The white metals all have a low melting point which facilitates the formation of the bearing by casting the metal from a ladle. This can be done with the shaft in position if necessary.

The reader will notice from the table below that some of the metals are composed mainly of tin whilst in others lead is the predominant constituent. These are referred to as *tin base* and *lead base* metals respectively and those with a tin base are often called *Babbitt metals*.

TABLE 8. WHITE BEARING METALS.

Tin.	Antimony.	Copper.	Lead.	Uses.
93	$3\frac{1}{2}$	$3\frac{1}{2}$	—	Big end bearings, motor and aero engines.
86	$10\frac{1}{2}$	$3\frac{1}{2}$	—	Main bearings, motor and aero engines.
80	11	3	6	Bearings for heavy loads and high speeds.
60	10	$1\frac{1}{2}$	$28\frac{1}{2}$	Bearings for engines and electrical machines, railways and tramways.
40	10	$1\frac{1}{2}$	$48\frac{1}{2}$	Heavy pressure and medium speeds.
20	15	$1\frac{1}{2}$	$63\frac{1}{2}$	Medium pressure and speed.
5	15	—	80	Long bearings with medium load.

Copper—Tin Alloys—The Bronzes

When alloyed with tin, copper forms a set of alloys called bronzes, which are important metals in engineering practice. *Gunmetal* contains 88% copper, 10% tin and 2% zinc. The zinc is added to cleanse the metal and increase its fluidity. The metal is used chiefly for castings which must be strong and resistant to corrosion by water and the atmosphere. Gunmetal is not suitable for cold working but may be forged at about 600° C. (just below red heat). Another common bronze is made of 5% tin, 5% zinc, 5% lead and 85% copper.

Phosphor-bronze. When bronze contains phosphorus it is called phosphor-bronze. The main function of the phosphorus is to act as a cleanser to the metal so that good sound castings can be produced. The composition of this metal varies according to whether it is to be forged and wrought or whether made into castings. A common type of wrought phosphor-bronze is copper 93·7, tin 6, phosphorus 0·3. This may be obtained as rod, sheet and wire. When it is severely worked cold as in the drawing of wire or the rolling of strip, it becomes very hard and springy and is used for springs. Its tensile strength is then in the region of 33 tons per square inch as compared with about 20 tons in the soft condition.

A variety of phosphor-bronze suitable for casting contains 11% tin and 0·3% phosphorus alloyed with copper. This is used for bearings which must carry heavy loads, worm wheels, gears, nuts for machine lead screws and many other purposes. It may be obtained in the form of cast bar which, for making bearing bushes, may be bought as a hollow tube. This saves the waste of boring out a large part of the metal when turning bushes. Castings of all types may also be made in this metal.

The bronzes, although fairly hard, can be machined fairly easily with good tools, and the chips come off in short pieces. The fracture of the metal has an earthy appearance and is yellow, with a greyish or reddish tinge depending upon the amount of tin it contains, high tin promoting the greyish appearance. When quenched from a little below a red heat it is softened somewhat and made more ductile.

Zinc

The chief ores of zinc are blende (zinc sulphide) and calamine (zinc carbonate). In the extraction of the metal the ore is first roasted in a reverberatory furnace to convert the sulphide to oxide, and in the case of calamine, to drive off carbonic acid and water. The ore is then mixed with some form of carbon and put into long retorts in a special type of furnace. The heat distils off the zinc in the form of its greeny-white vapour and this is condensed to molten zinc.

Zinc is a bluish-white metal which if nearly pure shows large, bright smooth crystals at its fracture. If it is contaminated with iron, dull spots may be seen on the crystal faces, and if much iron is present the fracture becomes granular. The metal may be obtained in rolled sheets, and in cast ingots, the metal in these generally being fairly brittle. The specific gravity of zinc is about 7·1 and its melting-point temperature. If this steel is used for cutting tools where the cutting temperature is likely to be high, softening will occur and the tool will be useless. It has been found that by adding tungsten to steel it is given the property of holding its hardness at a red heat, hence the name " high speed." The hardening technique for high-speed steel differs from that of carbon tool steel. The temperature before cooling must be round about 1300° C.—a white-hot, almost melting heat. From this temperature the tool may be oil quenched or cooled off in a blast of cold air. Most high-speed steels have their hardness and general properties improved by re-heating to about 400–600° C. after quenching. This is called *secondary hardening*. Owing to the poor heat-conducting capacity of this steel, and the time necessary for the structural transformations to take place, the initial heating must be done carefully. The steel should be brought gradually to about 850° in one furnace, and then transferred quickly to another furnace which is at the quenching heat. The tool is ready for quenching when small bubbles can be seen on its white-hot edge.

Because of its tendency to oxidise and scale when at the hardening

TABLE 10. High-speed Steels

Carbon. %	Chromium. %	Tungsten. %	Vanadium. %	Cobalt. %	Hardening Temperature. ° C.	Method of Cooling.	Remarks.
0·6	4	14	—	—	1250	Oil	⎫ Secondary harden at 500–600° C.
0·6	4	18	1	—	1280	Oil or Air	
0·7	4·5	17	1·5	4	1280	Air	

temperature, methods which exclude air are preferable when heat-treating high-speed steel. Two methods commonly used are, (1) using a salt bath furnace, where the steel is heated by immersion in molten cyanide, and (2) using a *controlled atmosphere* furnace in which oxygen is excluded from the furnace interior by introducing another gas (e.g. incompletely burned coal gas). This latter principle is also used in bright annealing furnaces where a heat-treatment is necessary for bright bars and strip, but which must not blacken or scale the bright surface of the steel.

When properly hardened this steel will cut at high speeds when the tool nose is at a dull red heat. High-speed steel may be annealed by heating at 850° C. for about 4 hours and then slowly cooling in the furnace. During the whole of this time it must be protected from the air or it will oxidise and scale badly.

To cope with the difficulties of machining the modern heat-resistant steels and alloys, and other materials coming into use (e.g. titanium alloys) certain properties of high-speed steel have been improved by adding more cobalt and vanadium. The 10% cobalt alloy has 0·82% carbon, 20% tungsten, 5% chromium and 10% cobalt. This has a higher hot-hardness at the expense of some loss of toughness and is useful for heavy continuous-turning. The high vanadium cobalt alloy has 1·5% carbon, 12·5 tungsten, 4·5 chromium, 5 vanadium and 5 cobalt, and possesses maximum wear resistance and hot hardness. Tools and cotters made from this possess good resistance against the highly abrasive action of the metals mentioned above.

" Substitute " High-speed Steel. Within limits the tungsten in high-speed steel may be replaced by molybdenum without seriously affecting the properties of the steel. During the last war, when tungsten supplies were seriously curtailed, it became necessary for us to use such molybdenum steels which became known as " substitute " steels. Two of the chief of these were " substitute 66 " containing 6% each of molybdenum and tungsten and " substitute 94 " which had 9% of molybdenum and 4% tungsten.

Alloy Tool Steels

For many tools the most important property required is to be able to quench them for hardening without fear of cracking. It is useless, after much expense and labour have been put into the construction of a tool, for it to crack in hardening, and carbon tool steel is very prone to this. A good *non-shrinking steel* for such purposes has the following composition : carbon 1%, manganese 1%, tungsten 0·5%, chromium 0·75%. It is oil quenched from about 800° C. and tempered up to 250° C. to suit requirements. This steel is useful for making dies and thin tools which should not distort or crack when hardened.

Hot working die steels are steels suitable for punches and dies which have to shape other metal when it is in the red-hot condition. Such treatment would soften ordinary carbon steel. A steel suitable for this purpose contains carbon 0·27%, chromium 1%, vanadium 0·15%, manganese 0·2%. It is hardened by water quenching from 850° C. and tempered for about 2 hours at 230° C. Special steels for drop forging dies are given in B.S.S. 224.

An alloy steel for chisels contains carbon 0·4% and nickel 3%. It must be oil quenched from 900° C. and no tempering is necessary. This material gives an edge superior to that on carbon steel chisels.

Sintered Carbide Cutting Alloys

We have seen that the use of tungsten as an alloying element gives steel the property of retaining its hardness at high temperatures, and this is due to the formation of carbides of iron and carbon in the structure of the hardened steel. This property of the carbides led to investigations which, in 1926, resulted in the successful preparation of *tungsten carbide*, an extremely hard material able to cut metal at much higher speeds than high-speed steel. The extreme brittleness and high melting point (2500° C.) of this material prohibit ordinary methods for its preparation, and it is made by mixing tungsten metal powder and lampblack (carbon) and then heating the mixture to about 1600° C. in an atmosphere of hydrogen. This results in the chemical reaction necessary to produce the carbide which, after the process, is crushed and ground into a powder. Tool tips and other shapes for use as cutting edges are made from this powder by mixing it to a paste with powdered cobalt metal (3% to 20% cobalt) and water, and then compressing the paste to the shape required. This is then rendered hard and homogeneous by a sintering process consisting of heating to about 1500° C. for about an hour in a non-oxidising atmosphere such as hydrogen. The development of tungsten carbide was followed a few years later by titanium carbide which also possessed similar hardness, but which either alone or mixed with tungsten carbide has been found more suitable for cutting certain metals.

Because of their high cost, low strength and difficulties of preparation, carbide cutting tools are always made by brazing a tip or block of carbide to a shank of medium carbon steel. Owing to their extreme hardness the carbides cannot be ground with ordinary grinding wheels and special wheels are necessary. In addition, the cutting edge must be lapped to a very high finish so that the grinding process for a tool generally consists of three to five grindings on progressively finer wheels with a final burnishing on a special wheel impregnated with diamond dust.

Tungsten carbide is most suitable for machining the non-ductile materials such as cast-iron, brass, bronze, stone, glass, etc. For cutting steel and ductile metals mixtures of tungsten and titanium carbides are most suitable. Cutting speeds up to three or four times those possible with high-speed steel may be used with up to ten times the life of the tool between re-grinds. Hard spots, scale, etc., which would ruin an ordinary tool, have no effect on this material, and its application has revolutionised cutting practice, not only in the machine shop but in other industries (e.g. stone cutting) where previously no material existed which would stand up to the conditions imposed.

High Tensile Steels

For many purposes in engineering, high strength and toughness are necessary, and there are many alloy steels having these properties. Some of these steels when properly heat-treated will give strengths as high as 120 tons per square inch. These high strengths are usually obtained by suitable heating and cooling, followed by tempering.

The elements most commonly put into such steels are nickel and chromium and for this reason they are called *nickel-chrome steels*. The $1\frac{1}{2}\%$ steel of this class contains carbon 0.4%, nickel 1.5%, chromium 1.25%. It is oil quenched from $840°$ C. and tempered up to $600°$ C. according to requirements. When tempered at about $250°$ C. it has a strength of about 100 tons per square inch. A high tensile *air-hardening steel* has carbon 0.34%, nickel 4.25%, chromium 1.25%. Hardening is effected by air cooling from $830°$ C. and tempering is carried out at $200–220°$ C. This steel is used for gears and other intricate parts which must have high strength, and where cracking or distortion caused by quenching must be reduced to a minimum.

Use of the "Rare" Metals

Recent nuclear power developments have created a demand for materials to withstand the stringent conditions imposed, and as a result some metals, previously considered "rare," may come into common use. The student should know of them and follow up the limited details given below.

Titanium is a light metal, used in a range of alloys with aluminium, vanadium, manganese, iron, chromium and tin. Some of its alloys reach a tensile strength of 60/70 ton/sq. inch, are highly resistant to corrosion and retain a good strength at high temperatures. These alloys are extremely difficult to machine as the metal galls up and work-hardens under the tool.

Uranium is used as a nuclear fuel and is radioactive. It can be machined readily, but severe safety measures are needed against radiation. Copious coolant is necessary when machining to minimise swarf ignition and keep down the dust which is particularly hazardous.

Thorium, also radioactive, has machining properties similar to uranium.

Vanadium is also of nuclear interest, and the pure metal has only recently become available. Its oxide is toxic and precautions must be taken to avoid swarf ignition when machining. Although it picks up rather badly, it can be cut at low speeds with high speed steel tools.

Ceramic Materials

Ceramics is the general term applied to a range of materials, basically sintered oxides, of extreme hardness that have been developed as cutting agents. The most common of these is aluminium oxide and it is used in two forms : (a) in its pure state and (b) mixed with small amounts of other compounds (e.g. chromic oxide) to impart some special desired property. In the preparation of the tool tips alumina powder is ball-milled and mixed to a paste with water. The blanks are then pressed to shape afterwards undergoing a long high temperature sintering process followed by slow cooling. The resulting tip is harder and more wear resistant than tungsten carbide but is much weaker in tension. For this reason tools and machines must be extremely rigid and free from chatter to prevent the ceramic tip from disintegrating.

Because of its nature no satisfactory method has been found for brazing the tip on to its shank so that some form of mechanical clamping is necessary. One of these is shown at Fig. 121 (c). Ceramic tips are extremely wear resistant and will cut at speeds in the range of 500–1500 ft. per min. They can only be ground up with diamond wheels but because of their low cost they are often discarded and replaced when the available cutting points have been used up (the tool shown has 8 cutting points).

The Preparation of Metals

Generally, when the metal is delivered for use in the workshop it is in the form of bar, strip, sheet, wire or some other shape most convenient for the starting-point in the job of forming it. A few notes on how it reaches these forms will interest the reader and extend his knowledge of the properties of material when in its various forms.

Hot Rolling

All steel in the form of bar, strip or sheet, having a non-polished reddish-blue surface, has been hot rolled. The process starts with the steel ingot as soon as it has solidified sufficiently for the ingot mould to be stripped from it. This ingot will be about 5 ft. long, slightly tapering, and approximately square in cross-section, sizes varying from about 12 in. to 20 in. square. When taken from the ingot mould or soaking pit, it will be almost at a white heat. The first operation to the ingot is carried out at the blooming mill, where it is reduced to blooms. The action of rolling is shown at Fig. 37 (a), and a mill consists of at least two rolls mounted on their necks in bearings and driven through the couplings as shown in Fig. 37 (b). When there are only top and bottom rolls the mill is a " two-high " mill.

(a) Diagram of Rolling.

(b) Two-high Rolls and Stand.

FIG. 37.—Hot Rolling.

If three rolls are mounted so that rolling may be done between the top, or bottom roll, and the centre one, it is called a " three-high " mill, whilst the combination of a two-high mill with each roll backed up by another roll for strengthening purposes is called a " four-high " mill (Fig. 38).

(a) Three-high Rolls.   (b) Four-high Rolls.

Fig. 88.

The size of the mill is expressed as the centre distance of the rolls, blooming mills ranging from 28 in. to 46 in. Where mills are used for rolling plate, the length of the rolls also is specified. Two-high mills are made reversing so that the metal being reduced may be fed backwards and forwards, being supported and fed into the rolls by rollers driven by the mill mechanism (Fig. 40).

The main rolls of a mill, which may vary from 7 in. to 48 in.

Pass N⁰

Bar Rotated 90° between Successive Passes

(a) Stages in Rolling 1½ in. Bar from a 4 in. × 4 in. Billet in 10 Passes

(b) Pair of Rolls for Producing a 4 in. × 3 in. T Section

Finished Section

First Pass

FIG. 39.

diameter, and from 1 ft. to 17 ft. in length, are generally driven by steam engine or by electric motor. They are cast from iron or steel, the cast-iron rolls being chilled on their outside for increased hardness against the extreme wear and service conditions. The manufacture of these rolls is generally a separate industry from that of steel making, and their design, casting, turning and grinding forms a very specialised and skilled trade. Fig. 41 shows a roll being turned.

To return to the reduction of the ingot; this will be carried out

FIG. 40.—25-in. Two-high Reversing Mill (outgoing side) showing Bloom cogging on the right and Billet finishing on the left.

FIG. 41.--Turning a Roll (finished weight 20 tons).

in a specified number of passes through the rolls, depending upon the cross-section of the blooms being produced.

The blooms are cut up in lengths convenient for the subsequent reducing process into billets * and bars, being re-rolled either in a mil' somewhat similar to the blooming mill where the bar being reduced is passed backwards and forwards through progressively varied and reduced roll openings, or it may be reduced in a continuous mill. This consists of a series of 10 or 12 stands of rolls spaced at distances varying from 12 ft. to 6 ft. apart and made up of two-high rolls about 14-in. centres with the rolls 15 in. to 18 in. long. The speeds of the rolls are adjusted so that the metal may travel faster as its length is increased by the reduction, and arrangements are made to turn it through 90° occasionally to secure correct reduction in all directions. Fig. 39 (a) shows the successive stages in the reduction of a billet to a round bar, whilst at (b) are shown the rolls for a T-section.

Plates and Strip. When the final product of the rolling mill is to be sheets, plates or strip, the output of the blooming mill is usually composed of slabs instead of blooms. These are of a flatter form and lend themselves better to re-rolling into flat shapes. The procedure for rolling plates and strip follows the same general lines as for bars, the rolls generally being parallel instead of having forms turned in them.

Cold Rolling

For many purposes, particularly where steel strip has to be blanked and formed in presses it is made by a process of cold rolling. The objects of cold rolling are : (1) to secure improved surface finish, (2) to obtain smaller and more uniform thicknesses than is possible in hot rolling, (3) to give the metal improved physical properties by combining the cold work of rolling with suitable heat treatment. Cold rolled strip can be produced to very fine limits of accuracy in thickness dimension (to within 0·001 in.) and uniformity. By combining a shearing operation for the edges of the strip, widths may also be controlled to within a few thousandths of an inch.

The raw material for cold rolling is hot rolled strip from the hot rolling mill, and in its general principles the method is similar to hot rolling except that roll pressures are much greater because the resistance of the cold metal to reduction is much greater than when it is hot. This fact encourages the use of four-high mills for cold rolling, the two outer rolls being of large diameter and serving as backing-up supports for the smaller working rolls. The strip is usually wound in a coil which is supported on a spindle at one side of the rolls. After passing through the rolls the strip is wound up on to another power-driven roll whose speed is so controlled that the strip is kept taut as it emerges from the reducing rolls. Cold rolling may also be done in tandem (two mills in line), or continuous.

Before the hot rolled strip can be put through the cold mill all the scale must be removed from its surface by pickling in dilute acid. If this were not done the scale (oxide) would be rolled into the metal

* A bloom is 6 in. square or over, whilst a billet has dimensions between $1\frac{1}{4}$ in. and 6 in. square.

during the process. Another problem with which the cold roller has to deal is that of annealing the strip. We have seen that when metal is cold worked it becomes work hardened, and unless it has to be supplied in the work-hardened, springy condition, as copper, brass and bronze often have to be, then it must be annealed after the final pass, and also, if several reductions are necessary, it may, after one or two passes, be too hard for further reduction and must be annealed to enable further rolling to be done. Since the polished surface of the strip must not be tarnished or scaled during the annealing process, it is necessary to exclude all oxygen from the metal whilst it is heated, and for this reason the operation is called " close " annealing. If the strip is annealed in coils, these are packed in iron boxes along with cast-iron borings, and put into the furnace in this way. The boxes and borings protect the strip from the ingress of air, and any oxygen which is present combines with the carbon in the cast iron, thus preventing oxidation of the surface of the strip. More recent developments in the annealing of bright strip employ annealing furnaces inside which the atmosphere is kept free from oxygen by maintaining a slight pressure of another gas such as coal gas or hydrogen.

Cold Drawing

All the wire that is made is produced by cold drawing through dies. This method of production is also used for making bright drawn bars which are extensively used for producing parts on capstan, turret and automatic lathes. As in the case of cold rolling, the raw material for drawing is black rolled bar from the hot rolling mill. When required for drawing into wire this may be in coils of metal, the coils being 18 in. to 2 ft. diameter and the metal ¼ in. to ⅜ in. diameter.

FIG. 42.—Principle of Drawing.

For the production of larger sized bars the black bar will be a small amount larger ($\frac{1}{32}$ in. to $\frac{1}{8}$ in.) than the finished bars into which it has to be drawn.

The principle of drawing is shown at Fig. 42. The metal to be drawn is reduced at the end (tagged) to a diameter small enough to pass through the die and of sufficient length for it to be gripped by that portion of the drawbench which pulls it through. The hole in the die is generally conical, and the reduction in diameter is effected by the pressure of the sides of the cone on the rod. This pressure is set up by the drawing pull on the wire, and at the instant of reduction plastic flow takes place in the metal. In view of the enormous pressure between the die and the rod being drawn it is necessary to lubricate the area of contact. In bar drawing this is effected by smearing the bar with a solid lubricant in the form of a grease. This is not a convenient procedure in wire drawing as the wire is coiled in long lengths on drums, and is drawn through the die by being coiled on one drum and uncoiled from the other. Wire drawing is either effected by the " wet " or the " dry " process. In the dry process the wire, after pickling, may be washed in lime-water, which on drying off leaves a thin layer of lime on the metal which serves as a lubricant. Alternatively, the wire on its way to the die may be passed through a box

Worm drive reduction unit   Change gear-box   Motor   Wagon (spare wagon also shown)

Die pedestal

Flexible coupling   Endless chain
[*The Wellman, Smith Owen Engineering Corporation Ltd.*]
Fig. 43.—Drawbench.

filled with dried soap. In the wet process the wire is passed through a solution of copper sulphate followed by a soapy solution. The copper sulphate deposits a thin film of copper which, when combined with the soapy solution, facilitates the drawing of the metal.

Bars are drawn on a drawbench which is a long bed with an endless chain running along the surface and returning underneath. The die is supported against a bracket at one end and a small wagon which carries the gripping jaws for the bar runs along the bed, being provided with a hook (" dog ") which can be engaged in the chain. When the tagged end of the bar has been threaded through the die and gripped, the hook is lowered (" dogging in ") so that the chain catches it and thus draws the wagon to the other end of the bench (Fig. 43).

The dies for drawing may be made of hardened tool steel, tungsten carbide, diamond or chilled cast iron (for large bars). The primary object is to obtain a die which is intensely hard, and resistant to the extreme wear which takes place.

Cold drawn steel has a smooth, bright surface, and for this reason is called " bright drawn." As in the case of cold rolling, the drawing work hardens the metal, and for wire, which has to undergo many reductions to bring it down to size, it is necessary to anneal from time to time during the process. Larger bars are generally only reduced sufficiently to correct out of roundness from hot rolling, and bring up the surface to a good finish. This confers a certain amount of work hardening and for some purposes (e.g. shafting) annealing is not carried out and the hardness is left in the metal. The hardening strains, however, are often left in also, and sometimes when the outer surface of such metal is removed (e.g. by cutting a keyway), the strains will be relieved, causing the bar to warp. Bright bars and wire can be drawn to very close limits as regards size and roundness.

The Production of Castings

After bar and sheet, the next most common form in which material is received for working is in the form of castings. The casting of metal into the intricate shapes that are possible is an immense advantage in engineering construction, and the work of the foundry and pattern shop is of great importance. Castings may be made in steel, cast iron, brass, bronze, aluminium, as well as in numerous other alloys. A description of sand casting, which is the most common method employed, will now be given.

A casting is produced by pouring molten metal into a mould made to the shape of the part required. In die casting this mould is made of metal, whilst in sand casting it is made in sand, its form being obtained by means of a wooden pattern having a shape similar to the part required. The first step, therefore, in making a casting, is that of making the pattern, and the patternmaker may be counted as one of the most highly skilled craftsmen in the engineering industry. It is he who first has to interpret a drawing, however complicated, into the solid shape it represents. His experience decides upon the method to be used in the production of the casting, a factor upon which quality and success often depend. We will give a simple and obvious example. When metal is cast it contains gases which rise up through it, leaving at the highest point. The top surface of a casting therefore is liable to be rather spongy with blowholes left by entrapped gases unable to escape before the metal solidified. Now, if a round bar is cast on its side, the chances are that on one part of its circumference it may be a little spongy, whilst if it is cast vertically on its end, the sponginess will be at one end. If we extend this simple case to a complicated casting, we can see that the method of casting has some control over which portions of the casting will be sound and which may be spongy, and this method is under the control of the patternmaker by the manner in which he disposes the pattern. In our round bar, if the curved surface was important we should wish to have any likely blowholes in the end, and the pattern would be made for vertical casting. On the other hand, importance of the flat ends would make side casting preferable. Very often, castings can be so made that the spongy metal is in the portion of the casting which has to be machined, and it is removed by machining.

The wood mainly used for patterns is a well-seasoned soft wood such as yellow pine, and the pattern is made to conform with the outside shape of the casting. To allow for the contraction which takes place when the casting cools, the pattern must be a little larger than the finished casting. The amounts that different metals contract are as follows :

Metal.	Contraction per foot.
Cast iron	$\frac{1}{10}$ inch
Brass	$\frac{1}{5}$,,
Steel	$\frac{1}{4}$,,
Aluminium	$\frac{9}{32}$,,

This contraction is allowed for by the patternmaker employing a special rule called a *contraction rule* (Fig. 44, *a*) with which to set off all the dimensions on the pattern. Since for cast iron a length of 12 in. contracts $\frac{1}{10}$ in., and cools to 11·9 in., a length of 12·1 in. will cool approximately to 12 in. On a contraction rule for cast iron, therefore, a length of 12·1 in. is marked as 12 in. and is then divided up exactly similar to an ordinary rule, so that when a patternmaker measures off a length with this rule, he automatically makes the length longer in the ratio $\frac{12·1}{12}$ and so allows for contraction. For brass and other metals, the rule length is compensated in the same way according to their contraction.

The finished pattern will be smoothed up as much as possible to facilitate its withdrawal from the sand when moulding, and to impart a smooth surface to the casting. This effect is further increased by the shellac varnish with which the pattern is covered. When the casting is of a simple nature the appearance of the pattern is similar to that of the casting, but when the casting is more complicated with holes and cavities it becomes necessary to resort to coring in the mould. This will be best explained when we are discussing the actual moulding process.

Let us commence by following the moulding of a bracket of the form shown in Fig. 45 (*a*). The patternmaker will be supplied with a drawing of this as it should be when finished, and on the drawing will be indicated those faces of the bracket which have to be machined. He will make the pattern, leaving contraction allowance, and will leave $\frac{1}{8}$ in. to $\frac{3}{16}$ in. extra on the faces marked for machining. At the foundry the pattern will be used to prepare the mould in moulding boxes, which are steel frames without top or bottom, provided with lugs and holes for lining up when several are put together and with handles for lifting (Fig. 44, *b*). The pattern will be placed face downwards on a board and a moulding box-section laid over it. After a little smooth facing sand mixed with coal dust has been sprinkled on the pattern, the box will be filled with moulding sand and this will be well rammed down with a wooden rammer shaped like a dumbbell. When the sand has been rammed sufficiently to have made a good impression from the pattern, the top of the box is trimmed off level and it will be like Fig. 45 (*b*). The moulding box is now turned over, another section placed on top of it and rammed with sand as before. A hole is now formed through the sand in the top box for pouring the metal (called the " pouring gate ") and the two boxes are parted again. The pattern is now carefully withdrawn from the bottom box, its impression is touched up with smoothing tools if necessary and the sides dusted with fine plumbago to assist the facing sand in giving a good surface to the casting. Channels (called " runners ") are formed to lead the metal from the pouring gate to

[*J. C. Chesterman.*

(*a*) A Contraction Rule.

[*Sterling Foundry Specialities Ltd.*

(*b*) A Pair of Moulding Boxes.

Fig. 44.

the mould and the top box is replaced. The mould is now ready for pouring and is shown at Fig. 45 (*c*). The top box is called the " cope " and the bottom one the " drag."

When casting takes place metal is poured in until it rises to the top of the pouring gate and this, together with the runners, is cut off the casting during the process of cleaning it up. To facilitate the withdrawal of the pattern from the cope, its sides are slightly tapered in the direction of moulding, the amount of taper usually being about $\frac{1}{8}$ in. per foot of length. The moulder also loosens the pattern for withdrawal by " rapping " it. To do this he screws a steel rod into its top face, and taps the rod in all directions so that the mould impression is slightly enlarged. When the bottom box has been turned over, and before the sand is put in the top box, a layer of dry parting

(a) Component to be Cast

(b) Bottom Box Rammed Up

(c) Mould Ready for Pouring

FIG. 45.—Moulding a Bracket.

sand is added. This preserves the joint, and prevents the sand in the two boxes from congealing into a solid mass which would make it impossible to separate the boxes for the purpose of withdrawing the pattern.

Cores and Core Boxes

It will be appreciated that there is a limit to the moulding which could be done by the simple method we have just discussed. Take, for instance, the casting of a bush, say, 4 in. outside diameter with a 2-in. hole and 6 in. long. If this is moulded on its side the pattern cannot be withdrawn if sand is to be left to cast a hole in the finished bush, whilst if cast vertically the pillar of sand left to cast the hole would be too weak to withstand the inrush of metal when pouring. When castings of this nature have to be made, a *core*, made of hard, dried sand and moulded in a *core-box*, is inserted in the mould. We will illustrate this by discussing an example which includes coring, and follow the moulding of the component shown in Fig. 46 (*a*).

The inside of this and the hole in the bottom would be formed by coring and the pattern would be as shown at (*b*). It will be noticed that the pattern is not only solid where the inside faces of the component should be, but is also provided with projections corresponding with the edges of the metal. These projections are called *core-prints* and are for forming recesses in the mould to locate the core. The core for this is made in a separate box called the core-box, which is

made by the patternmaker, and is auxiliary to the pattern. The core-
box is often made in two halves to facilitate withdrawal of the moulded
core and the one for our example is shown at Fig. 46 (c). At the
foundry a core would be moulded in the core-box from special core
sand and then this core would be dried in an oven until it was hard.
The moulding of the pattern in the cope and drag would leave an

Fɪɢ. 46.—Example of Coring in Moulding.

impression having a shape similar to the outside of the casting together with the impressions of the core-prints. The core itself is made
with extremities which just fit these prints when the cope and drag
are assembled and when the pattern has been withdrawn the boxes
are put together with the core fitted in. This completes the preparation of the mould which will be as shown at (d). The core-prints serve
an important function in keeping the core in its proper position relative to the outside of the mould. If it were not located properly, or
moved during pouring, the sides of the casting would not be of uniform
thickness, and the hole not in its proper position.

Split Patterns. To facilitate the moulding of some components,
the pattern, instead of being made in one piece, is split into two or
more parts. These are dowelled so that they may be fitted together
accurately to the finished shape. Such an example is given by the
flanged pipe shown at Fig. 47 (a) and its moulding would be carried
out as follows :

(1) Ram up one half in bottom box (Fig. 47 (c)).
(2) Turn over, fit the other half and ram top box.
(3) Remove pattern and insert core.

(a) *Finished Casting*

Core
Prints

(b) *Pattern, Showing Halves*
Separated

(c) *Bottom Box Rammed Up*

Core

(d) *Mould Complete, Ready*
for Pouring

FIG. 47.—Moulding a Flanged Pipe.

The completed mould ready for pouring is shown at Fig. 47 (d).

Plate Moulding. When large quantities of fairly simple castings are required they are produced several at once by a process of plate moulding. The form of the part is divided into two halves and patterns (often in metal) are attached to each side of a board. One side

1″ dia.

1″ dia.

1½″

(a) *Component*

Runners on
Top Side only

(b) *Plate with 8 Patterns*

(c) *Mould Rammed Up, Ready*
for Removal of Plate

FIG. 48.—Plate Moulding.

The left margin contains fragments of text:
a la
Wh
fied
boss
trac
by t
men
man
and
a su
show
oute
certa
T
and
make
of ca
stres
mach
that
worn
" sea
allow
the p
small
castin
and li
in the

CHAPTER 4

WORKSHOP PROCESSES REQUIRING HEAT.—FORGING, RIVETING, SOLDERING AND BRAZING

The hot forging of metals is an important subsidiary process to workshop production and possesses many advantages. We have seen how the hot working of metal is beneficial to its granular structure and how, if it is properly carried out, it may confer a strengthening effect owing to the directional property of the grains. In addition to these aspects, the use of forgings may save a great deal of time and expense, because instead of cutting the metal from the solid to give the shape required, it may often be forged to a shape very near to the finished one. This economises in machining time, and avoids an undue proportion of the metal being cut into swarf.

We may roughly divide forging into the processes of hand forging, machine forging and drop forging, the two latter processes being of types adaptable for large quantity production of similar articles.

Hand Forging

In hand forging the shaping of the metal is carried out under hand control, and accuracy depends upon the skill of the smith. For large work, some form of power-operated hammer or press must be used. We will deal with the smaller class of work first, and it will be advisable at the outset to consider the essential forging equipment, together with details of certain fundamental forming operations.

The Forge. For heating the metal some form of forge or furnace is necessary. For small work the blacksmith's forge is commonly used and consists of a hearth for holding combustible coke, a tuyère

(a)

(b)

[*Alldays & Onions Ltd.*

FIG. 50.—Smith's Hearth.

for leading forced air into the fire, a blower for supplying air under a slight pressure to the tuyère and a chimney for carrying away smoke and gases. Usually a " bosh " (tank) is also provided for holding water for quenching purposes. Because of the high temperature under which the tuyère operates, this is often surrounded by cooling water contained in a tank fixed at the rear of the forge.

The most substantial and satisfactory forges are brick built, incorporating a flue and chimney, but many in use are of the portable type and if these are well constructed they give satisfactory results. Fig. 50 shows the front and rear views of a cast-iron double smith's hearth where all the details mentioned above may be seen, together with the electric motor for driving the blast fan, and the blast regulating valves. To meet the requirements of the Clean Air Bill it is now customary to incorporate a grit arrester in the chimney of the forge. This is not shown in Fig. 50. The best fuel for forge fires is coke " breeze," which is gas coke crushed into small pieces about $\frac{1}{2}$ in. diameter. Small soft coal may be used but it should not contain sulphur, and when burnt should adhere into a mass and not fall to pieces. The temperature of the fire is governed by the amount of blast supplied and may be varied up to a white heat.

Forging Tools

The *anvil* (Fig. 51) is for supporting the work whilst it is being struck with the hammer, as well as providing means for other forging operations. The body of the anvil is of mild steel and, to give a hard top face, a piece of high carbon steel about $\frac{3}{4}$ in. to 1 in. thick is welded on. The beak is soft like the anvil body and its shape makes it useful for bending metal to rounded formations. The ledge between the beak

[*John Hall (Tools), Ltd.*
Fig. 51.—Anvil.

and the anvil face is also soft and may be used for resting metal when cutting through with a chisel ; the soft underneath metal does not damage the chisel edge. In the top of the anvil is a square hole to take the shank of various tools to be described later. Anvils vary up to about 3 cwt. and should stand with the top face about 2 ft. from the floor. This height may be attained by resting the anvil on a cast-iron or wood base.

Two kinds of hammer are used in hand forging :
(1) the *hand hammer* used by the smith himself ; and
(2) the *sledge hammer* used by the *striker*, the smith's assistant.

FIG. 59.—Blacksmith's Tongs.

the grip will not be secure. Hollow tongs for round work are shown at (b) and tongs for square bars at (c). In these three types there should, of course, be a variety of sizes suitable for dealing with the range of work to be undertaken. The tongs shown at (d) are for picking up round bars, but not for holding work during forging. To relieve the smith of the strain of holding the tongs during a long forging operation, means are often provided for clamping the tongs together, and one method is to drive a loop over the handles as shown.

Forging Operations

The formation of a shape by forging consists of a combination of two or more of a number of relatively simple operations which are as follows :

Upsetting (Fig. 60). This consists of increasing the thickness of a bar at the expense of its length and is brought about by end pressure. The pressure may be obtained by driving the end of the bar against the anvil, by supporting on the anvil and hitting with the hammer, by placing in swage block hole and hitting with hammer or by clamp-

FIG. 60.—Upsetting.

ing in a vise and hammering. The position and nature of the upsetting will depend on the heating, and upon the type of blow delivered. In general, the increase in lateral swelling will be greatest at the parts where the metal is hottest (most plastic), so that for upsetting the end of a bar only that end should be heated. If a short bar is heated uniformly over its whole length, heavy blows will cause a fairly uniform degree of swelling, but light blows will have a more local effect at the ends only.

Drawing Down is the process of increasing the length of a bar at the expense of its width or thickness or both (Fig. 61). A good method of drawing down square or rectangular bars is to use the edge or beak

(a) On Edge of Anvil   (b) On Beak of Anvil   (c) Between Fullers

FIG. 61.—Drawing Down.

of the anvil as shown, turning the bar through 90° if the thickness in both directions is to be reduced. When assisted by a striker, a pair of fullers may be used as shown. When the preliminary drawing has been done in this way the work may be finished off with the flatter.

When round bars have to be drawn down a considerable amount they should first be brought down to a square, drawn by the above method and then squared up again. The square is then taken to an octagon by taking off the corners and finally rounded and finished between swages. When reducing the thickness of metal care should be taken not to drive it outwards from the centre too rapidly or internal cracks will occur which will remain as permanent weaknesses in the metal.

Setting Down is a local thinning down effected by the set-hammer or set. Usually the work is fullered at the place where the setting down commences (Fig. 62).

Bending. Bending is an important operation in forging and is one very frequently used. Bends may be either sharp-cornered angle bends or they may be composed of a more gradual curve. Angle bends

Flatter

FIG. 62.—Setting Down.

may be made by hammering the metal over the edge of the anvil, over a block of metal held in the hardie hole or in a vise, or over a vise jaw itself, whilst the metal is being gripped (Fig. 63 (*a*)). When metal is bent the layers of metal on the inside are shortened and those

(a) Work Held in Vise

(b) Effect of Bending

Outside metal stretched

Centre layer unaffected

Inside of bend compressed and bulged sideways

(c) True Square Bend

(d) Metal Worked up to fill in Corner of Bend

Fig. 63.—Bending (Sharp Bends).

on the outside are stretched. This causes a bulging of the sides at the inside, and a radius on the outside of the bend as shown at (*b*). If a true square bend is required as shown at (*c*), additional metal must be worked to the place where the bend occurs as shown at (*d*). When this is bent the additional metal will go to make up the corner. If this is not done it may be possible to work up the square corner by blows

Taper Wedge for Clamping

Locknut

Stop Screw for Controlling Depth of Bend

Work

Fig. 64.—Simple Bending Fixture.

from a light hammer, working metal into the bend from nearby portions of the work. Whenever possible, a sharp corner on the inside of a bend should be avoided as it constitutes a weakness which may lead to a fracture of the corner. When double bends have to be made a simple bending fixture will often save time and enable more uniform results to be obtained. Such a fixture is shown at Fig. 64 and its operation is self-explanatory from the diagram.

Gradual bends may be made by using the beak of the anvil as a former as shown at Fig. 65 (*a*), or the metal may be bent round a bar

(*a*) Over Beak of Anvil   (*b*) Over Bar in Vise

FIG. 65.—Circular Bending.

of the correct radius held in a vise as at (*b*). When a quantity of bending has to be done, the use of some type of bending fixture will save time and produce better and uniform bends. At Fig. 66 the handle carrying the roller is swung round, causing the metal to be bent round the centre disc. Varying sizes of bends may be obtained by fitting different centre pieces and rollers to suit. For more complicated bending operations, bending tools of various types are used, one of such being shown at Fig. 67.

FIG. 66.—Bending Fixture.

Length of Material and Location of Bend.—We have mentioned that when a bend is made, the material on the outside is stretched and that on the inside compressed. At some intermediate layer there will be neither extension nor compression, and to find the length of material taken up by the bend we must find the length of this layer. For flat and round sections this neutral layer is at the centre,* so that

* For other sections see the treatment in the author's *Senior Workshop Calculations.*

[*Chas. Taylor Ltd. (Kennedy Products*).

FIG. 67.—Bending Fixture.

if we find the bent length of the *centre line* for such bars it will give us the length of material in the bend, and by adding the lengths of any adjoining straight portions we may obtain the total length of material required. Thus in Fig. 68 (a) the total length of material is 2 in. + $1\frac{1}{2}$ in. + (curved length AB) = $2 + 1\frac{1}{2} + (\frac{1}{4}$ of $\frac{5}{8}$-in. rad. circle) = $2 + 1\frac{1}{2} + (\frac{1}{4} \times 2\pi \times \frac{5}{8}) = 2 + 1\frac{1}{2} + \frac{5}{16}\pi = 4\frac{1}{2}$ in. approx.

FIG. 68.—Location of Bend.

The other point which deserves some attention is that of making the bend to come in the correct place, with 2 in. of straight at one end, and $1\frac{1}{2}$ in. at the other. This may be achieved by bending the bar over a shaped former held in the vise, and locating its position relative to the radius on the former. Thus in Fig. 68 (b) the bend must start at line CD and finish at EF. If line CD is set level with the commencement of the bend as shown at Fig. 68 (c), a line at GH will be level

with the top of the bending former if GH is distant from CD by the
inside radius.   Hence mark a line where the bend must commence,
and strike another line at a distance from it equal to the inside radius
of the bend.   Set this second line level with the top edge of the former
and then bend the bar over the former.

Punching and Drifting. As well as being used for its obvious
purpose of producing holes, punching may often be employed as a
shaping process.   When performed without a die, punching should be
carried out in two stages.   In the first operation the metal is held flat
on the anvil and the hole punched approximately half through.   The
work is then turned over and the hole completed by supporting the
bar as shown at Fig. 58 (c) (page 79).   If the hole is pierced right through
from one side a bulge is thrown upon the underside as shown at Fig. 69 (a).

FIG. 69.—Punching.

If a die is used having a hole with just clearance for the punch, the hole
may be pierced in one operation and the arrangement is shown at
Fig. 69 (b).   The taper in the die hole is to allow the punching to fall
through and a top plate may be added as shown, to align the punch
with the hole in the die.   After a hole has been punched it may be
opened out to any other size or shape by driving through it a
tapered drift, the large end shaped to the shape required for the
finished hole.

The application of punching as a preliminary for other shaping
processes is shown at Fig. 69 (c) and (d).   At (c) the slot in the lever
is first punched in a number of places as shown, after which it is cut
out with a hot chisel.   It may be finished by drifting or it may be filed
when cold.   For the component shown at (d) the hole may be punched
and then drifted out square, followed by cutting out the opening to form
the jaws.

Hand Welding

Wrought iron and mild steel may be welded by pressing together two surfaces of the metal after they have been raised to the correct welding heat. The welding heat for iron is at a temperature of about 1350° C., when the metal is white hot, and in a condition bordering on to the pasty stage. For mild steel the temperature should be a little lower than this, the best point being when its colour is yellow, and before merging to white. It is important that the temperature is correct ; if it is too low no amount of pressure or hammering will cause the weld to take place, whilst a temperature too high will ruin the metal by burning it. The second essential for a good weld is that the surfaces to be welded are perfectly clean. When iron or steel at a high temperature is exposed to the air it oxidises and becomes covered with a film of scale (oxide), and if this, or dirt and ashes from the fire, is allowed to remain on the surfaces to be welded, the result will be a failure. To counteract this a flux must be used which melts at a high temperature and dissolves the scale and ash to form a liquid slag, at the same time acting as a protective covering against any further oxidising action by the air. For wrought iron, sand is a suitable flux, whilst calcined borax serves the same purpose for mild steel. When the two parts of the joint have been fluxed and welding commences, the operation must be so controlled that the action commences at the centre and the joining of the metals proceeds outwards. By this means the slag and impurities are expelled outwards from the two surfaces and a clean, efficient weld is produced. If welding starts from the outside and spreads inwards the slag will be enclosed within the metal. In the case of wrought iron, the natural slag in the metal is influential in helping to flux a weld and form a liquid slag with the impurities.

Types of Joint. The three principal types of weld are : (1) the butt weld, (2) the scarf weld, and (3) the vee or splice. These are shown at Fig. 70 (*a*), (*b*) and (*c*). The *butt weld* is difficult to make by hammering because of the difficulty of bringing force to bear in the direction of the contacting faces, but it may be employed when facilities are available for pressing the faces together. This is made possible by employing a welding machine in which the bars are gripped, and their ends forced together by hand or power operation. Whilst they are so held, the sides of the weld may be smoothed up by hammering.

The *scarf weld* is the most straightforward one to carry out, and when preparing the ends of the pieces for welding they should not be flat, but should be rounded as shown at Fig. 70 (*d*). This ensures that the union of the metals commences at the centre and travels outwards, expelling the slag to the outside of the bar. If the ends were flat, or hollow, there would be the risk of slag being left in as explained above. When the ends have been prepared they must be raised to the welding heat in the fire and then sprinkled with a little flux to take up the scale and ash. They must then be pressed together and hammered, and the first few blows of the hammer should expel the slag, after which attention may be directed to the completion of the weld and its smoothing up.

(a) Butt Weld   (b) Scarf Weld   (c) Vee or Splice

(d) Ends Prepared
for Scarf Weld

(e) Preparation for
Splice Weld

Finished Weld

(f) Application of Splice Weld

FIG. 70.—Blacksmith's Welds.

The *vee weld* results in a very strong job and should be used where the thickness of the metal permits of preparing the vee. The scarfed end of the bar should be roughened as shown in Fig. 70 (*e*) and when hammered, the ends of the vee'd portion should be hammered over the shoulders of the upset end of the scarfed bar. This type of weld should be employed, if possible, when a bar must be welded to another bar as shown at (*f*).

Examples of Forging.

We have discussed in detail the forging operations because most jobs are produced by a combination of these processes. We will now consider the production of one or two typically shaped parts, and, as far as possible, convey the information by means of sketches. It must always be borne in mind, however, that forging is a skilled trade and cannot be learned from books. We can only indicate the lines on which the work should be done and leave its execution to patient practice on the part of the student.

EXAMPLE 1. *Upsetting a Head on a Bar* (Fig. 71).
(1) Heat one end of bar for a length sufficient to make the head.
(2) Jump up heated end on anvil.
(3) Flatten head by hammering against the end of a bush through which the shank will pass.
(4) Swage to size.
(5) Finish flatten.

EXAMPLE 2. *Small Lever with Boss* (Fig. 72).
Use material with section large enough to make the boss.
(1) Fuller on flat sides.
(2) Draw out lever leaving sufficient for final flatting.

FIG. 71.—Upsetting a Head on a Bar.

(3) Roughly flat faces of lever.

(4) With hot chisel take off corners of boss ; cut taper sides of lever and rough-shape end.

(5) Swage semi-circular ends of boss and handle.

(6) Finish flatting sides and edges of lever.

FIG. 72.—Operations in Forging a Lever.

(7) Punch hole in boss.
(8) Drift hole out square.
(9) Smooth up all over.

EXAMPLE 3. *Small Die Stocks* (Fig. 73).
Use material with section large enough to make the boss.
(1) Fuller on edges to just above thickness of handles.
(2) Draw down handles approximately to square.
(3) Trim boss roughly with hot chisel.

FIG. 73.—Forging a Small Set of Die Stocks.

(4) Flatten corners of handles, making them roughly octagonal in cross-section.
(5) Swage boss.
(6) Swage handles.
(7) Flatten boss faces and smooth up.
After forging, the handles would be turned smooth in a lathe, and the boss bored to suit the die.

Power Hammers

When forgings are large, and considerable volumes of metal have to be moved about, the work becomes too big for a sledge-hammer and has to be done by some form of power hammer. For very many years, considerable thought has been given to the introduction of mechanical hammers, so as to dispense with the need of a blacksmith's striker, and one of the first mechanical hammers was the " Oliver," a foot-operated contraption which gave an effect similar to a sledge wielded by a striker. The Oliver hammer is now almost extinct, but there are still a few working on special nut and bolt forging jobs in the Black Country, and Fig. 74 is a sketch of one of them. Following the principle of this hammer, various power-operated types have been developed and these are useful for lighter and more specialised classes of work.

FIG. 74.—The Oliver Hammer.

To meet the more general need for a heavier power operated hammer the upright type is now the most popular. This class of tool may employ a crank and spring, or steam pressure or pneumatic pressure as the means of delivering the blow. The last two types are the most common, and in their general layout they are similar, consisting of an anvil block for supporting the work, a tup (hammer) which strikes the work and which is connected to the piston by means of a piston-rod, the frame, and the mechanism for the control of the fluid pressure on the piston. The tup and anvil are faced with carbon steel palletts which may be changed for any special shaped tools that may be required. The size of one of these hammers is classed according to the weight of the tup, piston-rod and piston; a 5-cwt. hammer having the weight of these upper moving parts totalling 5 cwt. The anvil should be about 8 times the weight of the moving parts and on the larger hammers this unit is generally set upon a foundation separate from the main frame of the hammer. The foundation is important and should consist of thick wooden blocks set on a deep slab of concrete. For example, the foundation recommended for a 5-cwt. hammer is timber $10\frac{1}{2}$ in. thick set on concrete 4 ft. thick.

[B. & S. Massey Ltd.

FIG. 75.—Massey 5-cwt. Pneumatic Hammer (" Clear Space " Type).

The Pneumatic Hammer. A diagram of a Massey 5-cwt. pneumatic hammer is shown at Fig. 75, and in section at Fig. 76. Air is compressed on both upward and downward strokes of the piston on the right, and the method of feeding this air to the ram cylinder is controlled by the long valve between the cylinders, the valve being moved by the control lever.

FIG. 76.—Sectional View of 5-cwt. Hammer.

When the lever is in the " neutral " position as shown, the spaces above and below the pump piston are open to the atmosphere, so that the pump reciprocates idly and the ram piston rests at the bottom of its stroke with the top pallett resting on the anvil. Depressing the lever lifts the valve from its neutral position, closes the openings to atmosphere, and connects the spaces above and below the pump piston with corresponding spaces above and below the hammer piston until eventually, with the valve in its highest position for " full work," the hammer piston lifts as the pump piston descends, and vice versa (full stroke automatic blows). If the control lever is raised to its full extent from the neutral position the valve is lowered, the upper part of the hammer cylinder is opened to atmosphere and the lower part connected to the air reservoir. This lifts the ram to the top of its stroke and holds it there (hold up). Raising the lever just a little above the neutral position reverses this condition and holds the hammer down (hold down). Single blows may be obtained by moving the lever from the " hold up " to the " hold down " positions, the force of the blow depending upon the speed and extent of the movement.

On the Massey " Clear Space " hammers the strokes vary from 14 in. on the 2-cwt. to 42 in. on the 40-cwt. size, and the speed from 200 to 85 blows per minute for the same range of hammer sizes.

Tools for Power Hammers. The working of metal under a power hammer follows the same general principles as for hand forging, remembering of course that more and heavier blows are possible, and that the blow is delivered with greater precision. The tools used with a hammer

[B. & S. Massey, Ltd.

FIG. 77.—Smithy Tools (Power Hammer).

A, Spring swages; B and C, Top and bottom swages; D, Ring for dropping over anvil pallet for holding swages; E, Spring necking tools; F, Round necking tool; G, Vee tool; H, Flatting tool; J, Hot cutter; K, Cold cutter.

are different from those employed in hand forging and a selection of these are shown at Fig. 77. By making simple bending and forming blocks, the power hammer may be used efficiently for the production of large numbers of similar forgings.

Drop Forging

Hand forging is a useful and indispensable process, but it is not suitable for the production of large numbers of identical forgings such as are necessary in mass methods of manufacture. For one reason, it would be too slow and costly to use hand methods of production, and also the forgings would not be uniform enough in size to enable the subsequent machining operations to be performed by mass production methods. When large quantities of a certain shaped component have to be made, and the mechanical properties required are such that a casting would not be suitable, drop forging is a very common method of making the part. Drop forgings can be produced from nearly all qualities of steel, from some aluminium alloys and from certain brasses and bronzes. The hot working that is given to the metal makes for

[*B. & S. Massey, Ltd.*

FIG. 78.—4-ton Friction Drop Stamp.

soundness and high quality in its structure, so that drop forged parts are used in all cases where strength and reliability are the prime considerations.

Drop forgings are made by squeezing the metal at forging heat into shaped impressions cut in heavy steel blocks called dies. Generally half the impression is cut in one die and the remainder in the other, so that when the faces of the dies meet with metal squeezed into the cavities, a complete stamping has been formed. The method used for squeezing the metal is to allow one die to fall from a height of 10 to 20 ft. on to the other, with the metal in between, and it is from this that the name " drop " forging is derived. The dies for drop forging are made from large blocks of steel, the quality used being a medium carbon steel or one of the alloy die steels (B.S.S. Spec. No. 224), and the size of the drop stamp is expressed as the weight of the top die block (the tup). In practice, stamp sizes vary from 1 cwt. to 24 tons. A drop stamp consists of the bottom die, held by set screws on to the base, the top die carried on the tup, together with the mechanism for raising the tup and allowing it to fall. For raising the tup two methods are in general use : the English pattern, which makes use of a belt passing over a pulley, and the American type, in which a board, attached to the

[*B. & S. Massey, Ltd.*

FIG. 79.—Mechanism for raising the Tup of a Friction Drop Stamp.

tup, is raised when it is held between two rollers rotating in opposite directions. A general diagram of a belt lift drop stamp is shown at Fig. 78, and details of the method of raising the tup at Fig. 79. The friction drum (A) is keyed to, and rotates with, the shaft. The friction band (B), which is steel, lined with a friction material such as Ferodo, encircles the drum and can be caused to grip the drum by a cam operated from the cord D, attached to the cam lever E. The lifter arm (G), which carries the end of the belt, is attached to ends of the friction band and also to the guide pulley (H). When the cord is pulled, the grip between the friction band and the drum causes the arm, together with the guide pulley, to rotate, and thus winds the belt on to the guide pulley, raising the tup. The tup may be held at any position by operating the cord, and an attachment is often provided whereby it may be positively held at the top. Control is exercised on the speed of drop by manipulation of the cord. If it is released entirely, all the friction is taken off and the tup falls freely, but if the cord is only partially released, some friction still remains and the tup falls more slowly. Drop stamps are often erected in batteries of several in a row with one motor supplying the power for them all. A pair of dies for forging a component will have approximately half the shape of the component formed in each one, and the process of cutting these impressions is called *die-sinking*. Die-sinking is a very skilled trade and requires not only the skill and patience to do accurate work but also a thorough knowledge of all classes of bench and machine tool technique. In planning and making the dies for a particular forging the following conditions have to be looked after:

(1) *The size of the Forging and the Material of which it is to be made.*

This will determine what size of stamp must be used to produce it.

(2) *The Direction in which it may be Forged.*

For some articles, e.g. a flat disc, this is obvious, but for others a choice is possible (e.g. the component Fig. 80 (*a*) could be drop forged with the dies meeting on line **XX**, or on **YY**).

Fig. 80.—Drop Stamping a Lever.

The considerations which chiefly decide this point are (i) the relative efficiency with which the metal will flow to the alternative die impressions, and (ii) where taper may or may not be tolerated on the finished component. This is shown at Fig. 80 (*b*) and (*c*), where the taper that would be on the component sides is drawn rather exaggerated for illustration, and it can be seen that if, for example, the boss of the lever were required with flat faces, then it would have to be stamped on **YY**.

(3) *The pre-forming of the Raw Material for the Forging.*

Sometimes the bar or blank may be introduced between the dies without any previous shaping, but in many cases some preliminary forming is necessary if the die impressions are to be everywhere filled up. This would be necessary for Fig. 80 (*a*), and it can easily be imagined what would be the result if a parallel bar were stamped between the dies made for this component. Pre-forming may be carried out in impressions on the actual dies or it may be done separately under a power hammer.

(4) *The Number of Stampings to be Produced and the Life of the Dies.*

The life of a pair of dies is a variable factor depending upon the form of the impression, the importance of the forging, the material of the die and the material being forged. If large numbers of stampings

Stamping with Fin
before Trimming

Flash left
from Fin

Finished Stamping
after Trimming

Fig. 81.—Drop Forging a Fork End.

have to be made, long die life is aimed at and expense need not be spared on the material and finish of the dies. For small orders cost should be kept low and life is not so important. As a rough idea it may be taken that a pair of medium carbon steel dies stamping an average mild steel component will give a life of 20,000 to 30,000 stampings.

When the foregoing points have been settled satisfactorily, a special drawing of the stamping is usually made, being somewhat similar to the finished drawing of the component but having allowances made for machining and contraction, as well as taper shown on it. From this drawing the die-sinker will cut the impressions in the die blocks, using hand- or machine-tool methods as may be necessary. When finished, the impressions must be polished, as the forging will receive a good or bad outer finish according to the finish put on the dies. On the face of the die blocks and round the profile of the impressions are now cut shallow grooves or depressions. These are to allow a fin to be formed on the stamping round the line where the dies meet. The reason for this is that it is impossible to judge the exact volume of metal to fill the die impressions when the dies meet, and a little extra is allowed which is squeezed out into a fin or flash when the impressions have filled up. This flash is afterwards trimmed off by pressing the stamping whilst still hot through a sharp die having an opening the same profile as the finished stamping.

In the process of drop forging the metal to be forged, which may be in the form of bar, blanks or pre-shaped pieces, is heated in oil, gas or coal fired furnaces. (In the case of forging direct from bar, the end is heated for a sufficient length to make the forging.) The stamper controls the process, having one assistant to manipulate the controls of the drop stamp, and others if necessary to help in handling the work. The dies, having previously been set with a dummy stamping so that the two half impressions are an exact match, are now ready for their work, and according to the experience of the stamper the top die is raised and allowed to fall until the forging is completed. The stamping is finished off by trimming off the flash on a press, and if possible this should be done whilst the forging is still hot.

In Fig. 81 is shown a component, together with the dies for stamping it, and a sketch of the forging before and after finish trimming.

The Joining of Metals

Riveting

When plates have to be fastened together to form a permanent joint, riveting is a satisfactory method of making the joint and is extensively used on boilerwork, shipbuilding and structural construction. Rivets are classified according to the shape of their head, and Fig. 82 shows the usual types together with the general size proportions. The round (snap) head is the most commonly used, but if the projecting head is an inconvenience, the countersunk type enables flush head conditions to be attained but does not give such an efficient joint. Steel rivets put in and riveted up hot give the best results, but for light work, copper, brass or aluminium rivets may be used cold. For very light work, hollow and bifurcated rivets may be obtained, but these cannot be expected to give a joint as satisfactory as a solid rivet.

A good guide for the rivet size to use is to make $d = 1\frac{1}{4}t$, where d = rivet diameter, and t = thickness of plates being joined. For thin plates this will give a rivet too small and must be used with discretion. For riveting up the end of a snap head rivet a length equal to $1\frac{1}{2}d$ should be allowed, whilst d should be allowed on the length of a countersunk rivet.

Riveted joints to plates may be made either by lapping over the edges of the plates and fastening with one or two rows of rivets (lap joint), or the edges of the plates may be butted together and then completed by holding them together with one or two cover straps and riveting (butt joint). Examples of these joints are shown at Fig. 83.

When preparing the plates for the joint they should, if possible, be clamped together with the top plate marked out for the holes. The holes may then be drilled in all the plates at once and there will be no doubt about all the holes being in alignment for insertion of the rivets. If one plate already has holes, it may be clamped in position and the holes marked through for drilling in the other plate, or the holes used as a guide for the drill itself. The holes should be slightly larger than the rivet, an allowance of about $\frac{1}{16}d$ being about suitable (e.g. for a $\frac{1}{2}$-in. rivet; allowance $= \frac{1}{16} \times \frac{1}{2} = \frac{1}{32}$ in. clearance). In some classes of work rivet holes are put in the plate by punching with a punch and die. When this is carried out on the cold plate the edges of the holes are severely cold worked and the work hardening may be severe enough to start small cracks round the edges of the holes. This defect may be removed to a large extent by punching the holes a little smaller than their finished size and opening them out to size with a 3 or 4 flute drill. This removes the hardened metal and any small cracks that may have started in it.

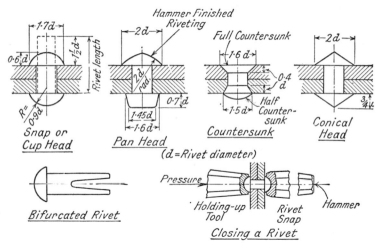

Fig. 82.—Rivets.

For countersunk rivets the holes in the plates must be chamfered on their outer edges until they are the same diameter as the rivet head, the angle of the chamfer being the same as that under the rivet head (see Fig. 82). This chamfering is called countersinking, and is usually done with a special fluted cutter.

When the plates are ready for riveting they should be clamped together and located with the respective rivet-holes in alignment. If hot riveting is being carried out the rivet should be at a forging heat, and the operation should be completed before it cools too much. For snap head rivets a punch, or tool (snap), having a half-spherical cavity similar to the rivet-head must support the head, whilst the plain end of the rivet is riveted over by a similar punch held to the rivet end and struck with a hammer (Fig. 82). If the work is small enough to be handled it may be rested on the supporting snap whilst the riveting is completed, otherwise an assistant (a " holder up ") must hold the supporting snap whilst the head of the rivet is closed. The aim in riveting should be to swell the body of the rivet by the hammering until it completely fills the hole and to complete the process whilst the rivet is as hot as possible. This avoids any risk of cold working (and brittleness) of the rivet, and as the rivet cools it contracts, drawing the plates tighter together. Care should be exercised to ensure that the rivet end is spread evenly in all directions, and not bent over one way. This is often helped by giving the rivet end a few preliminary blows with the

Double Riveted Lap Joint

Lap Joint with Single Row of Rivets

Double Riveted Butt Joint with Cover Plates each side

Butt Joint with Single Cover Plate. Single Riveted

Lap Joint in a Flat Bar or Strip

Butt Joint in a Flat Strip

Fig. 83.—Riveted Joints.

ball end of the hammer. Countersunk rivets may be held up with a flat-ended punch, and when only a few have to be dealt with the ball end of the hammer may be used for the initial spreading, followed by finishing blows with the flat end.

For cold riveting the closing of the rivet follows the same lines as when the rivet is hot, except that the metal is not as plastic, and more difficulty will be met in swelling it to fill the hole, also if the plates are not tightly together after riveting there will be no cooling contraction to pull them to.

When a considerable number of rivets have to be put in it is advisable not to start at one place and fill the holes in order from that place but to rivet the extremities first. For example, rivet holes in a line should have the end ones filled first, then the centre, after which the order does not matter much. If the formation is square, fill opposite corners first, then the other corners, followed by the remainder. By working this way the embarrassing effects of the plates creeping are eliminated. In the same way, if the rivet holes have to be drilled, the operation is facilitated by drilling and riveting two extreme holes first, afterwards drilling the remainder with the plates fastened together.

For structural work, boilermaking, etc., where large numbers of rivets have to be dealt with, there are various types of machines for closing rivets. The pneumatic riveter—probably known to readers by the noise it makes—closes the end of the rivet by a quick succession of blows. Other forms of machine such as the hydraulic riveter squeeze the rivet by hydraulic pressure.

Soldering

Soft Soldering

Soldering is a quick and useful method of making joints in light articles made from steel, copper and brass, and for wire joints such as occur in electrical work. It should not be used where much strength is required, or in cases where the joint will be subjected to vibration or heat, as solder is comparatively weak and has a low melting point. When joints must stand these treatments they should be riveted, welded or brazed.

When conditions are made suitable for molten solder to wet the surface of the metals being soldered, a thin layer of an alloy of the tin in the solder is formed with the metals, and this union, with the solder in between, causes a joint between the two metals. The conditions are shown in Fig. 84, which illustrates the joint between two copper

FIG. 84.—To Illustrate a Soldered Joint × 300 approx.

surfaces, the layer of metal where the solder joins the copper being an alloy of copper and tin. Now in order that this union shall take place, intimate union between the metal and the solder must be made possible by rendering them scrupulously clean. If molten solder is placed on the surface of an uncleaned metal it will not wet the surface, but will remain in a globular state. This is because the dirt and oxide film prevent the intimate union necessary for the solder to spread over and wet the surface to form the union required. For successful soldering then, the principal requirement is cleanliness, but however careful we may be in cleaning the surfaces to be joined, we should still be unable to make a joint because immediately a polished metallic surface is warmed a thin film of oxide spreads over it and this would prevent the solder from running.

Fluxes. To assist in maintaining the necessary cleanliness, a flux must be used to protect the cleaned surfaces from fumes and atmospheric action whilst the process is taking place. Fluxes are of two kinds : (1) those which not only protect the surface, but play an active chemical part in cleaning it, and (2) those which merely protect a previously cleaned surface. The first class of fluxes are the most efficient, the chief being zinc chloride (" killed spirits "), ammonium chloride, and zinc ammonium chloride, a combination of the two. In the " protective " group of fluxes (under (2) above) there are tallow, resin, vaseline, olive oil, etc., and in addition to these there are various patent fluxes of which " Fluxite " is a well-known example.

Killed spirits gives the best all-round results. It is prepared by adding zinc to hydrochloric acid until the acid will dissolve no more and some undissolved metal is left in the acid, the action taking some hours to complete. The main disadvantage to this flux is its corrosive after-effects, and joints made with it should be well washed with, or dipped in, a weak solution of an alkali such as ammonia to neutralise the acid.

For light, continuous work such as the soldering of electric connexions, the problem of fluxing is greatly facilitated by using one of the strip solders with the flux incorporated. One such solder is resin cored, being in the form of a small thin tube having a core of resin which melts and fluxes the work as the solder is consumed.

Making the Joint. A soldered joint may be made by heating and fluxing the parts to be joined and adding the solder, by dipping the previously fluxed parts into a bath of molten solder or by the use of a soldering iron. For the general run of work the use of a soldering iron is the most common, and irons are made of copper. This metal is used (1) because it is a very good conductor of heat and rapidly transmits heat from itself to the metal of the joint, and (2) it readily alloys with tin and this facilitates the operation of coating the end of the iron with a layer of solder, known as " tinning " the iron. A good way of heating an iron is by placing it inside an iron or steel box, open at the ends and bottom, and heated inside by the flames from a rectangular gas heater (Fig. 85). Electric and gas heated irons may also be obtained and are preferred by some people. Sketches of straight and hatchet-shaped irons are shown at Fig. 85, the hatchet type being useful where working with the straight iron is likely to be awkward.

The first operation is to " tin " the iron and this is done by heating it to a good temperature but less than a red heat, quickly cleaning its end with a file or emery cloth, dipping it in flux, and rubbing solder on it. If the temperature and other conditions are right, the iron will take on a thin film of solder, and if it is held against the stick of solder, a certain amount in the form of a globule will adhere to it (suitable solders have been discussed on page 51). The work must now be cleaned, fluxed

(a)Straight Type

(b)Hatchet Type

(c)Heater

Fig. 85.—Soldering Irons and Heater.

and tinned. With a file or emery cloth thoroughly clean the surfaces to be joined and cover them with a film of flux. Take the iron in one hand and a brush or spill containing flux in the other. Slowly stroke the surface with the tinned iron and if necessary with more flux until a thin film of solder spreads over the surface. When both surfaces have been tinned, place them together after adding a little flux, and slowly move the iron over them endeavouring to melt and fuse together the tinning on the surfaces, at the same time adding a little solder from the iron if this is necessary. The object should be to use the least amount of solder possible and to make the heat of the iron do the job after previous tinning rather than to feed a large amount of extra solder.

A good joint is characterised by a small amount of solder and perfect adhesion, rather than by large unsightly masses of solder, and the reader should practise making joints and pulling them apart, until he is satisfied with what he is doing. From tests made on joints it has been established that the best joints are those in which the thickness of solder varies between 0·003 and 0·006 in. Experimental work has also shown that the thinner the layer of solder, the higher is the soldering temperature necessary for maximum strength. Thus for a solder made up of 56% tin to 44% lead it was found that for maximum strength the relationship between joint thickness and soldering temperature was approximately as follows :

Joint Thickness.	Soldering Temperature.
0·001 in.	400° C.
0·004 in.	270° C.
0·007 in.	230° C.
0·010 in.	220° C.

The ideal then, in soldering, should be to start with a pair of perfectly clean and fluxed members, so that the solder will flow in under capillary action without much aid from the iron. The following additional hints are given in the hope that they may be useful.

(a) Always use an iron as large as can be handled and err in the direction of having it too hot rather than not hot enough (it should not, of course, be red hot).

(b) A better joint can be made if the work is warm rather than cold.

(c) Iron tinning is facilitated by having some blobs of solder in a tin lid with a little spirits, and touching both the spirits and the solder at the same time.

(d) Quenching the hot joint in spirits, or painting on spirits whilst hot, will often effect remarkably thorough cleaning.

Brazing

At its best, solder is only a soft metal with a strength of about 3 tons per square inch, so that where much strength is required an alternative form of joint must be used. This alternative is provided in brazing, where the joining metal employed is brass, a harder, stronger and more rigid metal than solder. As in the case of soft soldering, an alloy of the brazing metal and the metal of the joint is formed at the surface of the joint metal.

The brass used for making the joint in brazing is generally called " spelter " and its composition depends upon the metal being brazed because it is essential that the spelter shall have a lower melting point than the material being joined. The following table gives particulars of brazing spelters.

TABLE 11. BRAZING SPELTERS.

Metal being joined.	Melting Point.	Brazing Spelter.		Melting Point.
		Copper.	Zinc.	
Steel	1530° C.	65	35	915° C.
Copper	1080° C.	60	40	900° C.

Spelter may be obtained in the form of sticks, or in a granular state when it may be mixed with the flux before being applied to the joint. If it is used in this form the granules should not be too fine or they may fuse and oxidise away instead of melting into the joint. When buying spelter it is advisable to specify the material for which it is to be used, and, for the same reason, if brazing a delicate job with unknown spelter a test should be made to ascertain that the spelter will melt and run well before the work is too near its point of fusion.

Borax is practically the only flux used for brazing. It dissolves oxides which form on the surface of the work and when a red heat is attained the borax vitrifies and forms a film over the metal which prevents any further atmospheric action. When granular spelter is used the powdered borax may be mixed with the spelter, but if the spelter is in stick form the flux is best applied as a paste.

FIG. 86.—Blowpipe.

The heat for brazing is obtained by a blowpipe fed with coal gas, and air at a slight pressure. The air supply may be obtained by tapping off from the blower used for the blacksmith's hearth, from a compressor and pressure tank or, for a small installation, from foot bellows. The mixing of the air and gas is arranged for in the blowpipe, which may have separate air and gas regulating valves, or the gas only may have a valve. A diagram of a brazing blowpipe is shown at Fig. 86. When the heating of the work is taking place it is advisable to make the most of the heat given out from the blowpipe flame, and for this reason a small sheet-metal hearth containing firebrick or coke should be used. If the work is placed upon such a substance heat is reflected back on its underside and this conserves the heat during the operation. A brazing hearth, with motor-driven rotary blower, is shown at Fig. 87.

[Alldays & Onions, Ltd.

FIG. 87.—Brazing Hearth.

The rule of cleanliness applies with equal force to brazing as to soldering, and before commencing any brazing, the work should be clean and polished at all points where brazing is to occur. Where one part fits over another the fit should be neither too tight nor too loose, but just sufficient to allow a film of molten spelter to find its way between the surfaces. In cases where one tube has to be brazed on to another, if conditions will allow, an additional security is given by drilling, and driving one or more steel pegs through the two tubes before brazing. Having prepared the surfaces for brazing, they should be given a coat of borax paste, placed on the hearth, and raised to a red heat as quickly as possible. Care must be exercised when brass or copper parts are being brazed in order that they shall not be fused. When the correct temperature is reached a mixture of borax and spelter is applied to the joint and the spelter will melt and permeate the surfaces, forming a hard brazed junction. The work should be allowed to cool off normally, as quenching may lead to distortion of the joint or cracking of the spelter. When the borax is cold it becomes hard and glassy and difficult to remove without some chemical assistance. Pickling in weak acid or a hot solution of alum may be used for this, or salt may be sprinkled on after the spelter has set but whilst the joint is still hot.

Silver Soldering

This is a hard soldering process which may be classified in between soft soldering and brazing. The recommended range of silver solders is given in B.S.S. No. 1845, two common ones being as follows :

Type 4 . Silver 60–62%. Copper 27·5–29·5%. Zinc 9–11%.
Melting range 690°–735° C.
Type 5 . Silver 42–44%. Copper 36–38%. Zinc 18·5–20·5%.
Melting range 700°–775° C.

It will be seen that the melting point of this solder is considerably lower than that of spelter, so that it may safely be used for joining brass and copper. The process is carried out with a blowpipe in the same way as brazing, borax being used as a flux. Silver solder is usually supplied in thin strip so that some form of holder is necessary to feed it to the joint when the required temperature has been reached. The satisfactory execution of a joint by silver soldering is helped by pickling the joint in dilute sulphuric acid before starting.

CHAPTER 5

POWER, SAFETY AND CARE IN THE WORKSHOP

Before discussing the various workshop processes and operations we will note a few items which are of general interest to all who are connected with the shop.

Industrial Safety

Every day a large number of accidents occur in the factories of this country. These sometimes result in death, sometimes in permanent disablement and in many cases, fortunately, in nothing worse than a few days' or weeks' absence from work. Even if an accident does not render the victim unfit for work it makes him liable to infection, or any other of the ills which may be contracted as the result of injury and shock. On an average 3 people are killed and 750 injured *every day* in industrial accidents. The Government takes a very lively interest in these accidents, and, through the Factory Inspectors, exerts every means in its power to keep them as low as possible. Statistics gathered of the accidents show, in general, that of every three accidents which occur, two are caused by the personal element of the victim, and one by means beyond his control. To put it briefly, we may say that two out of three are the victim's own fault, and the third was his employer's fault for not making safe working conditions. We will discuss, first, accidents which are the worker's own fault and which might have been prevented by his own precautions.

Machines. Power-driven machines are always a fruitful source of accidents, however well the moving parts may be protected. An operator who is careful at first may gradually, through familiarity, take risks he ought not to take, and ultimately he will meet with a misfortune which he will call " bad luck." Confidence is a necessary part of our characters and without it we should be of little use in a machine shop. Over-confidence, however, is to be guarded against at all costs.

The first thing the operator of a machine should find out is the quickest way to stop the machine, and he should practise this until it can be performed instantly, and without thinking. If we are involved in an awkward situation on a power-driven machine, a fraction of a second may mean the difference between a humorous and a serious result. The rotating bolt on the driving plate of a lathe is a danger-spot, and if filing *must* be done on work between centres it is safer to file left-handed. (When the writer was learning his turning he was not permitted to have a file.) Rotating work, whether between centres or held in the chuck, is generally rather rough after a cut has been taken over it, the roughness often being sufficient to pick up rag, or waste held to it. If the waste alone is taken round no harm is done, but if the hand holding the waste cannot be disentangled in time the result is likely to be serious.

On many machine operations the work must be clamped to the

table of the machine. If the clamping has been carelessly done the work may move when the force of the cut comes on it. In drilling, particularly, we may imagine that a hole can be drilled with the work only lightly supported, or even held from rotating by the left hand, but sooner or later we shall regret it. Also the waste metal (swarf) which is removed by the cutting tool on machines should not be handled. Turnings particularly are sharp and ragged, being capable of inflicting deep and painful cuts. A good plan is to keep handy a metal hook or rake with which to handle these.

Driving Belts. Many machines are still driven by belts from overhead shafting. When these belts have to be moved from one pulley to another for the purpose of changing the speed of the machine, the belt should not be touched by hand when it is moving, but should be manipulated by a bar of metal or a spanner. In addition to the risk of the hand being entrapped between the belt and the pulley, there is the danger of a projecting part of the steel belt lacing catching the hand and tearing the flesh. The guarding of dangerous belts is the concern of the management of the works and is generally well looked after according to the advice of the Factory Inspector.

Loose and flapping clothing may at any time become entangled in a belt or moving part which is not adequately covered, and for this reason overalls without loose ends are to be recommended. If a pair of combination overalls is worn and the ends of the sleeves buttoned up fairly tightly, the risk of accidents through loose clothing is greatly minimised.

Non-mechanical Accidents

The presence of machines or moving belts is not the only cause of serious accidents. Badly fitting spanners may slip with disastrous results to the knuckles, and it should always be ascertained that a spanner fits well before putting the full load on to it. A loose file haft may result in the spike at the end of the file being driven into the hand if the haft slips off on the drawstroke of the file. Metal or tools struck with a hammer without sufficient regard to their support against the blow may cause the striker to wish he had been more observant.

The reader should cultivate the " safety-first " habit and then, if misfortune does come his way, he can truly say it was bad luck, but if he takes simple and elementary precautions it is unlikely that anything very serious will happen.

Accidents of all types are rendered more probable by overtime and tiredness, the speeding up of production beyond the economic rate, bad lighting, cold working conditions, etc., and especial care should be exercised under any such conditions.

Mechanical Accidents

Let us now examine some of the causes of accidents which are a result of dangerous working conditions, e.g. unguarded machinery, etc., and against which it is the responsibility of the management to provide safeguards. The Factory Acts administered by the Home Office through the Factory Inspectors contain elaborate and far-reaching provisions for the prevention of accidents, and in the limited space at our disposal we can only indicate the bare outline of these accidents. The reader's experiences may be concerned with rotating shafts, belts and pulleys, power presses, milling machines and lifting tackle. All these, as well as many other classes of machinery, are subjected to careful scrutiny by the Factory Inspector. That portion of the Act relating to the fencing of machinery states that " every part of the transmission machinery, and every dangerous part of any other machinery, must be securely fenced unless it is in such a position, or of such construction, as to be as safe to every person, as it would be if securely fenced " (i.e. if a shaft is high up in the air it is " in such a position as to be safe "). This part of the Act alone puts considerable burden and expense on the Management, in fulfilling its requirements.

However smooth a shaft may be there is always the risk of loose clothing being caught and wound up, and if there are rotating projections

[*By permission of H.M.S.O.*

FIG. 88.—Gate-type Guard for Power Press.

such as bolt or key heads the dangers are very much greater. If such shafts are in such a position as to be touched by clothing they must be guarded. Belting which may break and fall on persons underneath, open belt drives which may catch the clothing of passers-by, and any moving parts which are deemed to be dangerous, must be provided with some type of guard. The reader, if he uses his observation in the workshop, will see many such guards and he should take an intelligent interest in them, so that when his turn comes to manage a workshop, he will have the safety of his subordinates at heart.

Power presses and milling machines generally receive the attention of the Factory Inspector because they are considered as especially dangerous machines. When work must be put under a press by hand, it is not possible to fit a permanent guard, so that various safety devices have been devised which close as the press ram descends. These guards are so designed that in closing they would sweep the hands away if they were in danger. One example of such a guard is shown at Fig. 88, the functioning of which will be obvious. The vertical bar at the right-hand end of the gate is a rubber-cased spring to soften the blow should the gate strike the operator's hand.

The danger-point on a milling machine is the cutter, and Fig. 89 shows an example of a guard for keeping the hands away from this.

In connexion with cranes and lifting tackle the Act lays down that the equipment must be marked with its safe working load, that it must be examined within specified periods, that it must be tested and certified before purchase, and that the chains must be periodically annealed (see notes on work and strain hardening).

Besides the actual provision of guards, safety is promoted in various other ways, of which the following are examples :

(1) Foot actuated presses are operated by a clutch which trips out when the foot is removed from the pedal. If an accident were imminent, the operator would instinctively remove his foot from the pedal and so stop the machine.

(2) Very large presses operated by two attendants can only be set in motion by pressing two switch-buttons, one for each man. To reach his button each man must move well away from the danger-point.

[*Brayshaw Furnaces and Tools, Ltd.*]

FIG. 89.—Guard for Milling Cutters.

(3) The provision of inter-locked devices whereby the machine cannot be started until the guard is in position, or until the machine is safe, helps to reduce accidents. An example of this occurs in connexion with laundry machinery, where a horizontal revolving washing cylinder might be started when the operator has the cover off, and his arms inside the cylinder. To obviate this risk the cylinder cannot be run until the cover is in position. A similar device is incorporated in electrical switchboxes in which the front of the box cannot be opened until the switch is in the off position.

Electrical Accidents

One main difference between an electric shock and any other form of accident is that whilst some warning is given of ordinary accidents, the electric shock gives no warning—it just knocks you out. Electrical apparatus should always be treated with the utmost respect and never tampered with. If the wires seem frayed or loose, do not tamper with them but report the matter immediately. Apparatus should not be lifted or pulled about by the wires as the connexions are not made strong enough for such treatment. Electrical apparatus should not be used whilst the user is standing on damp or stone floors unless it has the special 3-core cable with earthing wire ; in fact it is now essential that all apparatus should be fitted with this arrangement.

All electrical apparatus should be fitted with an isolating switch in order that it may be completely switched off from the mains independently of the usual starting switch. If the appliance is plugged in with a loose length of wire, then this switch is located at the plug socket and it should be switched off before inserting the plug, and after withdrawing it. Remember always, that electricity is not a thing to be played with; its effects are sudden, extremely painful and sometimes fatal.

Power in the Workshop

The processes of cutting and forming metal generally require some power assistance so that the application of power to workshop processes is important. Energy is required in various forms by machine tools, e.g. reciprocating motion to a planer table, longitudinal feed to a lathe carriage, rotational motion to a drill, etc., but it is nearly always supplied to the machine in the form of rotational energy at the pulley. One of the functions of the machine is to convert the input of rotational energy into the various forms necessary for doing the work required. As supplied to most of our workshops, energy is in the form of electricity, and this is converted to rotational energy suitable for transmitting to the machines by means of an electric motor. Machines may be driven by either of two methods :

(1) Each machine may have its own electric motor which drives through belt, chain, gearing, or by direct coupling. This is usually termed *individual or self-contained* drive.

(2) The machines may be arranged in

[*H. W. Ward & Co., Ltd.*

FIG. 90.—Individual Drive adapted to a Capstan Lathe.

groups, each machine being driven from a *countershaft*, the countershafts being driven from the *mainshaft*.

Very often the mainshaft is set down the centre of the shop and belt drives are taken off to the machine countershafts which are arranged

Fig. 91.—Driving by Mainshaft and Countershaft.

on either side. Sometimes, when a machine is driven by a single pulley, and the stop and start arrangements are contained in the machine itself, the countershaft is dispensed with and the machine driven direct from a pulley on the mainshaft.

The mainshaft is driven from the electric motor by belt or chain,

(a) Fast and Loose Pulleys.   (b) Pulley with Clutch.

Fig. 92.

the motor being placed either on the floor (belt drive) or slung above (belt or chain drive). The use of shafting in workshops is rapidly declining since most of the machine tools now being installed are provided with individual motor drive.

Diagrams showing individual and countershaft drives are shown at Figs. 90 and 91. For disconnecting the drive and stopping the countershaft and machine, fast and loose pulleys, or a clutch, may be used (Fig. 92 (*a*) and (*b*)).

Machine Speeds

In order that they may be able to deal with a reasonable range of work sizes, it is necessary for most machines to have a range of speeds varying according to the work, and the type of machine. With a few exceptions electric motors run at a fixed, constant speed, so that speed-changing arrangements must be made, either on the machine itself, or somewhere between the mainshaft and the machine. Machines which are individually driven, and those driven by belt to a single pulley,

FIG. 93.—Cone Drive with Back Gear (Sectioned to show Details).

have the speed-changing arrangements incorporated in the machine itself—generally by means of gears. Those driven from a countershaft often obtain their speed range by making use of a *cone pulley* and a *back gear*.

A diagram of a 3-step cone pulley drive with back gear is shown at Fig. 93. The cone pulley is driven from a similar pulley on the counter-shaft, which is driven at constant speed by the mainshaft. By moving the belt on to each of the steps of the cone three speeds may be obtained. The other three speeds are obtained by the back gear as follows : Gear A is permanently fixed to and revolves with the cone pulley and gear B is keyed to the spindle. Gears C and D, which form one solid unit, rotate freely on the back shaft and may be moved into or out of mesh with A and B. If the locking plunger E is withdrawn, the cone pulley is disengaged from gear B, and is free on the spindle, otherwise the pulley is attached to B, and hence to the spindle. To obtain the first three speeds (i.e. without the back gear), E is engaged and the cone pulley drives the spindle via the gear B. The three back gear speeds are obtained by withdrawing E, and moving the back shaft so that gears C and D mesh with A and B respectively. Then the drive to the spindle is transmitted from A to C and D to B, the spindle running slower than the pulley because of the reduction effect of the gears. Many cone drives have a 4-step cone; we have sketched one with 3 steps for the sake of simplicity.

The All-gear Drive

An all-gear lathe head giving eight speeds is shown at Fig. 94. Gear A is solid with the pulley shaft, but this is free of the shaft to the right unless coupled, by sliding B to engage with A through a dog clutch. B, C and D are keyed to and slide on this shaft. E, K, G and J are keyed to the intermediate shaft, but L and M are free to

V-belt driven pulley (1170 R.P.M.) E(42T) A(21T) Change-speed lever L(24T) G(22T) C(21T) D(31T) Change-speed lever

N   F(53T)   M(46T) B(43T)   P   K(46T) H(73T) Main spindle   J(36T)

[*The Colchester Lathe Co., Ltd.*]

Fig. 94.—All-gear Head.

rotate on it as a unit. F and H are free on the main spindle, but either may be locked to it with the sliding clutch unit P. (The ribs on P are really rack teeth engaging with a gear underneath to effect the movement by a handle at the front of the head—see Fig. 227.) F and H are in constant mesh with E and G respectively. N is a gear for obtaining the reverse drive for the screw-cutting and feed motion. The eight speeds are obtained as follows (lowest upwards):

G driving H : (1) A to M, L to B, C to K ; (2) A to M, L to B, D to J ;
     (3) A locked to B, C to K ; (4) A locked to B, D to J.
E driving F : (1) A to M, L to B, C to K ; (2) A to M, L to B, D to J ;
     (3) A locked to B, C to K ;
     (4) A locked to B, D to J.

As an exercise the reader might calculate the speeds from the pulley speed and gear sizes given on the diagram. On this head starting and reversing are arranged by electrical switching of the motor, and a brake is incorporated in the pulley for quickly bringing the spindle to rest.

The all-gear head, either motorised or shaft driven, has now almost completely superseded the cone drive, which, in a few years, will probably be of historic interest only.

Amongst the advantages of the gear drive are :

(1) Easier and more efficient operation of machine, no belt changing, etc.

(2) The elimination of cumbersome and unsightly shafts and belts, giving more attractive surroundings and greater safety.

(3) Machines are more independent and when motorised may be set down in any position where an electric supply is available. If only one or a few machines are required it is not necessary to drive the whole shafting.

(4) Driving pulley runs at a constant speed giving a constant power input. On the cone drive the belt speed (and power input) is lower on the large cone steps.

Belt Driving

Since belt driving is so common, it is worthy of some attention. The drive from one pulley to another is caused by the frictional resistance between the belt and the pulleys. In practice a little belt slip takes place and there is a small amount of belt creep. In Fig. 95, if

Open Drive

Fig. 95.—Open-Belt Driving.

two pulleys of diameters d and D are connected, and if d makes N
R.P.M., then if we neglect slip and creep :

πd inches of belt pass over the small pulley per turn

or πdN inches per minute.

This length will also pass over the large pulley.

Hence, speed of large pulley $= \dfrac{\pi dN}{\text{Circum. of D}} = \dfrac{\pi dN}{\pi D} = \dfrac{N.d}{D}$;

i.e. pulley speeds are proportional to their diameters, with small pulleys
rotating faster than larger ones in the same drive.

EXAMPLE 1. *The drive to a machine is as follows : A 16-in. pulley on
the mainshaft drives a 12-in. countershaft pulley. From the countershaft
a 12-in. pulley drives a 9-in. pulley on the machine. If the mainshaft speed
is 250 R.P.M., estimate the speed of the machine (a) without belt slip, (b) with
5% slip.*

FIG. 96.—Drive for Ex. 1.

The drive is shown diagrammatically at Fig. 96, where A, B, C and D
are the pulleys, A and C being the drivers.

Then with no slip :

Speed of B (and C) $= 250 \times \dfrac{16}{12} = 333$ R.P.M.

Speed of D $= 333 \times \dfrac{12}{9} = 444$ R.P.M. Ansr. (*a*).

If there is 5% slip :

Speed of B and C $= 333 \times \dfrac{95}{100}$

$= 316$ R.P.M.

Speed of D $= 316 \times \dfrac{12}{9} \times \dfrac{95}{100}$

$= 400$ R.P.M. Ansr. (*b*).

EXAMPLE 2. *A machine with a 9-in. pulley is driven from a 12-in.
countershaft pulley. The countershaft pulley which takes the drive from the*

mainshaft is 15 *in. If the mainshaft speed is* 250 *R.P.M., what size of pulley must be fitted to drive the countershaft if the machine speed is to be* 320 *R.P.M. ?*

For 320 R.P.M. machine speed, the countershaft speed must be :

$$320 \times \frac{9}{12} = 240 \text{ R.P.M.}$$

We must now find the size of pulley running at 250 R.P.M. which will drive a 15-in. pulley at 240 R.P.M., and consideration tells us that it will be smaller than 15 in.

Hence mainshaft pulley diameter $= 15 \times \dfrac{240}{250} = 14\cdot4$ in. Ansr.

Types of Belt Drive

Being flexible, a belt may be twisted in more than one plane and this renders the belt drive suitable for connecting shafts which are not parallel. Sometimes guiding pulleys are necessary to direct the belt, but these present no disadvantages and may be used to adjust the

(a) Crossed Belt Drive

(b) Quarter Twist Drive

Jockey Pulleys

(c) Right Angle Drive as applied to a Drilling Machine

FIG. 97.—Belt Drives.

belt tension. Examples of common drives additional to the open drive are shown at Fig. 97 (*a*), (*b*) and (*c*). At (*a*) is the crossed drive used between parallel shafts to reverse the rotation, (*b*) and (*c*) are for drives where the shafts are not parallel. When shafts are parallel the pulleys must be lined up by a straightedge placed across their sides. Angular drives (as at (*b*)) must have the pulleys so disposed that the belt runs *on* to each in a line with the centre plane of the pulley at right angles to the shaft. The belt may run *off* at any angle but will remain on the pulleys if led on straight. When jockey pulleys have to be used as at (*c*), they should be as large as the smaller pulley of the drive, well balanced and rigidly held, but adjustable in position. Jockey pulleys have no effect on the speed ratio of the drive, which depends only on the sizes of the driving and driven pulleys.

General Notes on Belting and Drives

The most common types of belting are:

(1) *Leather* belts made from the " butt " of the hide. These are generally of single thickness but two or more may be cemented or sewn together. Single belts average from $\frac{7}{32}$ to $\frac{1}{4}$ in. in thickness and double ones from $\frac{11}{32}$ to $\frac{3}{8}$ in. The average breaking strength *per inch of width* for single leather belting is : solid leather 900 lb. ; at riveted joint 600 lb. ; at laced joint 350 lb.

(2) *Cotton and canvas* belts are woven and folded longitudinally to form the plies which are stuck together with cement or rubber solution. These belts are made in various thicknesses up to about 10 ply on the largest widths. When they have to pass through belt shifting forks the wear on the belt edges tends to cause the plies to come apart. The strength of this belting is about the same as leather.

(3) *Rubber* belts are useful out of doors and in damp places. This belting, in common with the cotton and canvas varieties, is not reliable

Fig. 98.—Jockey Pulley to increase Arc of Contact.

in the presence of oil and grease, as these cause the plies to come apart. The fastenings for woven belts require more care than those for leather, since the canvas is easily torn.

Leather belts should be kept supple, and free from cracks by applying some form of dressing. Tallow is good for this, or, alternatively, one of the patent dressings sold for the purpose. On no account should greasy dressing be applied to woven belting. If belt slip becomes troublesome there are many compositions on the market for increasing the friction between belt and pulley. A cheaper and better known remedy is powdered resin.

The centre distance between the pulleys should not be less than 3 times the larger pulley diameter, and the ratio of pulley diameter should not exceed six to one. If conditions are such that these ratios must be exceeded, a jockey pulley should be fitted to increase the arc of contact on the smaller pulley (Fig. 98).

Horizontal drives give the best results, and if the belt is open the driving side should be underneath. This brings the slack, sagging side of the belt uppermost and increases the efficiency because the belt is in contact with the pulleys over a longer arc. For this reason a crossed belt drive is superior to an open one, but wear is caused by the belt sides rubbing together.

Power transmitted by a Belt

When a belt is stretched over a pair of pulleys and the arrangement is stationary, the tension is the same in all portions of the belt. If one pulley is now rotated so that it drives the other and overcomes resistance, the tensions in the two sides of the belt re-adjust themselves to the requirements of the drive, more tension being in the driving (tight) side, and less in the free (slack) side. It will be appreciated that unless the driving side of the belt is more heavily loaded than its free run there is no difference of tension to drive the pulley, and it is this difference in tensions which is available to turn the driven pulley. The amount of this difference will depend, of course, upon how much resistance there is at the driven pulley; if this pulley is only lightly loaded the tension difference is small, but if it is very difficult to turn, the difference may be so great, and the tight side tension so high, that the belt will either slip, or break.

For average belting it is found that when the belt is driving normally without slip it can safely be loaded to a tension difference of about 50 lb. per inch of width. Knowing this and the belt speed, we may obtain an expression for the greatest horse-power that any given belt can transmit. For example, if the effective driving tension is 50 lb. per inch of width, then the total driving tension $= 50 \times w$ lb. ($w =$ width of belt), and if V ft. per min. is the belt speed :

$$\text{Work done per min.} = 50 \times w \times V \text{ ft. lb.}$$

and   Horse-power $= \dfrac{50 \times w \times V}{33000}.$

We can find the belt speed V from the size and speed of the driving pulley. If its speed is N R.P.M., and its diameter is d inch, then

$$V = \frac{\pi d N}{12} \text{ ft. per min.}$$

Our expression for horse-power now becomes

$$\text{H.P.} = \frac{50 w V}{33000} = \frac{50 w}{33000} \cdot \frac{\pi d N}{12}$$

$$= \frac{w d N}{2520} \text{ (taking } \pi \text{ as } \frac{22}{7}\text{).}$$

EXAMPLE 3. *Estimate the horse-power that can be transmitted by a leather belt $2\frac{1}{2}$ in. wide when driven by a 10-in. pulley at 350 R.P.M.*

We have $\text{H.P.} = \dfrac{w d N}{2520} = \dfrac{2\frac{1}{2} \times 10 \times 350}{2520}$

$$= 3 \cdot 5 \text{ H.P. Ansr.}$$

EXAMPLE 4. *What width of belt would be required to transmit 5 horse-power when driven by a 12-in. pulley rotating at 425 R.P.M.?*

We have that H.P. $= \dfrac{wdN}{2520}$ and transposing the formula for w gives

$$w = \frac{2520 \times H.P.}{dN}$$

Putting in the values: H.P. $= 5$; $d = 12$ and N $= 425$,

$$w = \frac{2520 \times 5}{12 \times 425} = 2\tfrac{1}{2} \text{ in. Nearest Ansr.}$$

Pulleys

Mainshaft pulleys are generally made of wood or pressed steel, which gives them suitable strength combined with lightness. They must be fixed rigidly to the shaft, and to facilitate their assembly they are made in two halves which are bolted together. The hole in the pulley is made large enough to accommodate the largest shaft likely to be

Pressed Steel Pulley   Wooden Pulley

Bushes for
Steel Pulley

FIG. 99.—Mainshaft Pulleys.

encountered, and adaptation to smaller shafts is made by using liner bushes made in halves (Fig. 99).

Countershaft pulleys which are narrower and often smaller than those on the mainshaft are made of cast iron (see Fig. 92 (*a*)). The tight pulley is keyed to the shaft and the loose one fitted with a bush which may be renewed when worn. To help the belt run on the centre of the countershaft pulleys their top diameter is made slightly larger than at the edges. This is called "crowning."

Shafting and Spindles—Couplings

The shafting used in machine shops is made of mild steel, and up to about 4 in. diameter it is generally supplied and used in the cold drawn or cold rolled bright condition. Above this size it must be turned. Cold drawn shafting is comparatively cheap and the drawing confers a certain amount of work hardening to the skin which is an advantage. This cold working, however, tends to leave internal stresses in the shaft which may be released by the cutting of a keyway

[*Buck and Hickman Ltd.*

(a)   (b)

(c)

[*Renold & Coventry Chain Co., Ltd.*

(d)

FIG. 100—Couplings.

or by the removal of the outer skin by wear or machining. The release of such stresses may cause the shaft to warp and result in worn or seized bearings if these are not flexible enough to accommodate themselves to the changed conditions of the shaft. Machine and motor spindles are not likely to suffer this defect since they are turned to size, and this will remove any stresses and correct their after effects before the spindle is put into service.

Shafting is supplied in reasonable lengths, and to make up a long length for a workshop several pieces may be joined together by couplings. When a length of shafting is supported in bearings and coupled up in this way the coupling should preferably be near to a bearing (see Fig. 91) and should support and align the two ends of the shaft rigidly so as to give an effect as near possible equivalent to a solid shaft. The muff coupling at Fig. 100 (a) envelops and grips the ends of the shafts, whilst the flanged coupling at (b) relies upon the bolting up of the flanges to give stiffness. When two spindles each carried on two or more independent bearings are coupled in line, it is necessary to introduce slight flexibility in case a rigid coupling might cause excessive bearing wear when there is a slight mis-alignment of the two shafts. Examples of this practice occur when a motor shaft is directly end coupled to the machine shaft it is driving, and for such purposes couplings having some degree of flexibility are used. Each member of the chain coupling at Fig. 100 (c) has a chain wheel cut on a flange at its end and the pair are coupled by a length of double roller chain which just encircles the cut teeth. This type allows for a slight mis-alignment and has the advantage that the two halves of the coupling may easily be disconnected by removing the chain. In the flexible coupling shown at (d) the drive is transmitted between the projecting pins through the laminated rubber disc, which absorbs minor irregularities in the drive as well as allowing for slight mis-alignment.

For the satisfactory operation of all couplings consisting of an end-flanged member fitted to each shaft it is essential that each of these should be a very good driving fit on its shaft before being keyed.

Bearings and Support for Shafting

Shafting must be carried in bearings spaced at suitable distances and these are supported by brackets or hangers according to the prevailing conditions. The bearings may be in the form of plummer blocks or pedestals or some form of housing to accommodate the bearing bush or ball races, this housing then being clamped to the supporting bracket or incorporated in it. Fig. 101 shows at (a) a plain bearing plummer block and at (b) a ball-bearing pedestal. The suspension of a length of shafting from beams by hangers is shown at (c), and a length being carried on columns by brackets at (d). It is always preferable for the bearing itself to be capable of a small swivelling movement in all directions so that it may accommodate itself to slight deviations in the shaft. With plain bearings this is often achieved by clamping the bearing housing between large spherical-ended plugs in the hanger or bracket. Ball race bearings are made self-aligning by making the outer ball race shaped to a portion of a sphere, thus allowing the inner member carrying the shaft to rotate on its own axis. The use of plain bearings for shafting is giving way to anti-friction bearings of the ball and roller

[Crofts (Engineers) Ltd.

(a) Plummer block (ring oiled).

Locking Device

[Hoffmann Manufacturing Co., Ltd.

(b) Ball-bearing pedestal.

(c) Shafting carried on hangers.

[Hoffmann Manufacturing Co., Ltd.

(d) Shafting carried on brackets.

FIG. 101.

types as the latter have various advantages. The frictional loss in a ball race is only a fraction of that in a plain bearing and its resistance against starting from rest is negligible. When properly designed with felt-retaining washers the anti-friction unit when packed with grease will operate for long periods without attention. Normally ball races are used for shaft sizes up to about $2\frac{3}{4}$ in. with roller races for sizes above that.

The Vee Belt Drive

When a machine is driven by its own individual motor it is necessary, in the interests of compactness, to mount the motor on, or inside the machine, as close as possible to the driven pulley. Such an arrangement necessitates pulley centre distances much less than the minimum satisfactory distance mentioned above for a flat belt, and for these conditions such a belt would generally be unsuitable. This has led to the development of the vee belt drive using endless belts of a rubber and canvas composition, working at pulley centre distances in general of not less than the larger pulley diameter, nor more than the sum of the two pulley diameters. Details of the most usual belt sizes are given in Table 12.

The belt runs in 40° vee grooves turned in the pulleys and according to the power and speed several belts may be used for any given drive. Since the belts are endless and fixed in length, adjustment is necessary for the motor position to obtain the correct tension and to allow for stretch. When calculating speed ratios for vee belt

[*Crofts (Engineers) Ltd.*
FIG. 102 (*a*).—A Vee Belt Drive.

TABLE 12.—DETAILS OF VEE BELTS.

Section of belt		$\frac{1}{2}$	$\frac{21}{32}$	$\frac{7}{8}$	$1\frac{1}{4}$	$1\frac{1}{2}$
	A(in.)	$\frac{1}{2}$	$\frac{21}{32}$	$\frac{7}{8}$	$1\frac{1}{4}$	$1\frac{1}{2}$
	B(in.)	$\frac{5}{16}$	$\frac{7}{16}$	$\frac{17}{32}$	$\frac{3}{4}$	1
Max: horse-power at 2000 ft./min. belt speed*		1·7	2·3	5·5	10	14

*Power at other speeds approximately in proportion

drives it is advisable to assume pulley diameters measured to the centre of the belt, since contact between belt and pulley extends over an appreciable distance.   Fig. 102 (*a*) shows a vee belt drive.

The Roller Chain Drive

The reader will be acquainted with the roller chain drive on a bicycle or motor-cycle and will know it for a reliable and efficient method of transmitting power.   In its industrial form this drive has various applications in the works and gives a compact method of driving when the shafts are not too far apart (range of about 30 to 80 times the pitch of the chain used).   This drive, as for a pair of gears, gives a rigid link between the shafts it connects, and lacks the flexibility of the belt which will slip in the event of an excessive overload.   For some purposes this is an advantage since a slipping belt may prevent what would be an expensive smash if the drive were solid.   There are occasions, however, when a large amount of power has to be transmitted in a restricted space, where a belt drive would be cumbersome and impracticable, or where a fixed ratio has to be maintained between the driver and driven shafts.   For such cases the chain provides a drive which will operate for long periods without attention.   The speed ratio between the shafts depends on the teeth in the chainwheels employed and is determined in the same way as we discuss for gear driving in the next paragraph. A roller chain drive is shown at Fig. 102 (*b*), and the component parts

[*Renold and Coventry Chain Co., Ltd.*

FIG. 102 (*b*).—Roller Chain Drive to Special
Purpose Lathe.

(¾-in. Pitch Triplex Chain.   Ratio 4 : 1.   Motor 15 h.p. at
1,460 r.p.m.)

of the outer and inner links at (c).   As the chain articulates motion occurs between the plate sides, between the bearing pins and bush bores and between the roller bores and bush diameters.   For this reason the protection and lubrication of these chains is important and the best condition is when they are totally enclosed in an oiltight case with bath lubrication.   As wear occurs at the joints the chain stretches and means must be provided for this to be taken up.   This can be done either by a movement of one of the sprocket shafts or by providing a spring-loaded jockey sprocket which presses on the chain somewhat in the same way as the belt tensioner shown at Fig. 98.   Normally a chain should be replaced when its length has increased 2% by wear.

FIG. 102 (c).—Component parts of a Simple Roller Chain.

Gear Driving

A geared connexion between two shafts gives a solid drive and a fixed speed ratio.   It is not flexible in the same way as the belt, and whilst this property of the gear drive is necessary when a fixed unvarying ratio is required such as in screw-cutting, the solid property of the drive is sometimes the cause of trouble.   If anything occurs to make one of the shafts in a gear drive become locked the drive cannot slip, so a smash-up takes place somewhere ;   in a belt drive the belt would merely slip off.

The speed ratio between the shafts carrying a pair of gears depends upon the numbers of teeth in the gears and, as in the case of a belt drive, the smaller wheel turns the faster.

For example :   If a 20-tooth gear were driving a gear of 50 teeth the smaller gear would need to turn $2\frac{1}{2}$ times, or $\dfrac{50}{20}$, to cause the larger one to make 1 turn.

Thus if t and T represent the number of teeth in the small and large gears respectively, we may say

$$\frac{\text{Turns of small gear}}{\text{Turns of large gear}} = \frac{T}{t}$$

EXAMPLE 5.   *If, in the back gear arrangement shown at Fig. 93, the two small gears had 25 teeth, and the large ones 80 teeth, find the reduction given by the back gear.*

When the gear is engaged, 1 turn of the cone pulley will cause the gears on the backshaft to make $\dfrac{25}{80}$ turn.

1 turn of the backshaft gears will also turn the large gear on the spindle $\dfrac{25}{80}$;   so that for $\dfrac{25}{80}$ of the backshaft the spindle will turn $\dfrac{25}{80} \times \dfrac{25}{80} = \dfrac{25}{256}$;

i.e. for 1 turn of the spindle, the cone pulley must turn $\dfrac{256}{25} = 10\frac{6}{25}$ turns.

EXAMPLE 6. *A gear of 22 T. drives another of 46 T. Attached solidly to the second gear is a 32 T. which drives a gear of 80 T. If the first gear makes 100 R.P.M., find the speed of the last one.*

The drive is shown at Fig. 103. The middle shaft turns at

$$100 \times \frac{22}{46} \text{ R.P.M. and the last}$$

gear makes

$$100 \times \frac{22}{46} \times \frac{32}{80} = 19\frac{3}{23} \text{ R.P.M. Ansr.}$$

FIG. 103.—Gear Drive for Ex. 6.

Bearings and Lubrication. A bearing consists of two members, the moving member, and the stationary one which supports it and carries the load. The surfaces of bearings are generally flat or cylindrical in form and they may consist of metal surfaces (plain bearings) or hardened races supported by balls or rollers. When a bearing supports a cylindrical shaft it is called a *journal* bearing, and the bearing which takes the longitudinal load on a shaft is called a *thrust* bearing. Flat bearings have many forms and the reader may study these for himself by observing the bed and carriage of a lathe, the table of a planer, the ram and slides of a shaper, and so on.

Fig. 104 shows some of the more common examples of bearings. In a journal bearing the bush which supports the shaft may be made as a complete bush (solid bearing) or it may be made in two halves (split bearing). The reason for making a bearing split is for purposes of assembly, e.g. a shaft with a bearing at each end and an enlargement in the centre could not be assembled in two solid bearings. If the reader examines the machines in the shop he will find many examples of bearings and he should make careful note of the relative sizes of various bearings on a machine, the metals of which they are composed, how they are lubricated, and so on.

Materials for bearing. Generally, the only portion of a journal bearing for which we have a choice of materials is the bush. The shaft, almost without exception, is of steel, and may be soft or hardened according to the conditions it has to encounter in service. From a given shaft, then, we have to decide upon the most suitable mating material for the bearing bush, and the materials available are cast iron, bronze and one of the white metals.

For moderate speeds and loads cast iron makes a suitable bearing

(a) Plain Journal Bearing

(b) Ball Race Journal

(c) Plain Thrust Bearing

(d) Ball Thrust Bearing

(e) Flat Bearing (e.g. on Shaping Machine)
(" " " Bearing Surfaces)

Fig. 104.—Types of Bearings.

metal if the lubrication is not neglected. It has the property of taking on a surface which lasts a long time without any appreciable wear. It is cheap and easily obtained.

Bronze is an excellent metal for lining bearings which have to carry high loads at medium speeds, and gives good results if the metal in the shaft is not too soft.

White metal bearings are commonly used for high-speed hard or soft shafts, especially if of fairly large diameter. If the loading is high, care should be exercised to get a suitable white metal as a soft one may be squeezed out of the bearing under the load. The soft nature of the metal enables it to adapt itself more closely to the shape of the shaft, and if the bearing does become overheated the metal melts and runs, leaving the shaft undamaged and giving warning of the happening. White metal bearings are commonly made of the split type and the white metal is run in as a thin lining to a shell of cast iron, steel or bronze (preferable). To help anchor the white metal to the liner, grooves or holes are made into which the metal secures itself (Fig. 105). After the lining shells have been cleaned, tinned and fluxed the assembly may be set up with the shaft in position, and the molten metal poured in from a ladle.

The materials forming a sliding bearing such as a planer table or shaper ram are the cast iron of which the mating components are made. Fortunately, two cast-iron surfaces will run together and make an excellent bearing; if it were not so, the construction of our machine tools would be rendered much more difficult and expensive. In this property cast iron stands almost alone (i.e. no other metal will run

Fig. 105.—Dovetail Grooves for anchoring White Metal to Liner Bush.

with itself as a bearing), and it is probably due to the free graphite in its structure which helps as a lubricant.

The action in ball and roller bearings is not that of rubbing, but of rolling between the balls or rollers and their races, the inner of which is fixed to the shaft, and the outer to the housing supporting the bearing. These bearings are made from high-grade hardened steel and their manufacture is a highly skilled trade, to be undertaken only by those who specialise in it.

Wear of Bearings. During the course of its service a bearing wears and must ultimately be renewed. The rate at which wear takes place, and the amount that can be tolerated before renewal is necessary, depend upon each individual bearing, and no hard-and-fast rule can be laid down. For example, a small amount of wear in the main bearing of a lathe headstock would render the machine unserviceable on account of chattering, and lack of accuracy in the work produced, but the end bearing supporting the feed-shaft of this same machine could be very badly worn without affecting the operation of the machine hardly at all. The rate of wear will depend upon the loading conditions, but chiefly upon the efficiency with which the bearing is lubricated, a question we will discuss directly.

The renewal of a bearing generally means making a new bush, but very often that only constitutes a small part of the work. A large amount of stripping down may be necessary to get at the bush; the shaft itself may be scored or worn, needing a new surface turning or grinding on it; the shaft may have been taking its bearing in a solid casting which must be bored out before a bush can be fitted, and so on. These are aspects of his work which the reader must learn from observation, experience, and from the advice of others.

When the flat bearing surfaces of machine tools become worn they lose their flatness and accuracy. According to the arrangement and service conditions of the bearing the wear may be fairly uniform or it may be local. For example, the table of a planing machine which slides on a bed longer than itself will wear fairly uniformly on its whole length, but the bed will have the greatest wear at the centre portion, where, for the majority of the work, the table is located. In the same way the bed of a lathe will wear hollow in the centre, because the carriage is used at that position much more than anywhere else. The wear of such flat bearing surfaces can only be corrected by machining, grinding or scraping the whole of the surface until it is brought back to its flat condition.

Lubrication of Bearings. Efficient lubrication plays such a vital part in the reduction of wear that its importance cannot be overstressed. The object of lubricating bearings is to eliminate the solid friction between the metal surfaces and to substitute a fluid whose internal friction is much less. When a bearing is properly lubricated a thin film of oil separates the two metallic surfaces and the upper surface actually floats on this film. When this occurs there is not the metallic wear and damage there would be if the metals were actually in contact, and if the metals do come into contact for any length of time, the bearing very soon seizes up. A good lubricant is one which is able to maintain this film and not be squeezed out by the load on the bearing, whilst at the same time it must not offer undue internal resistance to the motion. This second property depends upon what is called the *viscosity* of the oil ; a thick oil has high viscosity and offers greater resistance to motion than a thin one. We might imagine that a thick oil would be less likely to have its film broken and be squeezed out of a bearing than an oil of thinner consistency, but this is not so. The oil film is very thin—probably less than $\frac{1}{1000}$ in.—and there are qualities besides its " body " which make an oil efficient or otherwise in maintaining the film under load.

Action of Journal Bearing. When a shaft is at rest it will lie in contact with the bush at the side farthest from the load on the shaft (i.e. at the bottom if the shaft load is on top), and as soon as it is started up it will climb to a position which will depend on the fluid friction in the bearing. If friction is high the shaft will climb higher than it would for low friction. Between the two surfaces will be a thin film of oil, and in the regions of closest contact there will be a considerable fluid pressure. At the portions of the bearing opposite to those of greatest pressure there will be very little pressure—in fact there might be a slight vacuum—and it is in this region we must feed the oil to the bearing (Fig. 106).

Oiliness. The oil film is induced by the motion of the shaft, so that when this is at rest, and is stationary at the bottom of the bush, the film is squeezed out, leaving the metals in contact but having on them an oily wetness. When the shaft is started up, and before the film is formed, it is this wetness which must lubricate the bearing, and the efficiency with which it performs the task depends on the capacity of the oil to leave an oily skin on the metals or its " oiliness." It is during the few moments after starting up that the greatest wear is liable to occur in a bearing, so that the " oiliness " of a lubricant is an important property.

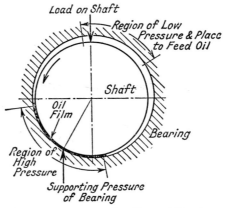

FIG. 106.—Action of a Journal Bearing.

Methods of applying Lubricant. In view of the necessity for efficient lubrication, the methods employed for it are worthy of our attention. Broadly classified, these methods may be divided in (*a*) gravity feed, (*b*) force feed, and (*c*) splash methods. Force and

FIG. 107.—Lubricators.

splash feed methods are much more efficient than gravity, and should be used on the important bearings of a machine tool.

(a) *Gravity Feed.* There are numerous methods employing this principle, varying from the simple oil hole to the more elaborate wick and glass sided drip feed lubricators in which the flow of oil may be controlled, and observed through the glass. A selection of these lubricators is shown at Fig. 107, the most efficient being the wick, and drop feed types. Every oil hole should be provided with a lubricator of

Oil Pipes leading to bearings.

Pipes to Bearings

Pump.

Pump

Driving Motor.

(a) Motor-driven Tecalemit Brantford Oil Pump with Oil Flow Indicator.

(b) Hand Pressure Feed (one Shot).

(c) Grease Gun and Nipple.   [*Tecalemit Ltd.*

Oil Filler

Felt

Liner Bush

Ring   Oil Well

(d) Ring Oiling.

FIG. 108.

some description, as otherwise the hole becomes blocked with dirt, and then takes no further part in lubricating the bearing.

(b) *Force (pressure) Feed.* There are various systems of lubrication employing a pressure feed to the lubricant and they may be divided roughly into the following :

1. Continuous feed of oil under pressure to each bearing concerned. In this method an oil pump driven by the machine delivers oil to the bearings, the oil then draining from the bearings to a sump from which it is drawn by the pump (Fig. 108 (a)).

2. Pressure feed by hand pump in which a charge of oil is delivered to each bearing at intervals (once or twice a day), by the machine operator (Fig. 108 (b)).

3. Oil or grease gun method. The oil hole leading to each bearing is fitted with a nipple and by pressing the nose of the gun against this the lubricant is forced through to the bearing (Fig. 108 (c)).

The first method is the most efficient as (b) and (c) depend on the human element for the regularity with which oil is delivered.

(c) *Splash lubrication.* In this method the shaft, or something attached to it, actually dips into the oil and a stream of lubricant is continually splashing round the parts requiring it. This method is employed for the gears and bearings inside all gear drives, the lower parts of the gears actually dipping in the oil. The oil must be maintained at the proper level, and this is ensured by a filling spout which must be filled up until no more oil can be poured in. A common method of employing splash lubrication is in *ring oiling.* In this method the bearing is cut away in the centre, and a ring passes over the shaft and dips into a reservoir of oil. As the shaft rotates it causes the ring to turn also, and the oil adhering to it is brought up and deposited in the bearing, from which it is led back into the reservoir (Fig. 108 (d)).

Grease. Ball and roller bearings, as well as certain other parts of machinery, may be lubricated by grease. Only those plain bearings which move at low speeds and do not carry heavy loads should be lubricated this way, and care should be taken to use grease having a quality beyond question. Thick and unknown greases may set hard in the course of time, and lead to the destruction of those bearings relying upon them for lubrication. It is a popular delusion that a good thick grease is an efficient lubricating agent, but with his knowledge of oil film lubrication, the reader should now realise that it is a delusion. Grease may be applied to bearings by means of a grease gun and nipples, or by a screw-down greaser which is filled, and the top screwed down, forcing the grease into the bearing. Caution should be exercised not to force grease into nipples or lubricators intended for oil, or to use grease of an unsuitable grade ; where doubt exists err on the safe side and use oil.

Theoretically, the rolling action of ball and roller bearings requires no lubrication, but they should be kept supplied with a thin grease principally to lubricate the cages which space the balls apart.

It will be well to close this section by warning the reader against using cheap unknown qualities of oil. The leading oil refiners have built up a high reputation by the quality of their products, and it is false economy, when such oils are available, to use an inferior grade.

Two defects which may develop in an oil after it has been in use for a time under warm conditions are : (1) it may go gummy, and (2) it may turn slightly acidic.   If the first fault develops the oil will lose much of its lubricating power and may clog the hole leading to the bearing. Free acid in the oil will corrode the bearings, and the oil may be tested for this as follows : soak a string in the oil and wrap it round a highly polished bar of steel.   Leave the string on the bar for several weeks, and if any acid is present, a permanent mark will be left on the bar when the string is removed.

Care and Order in the Workshop

At the beginning of this chapter we discussed the safety and care of the reader's person when working in the shop. As a contributory factor towards his ultimate emergence as a skilled workshop engineer, the care with which he utilises his tools is of no less importance.   We cannot convey by the written word the niceties of control and touch which go to make up the expert user of a pair of calipers, a hammer and chisel, or even a spanner.   Such instincts can only come as the result of long years of thoughtful experience, with the early days often being filled with delusions and disappointments.   However, let the reader maintain a good heart and a sense of humour amidst such apparent setbacks, and providing he thoughtfully learns the lesson of his early failures he will live to look back on his first efforts with a well-earned degree of pride.

Even although we cannot convey the instinct necessary for such a simple job as tightening a nut, we can offer a few words of advice on matters of a more tangible nature and do so in the hope that they may help to form the right type of habits to commence with.   If good habits can be formed early in one's career, they are never left behind and their value cannot be estimated.

Tidiness

Habits of tidiness are no less important in the workshop than in any other aspect of life, and one may form a very reliable judgment regarding the capabilities of a workman by the tidiness and order or otherwise of his methods of working.   When we say tidiness we mean more than the obvious habits of tidiness exhibited by keeping one's tools in their proper place, replacing a tool as soon as it is finished with, and so on.   Tidiness implies such order, cleanliness and method in one's working that the job seems to proceed smoothly without any obvious effort.   Amongst the workshop associates of his younger days the writer still carries the memory of two tool-turners with whom he worked.   Both were rather stout and slow of moving, and neither ever appeared to be in a hurry.   If one watched them carefully, however, it was obvious that they wasted neither a movement of their body nor a second of time.   Their tools were always where they looked for them, they were fastidious in the cleanliness of their machines, and their job never seemed to go wrong—in short, they were two first-class artisans who had trained their minds and hands to lathework.

A first-class mechanic should regard soil, dirt or superfluous articles about his machine, tools, or work with as much concern as if they were on his own person. If he has developed orderly habits it will not be necessary for him to fritter his energy looking for tools, or clearing unwanted articles, he will have his mind clear for attending to the job, and at the end of the day he will be fresher than another of untidy habits who probably has not done nearly as much useful work.

The Care of Tools and Machines

From the very start of his career the reader will need the help of tools and machines in his work, and as he advances these will get more numerous and costly. Some of the tools will belong to the employer, others will be the reader's own property. To the employer, the equipment he provides represents so much capital being used in the business for obtaining output, and earning profits, whilst to the worker, the equipment represents the means of earning his living, and a better living may be earned if the equipment is kept in good condition. We have already discussed cleanliness, but we might add that the accuracy and life of a machine tool is helped exceedingly if it is kept clean. Machines are fitted with accurately made spindles and slides, and it is upon their accuracy that the quality of the work depends. The cutting done on such machines releases grit and other foreign matter from the metal, and unless the machine is cleaned regularly, this grit finds its way into the working parts of the machine and acts like sandpaper.

Spanners, files and other heavy objects should not be dropped on to the machined surfaces of tables and slides. If we must store spanners and tools on a machine bed a piece of board placed under them will look more tidy, and leave the machine undamaged.

Often it is necessary to use a hammer to loosen, tighten or withdraw some part of a machine. If possible a lead or copper hammer should be used to avoid bruising the part being hit. Failing that, a block of hard wood or soft metal interposed between the hammer and the part being hit will save damage. It is a shame to see, in some workshops, parts of machines mutilated by constant hammering ; the handles of vises and jigs are particularly unfortunate in this respect ; actually these are hammered up far more than they need be to hold the work securely.

Grinding Tools

In every machine shop a considerable amount of capital is locked up in cutters, cutting tools, drills and various other cutting equipment, and when we consider that these are made from steel costing up to 10s. per lb. we realise that the annual cost of them must be heavy. Because they do not have the appearance of being worth much, and because they are the general property of everyone, they are not always treated with the respect due to them. As a tool is used its edge gradually becomes dulled and needs re-sharpening. If this is delayed the tool rapidly deteriorates and might in a short time be ruined. The reader should learn as soon as possible the proper methods of grinding tools, as a tool may be as easily spoiled by faulty grinding as by being left unground. We must leave the technique of the actual holding and shape grinding of the tool for the reader to learn from being shown, but we might advise that a tool should either be ground with a *heavy* stream of water flowing on it or it should be ground gently with no water at all. When a tool is being ground, a large amount of heat is generated, and if plenty of water is flowing it carries the heat away, thus preventing the tool from overheating.   If the tool is ground gently without water the heat is not generated as rapidly, and has time to be conducted away to the body of the tool before the edge becomes burned. If the supply of water is sparse and intermittent the outside of the tool becomes heated, and when a splash of water falls on to it a sudden local quenching takes place leading to minute cracks which sooner or later will lead to the failure of the tool.   Grinding a tool dry, and plunging it into cold water from time to time, will lead to similar effects, and is equally as bad as using an insufficient supply of water.   A general purpose pedestal tool grinder is shown at Fig. 118.

Tool Failure in Cutting

A frequent cause of tool failure is running the machine too fast. This causes rapid overheating and deterioration of the cutting edge, and if the tool seems to be making hard work of its job the speed should be reduced and plenty of cutting lubricant applied to the tool.   Cast iron should not be cut with a lubricant, but can generally be machined if the first cut gets well beneath the hard outer scale.   If the tool is allowed to ride over the hard scale its nose will be rubbed away.

Some of the special steels which we have to cut have the property of hardening up under the action of the tool.   This is accentuated if the tool is allowed to " loiter " on its job, and if the tool is kept well up to its work on a low speed, it will bite into the material and cut efficiently.

We might close this chapter by urging the reader, in matters of safety and care, not only to develop good habits himself, but also to take initiative in persuading others of the importance of such questions. If everyone who reads these notes can claim a convert to their principles, he will have achieved a creditable piece of work.

CHAPTER 6

METAL CUTTING

A large portion of the training and skill of a workshop engineer is devoted to the shaping of metal, and to stopping the process at the proper time. In the workshop, most of the shaping involves cutting the metal, and stopping this at the correct place involves a knowledge of measurement. The next two chapters, then, deal with two very important fundamentals of our knowledge.

The Cutting of Metal. The usual conception of cutting suggests cleaving the substance apart with a thin knife or wedge, as represented in Fig. 109 (a). When we cut metal, the action is different from this,

(a) Cutting with a Sharp Wedge   (b) Cutting Metal with a Tool

Fig. 109.

being more in the nature of a tearing than a cutting process. A diagram of a metal chip being removed is shown at Fig. 109 (b). When the cut is under way the chip presses heavily on the tool at A, some little distance back from the extreme point. The pressure of the tool on the chip in the direction of the arrow tears the chip from the body of the metal, the tear being continuous and taking place along the crack marked B. At the same time the chip suffers severe pressure and shearing force, being sheared and compressed up to a much shorter length by the time it leaves the tool. The tearing of the chip from the work naturally leaves the surface of the latter in a torn and rough condition. It is at this point that the extreme tip of the tool does its work by trimming off the irregularities and leaving the surface in a reasonably smooth condition. The occurrence of the heavy pressure of the chip a little way back from the edge can often be verified by examining the nose of a tool which has been cutting for a long time without having been reground. A small cavity may be observed which has been worn in the hard tool by the severe rubbing of the chip.

It will be seen from Fig.109 (*b*) that the tool has not the shape of an ordinary cutting knife as in (*a*), being too blunt of form for cutting in the usual conception of the term.

Rake and Clearance. If we observe the tool nose shown at Fig. 109 (*b*) we shall see that it does not quite make a right angle, but is cut away to a slight angle both on its top face and on its front. These angles are shown again at Fig. 110 (*a*) and are called the *rake*

Fig. 110.—Cutting Tool Angles.

and the *clearance*. The clearance is put on so that every part of the tool except the point clears the work, thus allowing the tool to cut; if there were no clearance the tool would not cut but would only rub the work. The rake gives the tool nose a more wedge-like form and is varied according to the metal being cut. Soft and ductile metals are cut with more rake than hard and brittle ones. The rake we have shown is the slope back from the front of the tool and is called *front* or *top rake*. Sometimes a tool nose is sloped sideways as well, the slope in this direction being called *side rake* (Fig. 110 (*b*)).

The fundamental cutting form we have just described occurs in principle, on every type of cutting edge used for metal cutting. Sometimes it is not very obvious at first, but upon more detailed examination the fundamental rake (or rakes) and clearance may be picked out. It will be well for us to discuss a few of the more common cutting tools.

The Flat Chisel. A diagram of a chisel point in the action of cutting is shown at Fig. 111 (*a*), where the angles of rake and clearance

Fig. 111.—Cutting with a Chisel.

are indicated.   If, as is usual, the point is ground symmetrical, the
rake and clearance will depend upon the angle of inclination (A) between
the chisel and the work.   A clearance of about 10° would be suitable,
so that for a 60° point angle it would be necessary to hold the
chisel with angle $A = 10° + 30° = 40°$ and the rake would then be
$90° - (40° + 30°) = 20°$.   This is shown at (b).   Since cutting hard
and brittle metals calls for less rake than soft metals, the chisel angle
must be less for the softer metals, and the following table gives suitable
values for the angles :

TABLE 13.   CHISEL ANGLES

Metal being Cut.	Angle of Chisel Point.
Cast steel	65°
Cast iron	60°
Mild steel	55°
Brass	50°
Copper	45°
Aluminium	30°

As an exercise, the reader should calculate the angle (A) at which
each of the above chisels should be sloped to give a clearance of 10°,
and then find the cutting rake.

Hacksawing.   An enlarged view of the tooth of a 12-in. " Eclipse "
saw blade, having 10 teeth per inch, is shown at Fig. 112, together with
a diagrammatic view of a chip in the action of being cut.   As the tooth
is cutting relative to the line AA, it will be seen that this tooth is
cutting with little or no rake.   The clearance face is the portion BC

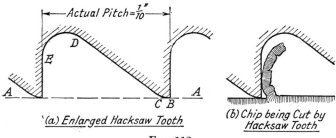

(a) Enlarged Hacksaw Tooth   (b) Chip being Cut by
                                                      Hacksaw Tooth

FIG. 112.

of the tooth, and then its profile is sloped more sharply to give the
form BCDE.   This is necessary because if the tooth were formed by
continuing line BC to the next tooth, the space between the teeth
would be too shallow, and would become clogged with chips of the
metal being cut.   On the other hand, if the portion BC were omitted,
and the back of the tooth formed by taking it from the sharp edge
down the slope CD, the tooth would lack strength.   In the same way
the tooth would be weakened by adding much rake.   The part BC is

only about $\frac{1}{64}$ in. long, but it is very influential in giving strength to the back of the tooth. The radiussed portion DE also adds strength.

Saw-blade teeth are very small and thin, and as they are generally used on every kind of metal, the makers of them do their best to design the most durable tooth possible under the circumstances, rather than try to suit any particular metal.

The File. File making is a highly specialised trade, the cutting of the teeth calling for much skill and experience. The teeth on a file are cut with a sharp chisel having a point angle of 55° to 60°, and the operation may be carried out either by hand or machine methods. The most usual form of file is that with *cross-cut* teeth, the grooves in the face of the file running in two directions and dividing it up into small diamond-shaped teeth. In the *single cut* file there is only one series of grooves. The operation of cutting files consists first of cutting a series of grooves sloping at an angle of about 45° to the file edge, and marked " 1st cut " on Fig. 113. The extreme tip of

FIG. 113.—Angles of Grooves to form File Teeth.

the teeth is then filed off and a second series of grooves cut at an angle of 70° to the edge (marked " 2nd cut "). The result of the two sets of cuts is to raise teeth in the form of small pyramids with edged tops turned back towards the direction in which the file must cut. When one side of the file has been cut it is turned over, embedded in a block of soft metal, and the process repeated on the other side. An enlarged photograph of the teeth of a file is shown at Fig. 114 (a), and a section through one of the grooves at (b). It will be seen from (b) that the normal cutting point formation is again in evidence, but obviously, with such small teeth, we cannot expect to see precise rake and clearance faces. It will be noticed that the grooves being cut at an angle, instead of perpendicular to the length of the file, gives the teeth side rake when the file is moved in the direction of its length.

For many years all file teeth were hand cut and these were found to be greatly superior to the early machine-cut files. This was found to be due to the fact that the irregularity of hand-cut teeth gave them a higher cutting efficiency than the perfectly spaced teeth of machine cutting. In later developments of machine cutting the teeth were purposely made with irregular spacing.

The Twist Drill. It is difficult, on first looking at the point of a twist drill, to see where the rake and clearance enter into its action. We know, however, that even if a tool will cut without rake, it cannot do so without clearance, so let us first examine a flat drill, a tool used for boring holes long before the twist drill. One of these is shown

[*Samuel Peace and Sons, Ltd.*
(a) Enlarged Photograph of File Teeth.

(b) Enlarged Form of Grooves cut to form File Teeth.

Fig. 114.—File Teeth.

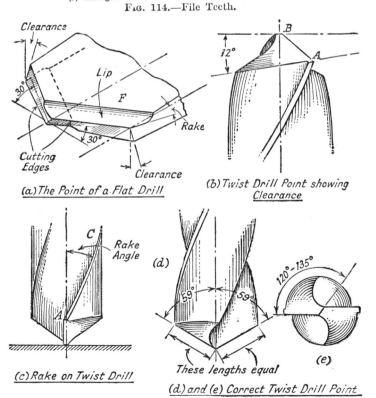

(a) The Point of a Flat Drill

(b) Twist Drill Point showing Clearance

(c) Rake on Twist Drill

(d)

(d) and (e) Correct Twist Drill Point

(e)

Fig. 115.

at Fig. 115 (*a*), and each of the two cutting edges is bevelled off to give clearance as shown. If the front face (marked F) is left quite plain, the tool has no rake, but if it is ground to a lip as shown, then the rake angle is as indicated. It would cut without rake, but for soft metals the addition of rake improves the action.

A side view of a twist drill is shown at Fig 115 (*b*), and here, as before, the metal behind the cutting edge AB slopes away. The correct angle for this slope is 12° at the outside diameter of the drill. In Fig 115 (*c*) a sketch is shown looking level with the cutting edge AB, and it will be seen that the effect of the twist formation of the drill (AC) is to give cutting rake. The rake angle is that indicated, and it is altered by making the " twist " quick or slow; if the flutes were straight, then there would be no rake; if they were left-handed instead of a right-handed helix the rake would be negative. As well as the cutting clearance on the point of a twist drill, there are two clearances on its body : (*a*) the body of the drill is made slightly less in diameter, leaving a narrow " land " of the full diameter running down the front of each flute. This is sometimes called the *body-clearance*; (*b*) a slight taper on the diameter of the drill (about 0·00075 in. per inch of length) from point to shank, the shank end being smaller than the point. This allows all parts of the drill behind the point to clear and not rub against the sides of the hole being drilled.

Drill Grinding. When properly ground the drill point should be central and the lip angles equal (Fig. 115 (*d*)). The metal behind the lip should be as Fig. 115 (*b*) and the line across the centre of the web should be as shown at (*e*).

(a) *Lips at Different Angles*   (b) *Lips of Different Lengths*

FIG. 116.—Effects of Errors in Drill Grinding.

The errors that may occur in the grinding of a twist drill are : (*a*) lips at unequal angles, (*b*) lips of unequal lengths, (*c*) lips having both unequal angles and unequal lengths, and the effect of these on the working of the drill are shown at Fig. 116. In each case the cutting is unequally shared between the two cutting edges and the hole is

(a) Gauge for Lip Angle   (b) Gauge for Checking Drill
Point Corners

Fig. 117.—Drill Grinding Gauges.

drilled oversize. For checking the grinding of a drill point the two
simple gauges shown at Fig. 117 are useful. That shown at (a) is for
the lip angle, whilst the one at (b) checks the points. The drill is supported on its centre at A, whilst a mark is made with each of the lip

[T. S. Harrison and Sons, Ltd.

Fig. 118.—Pedestal Grinder with Enlarged Diagram of Drill Grinding
Attachment.

corners on the back face B, which should be smeared with chalk. Any difference in the level of the corners can be seen immediately from the two marks made.

The only correct way to obtain the complicated form necessary for the clearance faces of a twist drill is by grinding them with a proper drill grinding attachment (Fig. 118). Unfortunately, many people do not see the wisdom of this, so that grinding attachments are not as common as they should be, and it is likely that the reader may have to learn how to grind drills by hand. In order to obtain the correct clearance it must be ground in a path similar to that which it follows when being fed into the work (i.e. points nearer the centre travel in shorter paths than those further out). To attain this the drill must be rocked about an axis AB (Fig. 119 (a)) such that radius C is *less* than D. The conditions shown at (b) and (c) are incorrect.

Point Thinning. The metal at the centre of a drill (called the web) tapers and gets thicker towards the shank. This causes the centre of the drill point to get thicker as its length is reduced by grinding, and to prevent this thick edge from reducing the efficiency of the drill it should be ground thinner. A diagram showing this is given at Fig. 120.

Miscellaneous Drilling Hints

(a) For soft metals use a drill having a quick twist to its flutes, and vice versa for hard metals. For chilled iron a flat drill gives best results.

(b) Cut with soluble oil for steel and malleable iron, kerosene or turpentine for very hard steel. Cast iron or brass should be drilled dry, or with jet of compressed air.

(c) If the corners wear away rapidly, the speed is too high.

(d) If cutting edges chip, reduce feed or grind with less clearance.

(e) If drill will not start drilling there is no clearance on lips.

(f) Examine relative sizes of turnings issuing from each flute. They should be approximately the same, and if not, the drill is wrongly ground with one lip doing more cutting than the other.

(g) Drill breakage may be caused by point wrongly ground; feed too great; not easing drill at " break through "; binding in hole due to lands being worn away; drill choked in a long hole.

(a) Correct. Rad.C less than Rad.D

(b) Wrong. Rad.C greater than Rad.D

(c) Wrong. Rad.C equal to Rad.D

Face of Grinding Wheel

AB = Axis upon which drill is rocked

Fig. 119.—Drill Grinding.

(*h*) The blueing of a high-speed steel drill is not detrimental but it is fatal to a carbon steel drill.

(*k*) A hard spot encountered may be removed by reducing speed and using turpentine.

(*l*) When drilling deep holes release feed occasionally and withdraw the drill. Remove chips from bottom of hole with an old round file that has been magnetised.

Fig. 120.—A Point-thinned Drill.

(*m*) When opening out holes only slightly less in diameter than the drill be careful of points digging-in. For large holes use a 3- or 4-flute drill.

Turning, Boring, Shaping and Planing Tools

The single-point tools used for these processes may have a solid shank as shown at Fig. 121 (*a*), be made of a tool bit held in a holder as at (*b*), consist of a small tool carried in a bar as at (*c*) (chiefly for boring), or consist of a shank to which a tip of the cutting material is brazed or clamped (*d*) and (*e*). Before we proceed to the

(*a*) Solid Tool.

Clamping Screw   Tool 'Bit'

Rake angle given by slope at which insert is set

(*b*) Holder with Inserted Tool.

Tool (square or round section)

Square End for Clamping in Toolpost

Clamping Screw

(*c*) Boring Bar

[*English Steel Corporation.*
(*d*) Ceramic Tool Holder and Insert.

[*Wm. Jessop and J. J. Saville Ltd.*
(*e*) Carbide Tipped Tool.

Fig. 121.—Single-point Tools.

(a) Greatest Slope on a Tool.
(A, B, C & D are in same Horizontal
Plane. A, B, E is a Vertical Plane)

FIG. 122.—Effect of Cut Disposition on Rake Value.

shapes and applications of these tools it will be well for us to examine
the disposition of the cutting angles as they may be influenced by the
type of cutting being done.

Rake. Let us consider a tool such as that shown at Fig. 122 (a)
having 15° front rake and 15° side rake. The line of greatest slope
on the face of this tool will be the line AE and it will be inclined at
an angle of about 21° with the horizontal. If, now, this tool is made
to cut by feeding parallel to its length it will cut with a top rake of
15°; if fed perpendicular to its length it will cut with a top rake of 15°,
and if fed at 45° to its length the top rake will be 21°. Then conditions are shown at (b), (c) and (d), and we see that the disposition
under which a tool must cut influences the effective values of its rake
angles. For example, at (b) the side rake has very little effect on the
tool action and could be omitted, whilst at (c) the tool would cut
almost the same without any top rake. These considerations are
important when a tool such as a side tool is used for more than one
purpose. In Fig. 123 (a), (b), (c) and (d) are shown four possible
methods of cutting with the same tool and the best cutting conditions
will be obtained when the line of greatest slope on the cutting face
is approximately according to the arrow shown. When tool bits are
used in holders the bit is generally set with an initial back slope as
shown at Fig. 121 (b). This gives to a flat-topped tool a front rake
equal to the slope angle of the tool and should be taken into account
when grinding the tool bit.

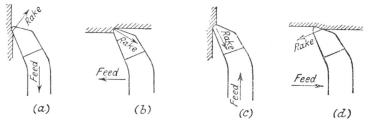

FIG. 123.—Approximate Direction of Rake necessary for different
Cutting Conditions.

Clearance. The remarks we have just made about rake apply in general terms to clearance. The tool must be provided with sufficient clearance *relative to the surface being machined,* and if this is not achieved the tool will be prevented from a free cutting action by its front rubbing against the metal. In Fig. 123 the clearance for the four examples shown must have its general direction inclined towards the arrow, and clearances should be ground in planes parallel and perpendicular to the surface being machined. The amount of clearance should be no more than is necessary to permit the tool to cut cleanly, and 5°–10° is usually sufficient. If more than this is allowed the tool point is made sharper and robbed of metal which would otherwise help it to survive and conduct away the large amount of heat generated when cutting.

A little more clearance is generally necessary for flat facing, boring,

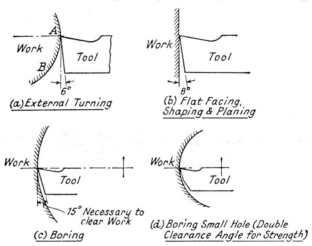

Fig. 124.—Effect of Cutting Conditions on Tool Clearance.

shaping and planing tools, than for external turning. This is shown at Fig. 124, where it can be seen that in external turning (*a*) the surface AB slopes away from the tool immediately below the centre line. For flat facing, shaping and planing (*b*) the surface does not change in direction, whilst for boring (*c*) it slopes towards the tool. Sometimes, when boring a small hole, a double clearance angle as at (*d*) helps to strengthen and leave more metal round the tool nose. On toolholders where the tool slopes back the clearance which must be put on the tool is the sum of the clearance required, and the slope angle of the tool (see Fig. 121, *b*).

Turning off Centre. When a bar is being turned the cutting takes place relative to a radial line drawn from the tool point to the centre of the work as OA in Fig. 125 (*a*). If the tool point is on the centre, this line is horizontal, and the rake and clearance angles are operative under their values as ground on the tool. If the tool is placed above centre without being rotated as at (*b*), it is now cutting

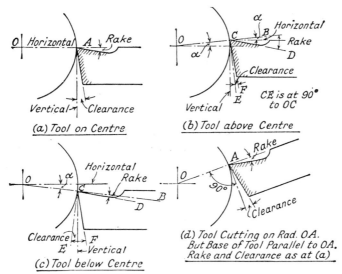

FIG. 125.—Effect of Tool Setting on Angles.

relative to OB ; the rake is now the angle BCD, or greater than before by the angle α and the clearance is angle ECF. We thus see that the rake is increased, and the clearance decreased, by α. Fig. 125 (c) shows the effect of putting the tool below centre where the reader will see opposite effects to those above. It should be noticed that the tool need not be horizontal for it to be cutting with its normal rake and clearance angles. It may be swung round to any position such as (d), where, provided it is correctly located relative to the radial line to its nose, it cuts just the same as if it were horizontally on the

TABLE 14. RAKE ANGLES FOR CUTTING VARIOUS METALS

Angle given is that of the true rake on the tool (see Fig. 126)

Metal being Cut.	Hard Brass, Bronze and Cast Iron.	Hard Steel, Medium Cast Iron, Brass and Bronze.	Medium Steel, Soft Cast Iron, Brass and Bronze.	Mild and Soft Steel.	Aluminium and light Alloys.
Rake . .	0°	8°	14°	20°–27°	40°

CLEARANCE

This should be no more than is necessary to allow the tool to cut efficiently and may be approximately as follows :

External turning, 6°–10°.

Facing, shaping and planing, 8°–17°.

Boring, sufficient to allow heel of tool to clear.

centre. This can be seen by turning the diagram round until the tool is horizontal.

The table on previous page will give an idea of the rake which should be used for cutting various metals. The angle given in the table is that of the line of greatest slope on the tool as explained in Fig. 122. Depending upon the conditions of cutting (see Fig. 126), this angle may be obtained by a combination of front and side rake (for ordinary surfacing, e.g. Fig. 122 (a); by front rake only, e.g. for a parting tool; or by side rake only, e.g. for a knife tool).

FIG. 126.—Top Profiles of Tools.

Plan Profiles of Tools

The top profiles of the more usual tools are shown at Fig. 126, and an indication of their uses is as follows:

(a) Straight Rougher: General surfacing work.

(b) Side Tool: Surfacing up to a corner facing down a side.

(c) Knife Tool: Facing ends of bars in lathe. Finish facing generally.

(d) { Parting Tool: Parting off in lathe, cutting grooves.
{ Cranked Parting Tool: Parting off near chuck; grooving near another face.

(e) Broad Finishing Tool: (Planer and shaper only.) Surface finishing on cast iron with broad feed.

(f) Boring Tool: Boring in the lathe.

The tools for lathes, planers, etc., should have a good solid shank and should be well supported by not protruding from the toolholder any more than is necessary.

Cutting Speed

The cutting speed for a cutting operation is the speed at which the cutting edge passes over the material, and it is usually expressed in *feet per minute*.

Cutting Speed for Turning. For turning, the cutting speed is the surface speed of the bar being turned. To find it we must multiply the circumference of the bar (in feet) by the speed in R.P.M. Thus if d = diameter of work (inch) and N = speed (R.P.M.), Circumference (feet) $= \dfrac{\pi d}{12}$,

Cutting speed (feet per minute) $S = \dfrac{\pi d N}{12}$. (See Fig. 127.)

We often require to find the R.P.M. when we are given the cutting speed (S) and the work diameter (d), and by changing the above formula we get

$$N = \frac{12S}{\pi d}.$$

For example : The R.P.M. for a 2-in. bar to cut at 80 ft. per minute,

$$N = \frac{12 \times 80}{\dfrac{22}{7} \times 2} = \frac{12 \times 80 \times 7}{44} = 153 \text{ R.P.M.}$$

Fig. 127.

The speed at which material may be turned depends upon the following factors :

(1) The material being cut. Hard, strong metals require a lower speed than soft and ductile materials.

(2) The rigidity and condition of the machine and tool; the rigidity of the work. An old, loose machine working with a poorly supported tool on a thin bar will not cut at such a high speed as a good machine with a rigid tool operating on a well-supported bar of reasonable dimensions.

(3) The material of which the tool is made. Special cutting alloy and high-speed tools will cut at much higher speeds than low tungsten or carbon steel tools.

(4) The depth of cut and the feed. A light finishing cut with a fine feed may be run at a higher speed than a heavy roughing cut.

The following speeds may be taken as a guide for the initial setting of the machine.

TABLE 15. Cutting Speeds for Turning

(The speeds given are for average cuts with high-speed steel tools)

Material being Cut.	Cutting Speed (feet per min.).
Mild steel	70–90
Cast iron	60–80
High carbon steel . .	40–60
Brass	150–300
Bronze	50–70
Aluminium	Up to 1000

(It may be possible to exceed these speeds for light finishing cuts. For heavy roughing cuts they should be reduced.) One formula for cutting speed in which the cut and feed are taken into account is as follows :

$$\text{Cutting Speed (S) feet per minute} = \frac{C}{\sqrt[3]{A}},$$

Where A = Area of cut = Feed × Depth of cut,
C = A Constant.

Values of " C " :

Material being Cut.	Soft Steel.	Hard Steel.	Cast Iron.	Bronze.	Brass.
C . . .	9	5	7	8	18

Example : To find the cutting speed for mild steel working on a cut of $\frac{1}{16}$ in. with a feed of $\frac{1}{32}$ in., using the above formula and taking C = 9.

We have $S = \dfrac{C}{\sqrt[3]{A}}$. Where C = 9 and $A = \frac{1}{16} \times \frac{1}{32} = \frac{1}{512}$.

Hence $$S = \frac{9}{\sqrt[3]{\dfrac{1}{512}}} \quad \text{and} \quad \sqrt[3]{\frac{1}{512}} = \frac{\sqrt[3]{1}}{\sqrt[3]{512}} = \frac{1}{8}$$

$$\therefore S = \frac{9}{\frac{1}{8}} = 9 \times 8$$

$$= 72 \text{ ft./min.}$$

Cutting Speed for Shaping and Planing

In turning, the material passes over the tool at a uniform rate, but in shaping and planing, for each double stroke of the machine the following takes place :

Cutting Stroke. The tool starts from rest, attains a maximum cutting speed and slows down to rest again.

Return Stroke. The same as for cutting except in a shorter total time.

This renders the estimation of a machine speed rather difficult, but the following method may be used as a guide in setting the machine :

Divide twice the length of the stroke (in feet) into the lowest speed given in Table 15. This will give the number of double strokes per minute.

Thus, for planing cast iron with a table travel of 18 in., the number of double table strokes per minute will be:

$$\frac{60}{2 \times 1\frac{1}{2}} = \frac{60}{3} = 20 \text{ double strokes of the table per minute.}$$

Cutting Speed for Drilling. The formula given on page 149 for the cutting speed in turning will apply to drilling if d is made to represent the drill diameter instead of the work diameter.

Thus for a $\frac{1}{2}$-in. drill to cut at 40 ft. per minute

$$\text{Speed of drill (R.P.M.)} = \frac{12 \times 40}{\frac{22}{7} \times \frac{1}{2}} = \frac{12 \times 40 \times 14}{22}$$

$$= 305 \text{ R.P.M.}$$

For drilling speeds use about $\frac{2}{3}$ of those given in Table 15.

Cutting Speed for Hacksawing. The conditions under which a hack-saw operates are much the same as for shaping and planing. Suitable speeds for sawing operations are as follows:

TABLE 16. SAWING SPEEDS

Operation.	Light Cutting Dry.		Medium Cutting with Cutting Lubricant.	
Metal being cut .	Hard steel	Mild steel Soft metals	Hard steel	Mild steel Soft metals
Double strokes per minute . . .	40–50	50–60	60–80	100–110

Beginners at hand-sawing nearly always operate the saw much too fast. This results in undue wear of blades.

Cutting Speed for Filing. The file, wielded by human energy, cannot be fitted in to hard-and-fast rules of cutting speeds. There are so many variable factors to be taken into account, such as material being filed, type of work, rate at which material is being removed, strength and endurance of the worker, and so on. It has been found that the range of speeds over which experienced users of the file operate varies from about 45 to 85 strokes per minute, with an average of about 65 strokes per minute.

Cutting Feeds

A metal-cutting operation consists of causing the tool to travel relative to the work and feeding it in such a way that it cuts the metal. In shaping, for example, the tool reciprocates backwards and forwards, and just before each cutting stroke the work is fed a small distance along.   We have already discussed the speed at which the work must travel past the tool and must now study the rate at which the tool is fed.

Turning.   In turning, the tool is fed along the bar for turning a cylinder, and across for a flat face.   This gives the effect of removing the metal by turning a very fine thread as shown in Fig. 128.   The *feed* of the tool is the distance it moves along for each revolution of the work, and it may be expressed either as a fraction of an inch per revolution of the work (e.g. $\frac{1}{32}$ in. per rev. as shown), or as the number of turns the work makes whilst the tool travels one inch (e.g. $\frac{1}{32}$ in. per rev. would be 32 feeds per inch).   The feed that should be used for turning or shaping depends on the following :

(*a*) The smoothness of the finish required.   A coarse feed will give wider and deeper machining marks, and an inferior finish to a fine

Fig. 128.—Turning with a Feed of $\frac{1}{32}$ in.

feed.   The shape of the tool enters into this as well because a blunt-nosed tool will give a better finish than a sharp tool for the same feed.

(*b*) The power available, the condition of the machine and its drive. The product of the speed, feed and depth of cut gives us the amount of metal that is being removed, and hence the power necessary.   A coarse feed on a poor or badly driven machine may be too much for the machine or tool, or cause the drive or belt to slip.

These two considerations must guide the reader in his choice of a feed.   As a general rule, when roughing a job down, give the coarsest feed that the machine will stand because finish is unimportant.   When finishing adjust the feed so that it is fine enough to give the class of finish required.

Shaping and Planing.   The remarks we have just made for turning apply in a general way to these two methods of machining.

Drilling.   The feed for a drill is expressed in thousandths of an inch per revolution of the drill (e.g. ·010 in. per revolution, or ten thousandths per revolution).   For a drill, the feed depends on the drill for the small sizes, and upon the machine for large drills.   To make this a little clearer the reader will appreciate that if we overfeed a $\frac{1}{4}$-in. drill it will break, but if we overfeed a $1\frac{1}{4}$-in. drill we may either break the machine, or cause the belt to slip off ; it is unlikely that we shall break the drill.   The dividing line between these two cases occurs for about a $\frac{3}{4}$-in. drill ; below that the drill is the weaker member and, above it, the machine.   The following table gives a guide as to twist drill feeds :

TABLE 17. TWIST DRILL FEEDS

Diameter of Drill (in.) Feed ($\frac{1}{1000}$ths inch per revolution) . . .	$\frac{1}{8}$	$\frac{1}{4}$	$\frac{5}{16}$	$\frac{3}{8}$	$\frac{7}{16}$	$\frac{1}{2}$	$\frac{5}{8}$	$\frac{3}{4}$	$\frac{7}{8}$–1	$1\frac{1}{4}$
	3	5	6	7	8	9	10	11	12	15

Sawing. In sawing and filing the saw or file is moved over the work and is fed into it by the pressure put on. This pressure, then, really determines the rate at which metal will be removed and average suitable pressures are approximately as follows :

SAWING

Blade thickness (in.) . .	0·027	0·032	0·065
Pressure (lb.)	12	20	65

Filing. As we have stated, filing is such an individual and variable operation that we cannot state hard-and-fast rules, but can only give figures, more for the reader's interest than anything else.

Filing involves a vertical pressure on the file and a thrust to cause it to move over the metal. These will not only vary according to the file, and the material being filed, but also according to the physique and habits of the workman. For example, a strong man will exert more force than a weaker one, and a filer who habitually files large articles will press harder than one who is always working on thin, fragile parts. Another factor in filing is that the pressure varies throughout the stroke, being greatest just over half-way. Tests on six experienced filers showed that the maximum pressure they exerted (sum of both hands) varied from 30 lb. to 48 lb., and the average pressure from 21 lb. to 38 lb. The thrust required to push the file forward will itself depend on the pressure, on the material, file condition, etc. For example, in a series of tests with new files, the average values of the ratio : $\dfrac{\text{Forward Thrust}}{\text{Vertical Pressure}}$ were found to be as follows :

Metal being filed.	Steel.	Cast Iron.	Copper.	Brass.
Average of thrust pressure	1·3	1	1·6	1

The Lubrication of Cutting Tools

The machining of most metals is greatly improved by the use of a cutting lubricant. Cast iron should always be machined dry ; brass, bronze and aluminium may be cut dry or wet, whilst steel may always be machined with a lubricant. The improvements effected by using a lubricant are as follows :

(*a*) The tool and work are cooled and higher cutting speeds may be used.

(*b*) The cutting fluid helps in lubricating the severe rubbing action taking place between the chip and the top face of the tool. This effects some saving in power, prolongs the life of the tool and promotes a better finish. (Many readers are probably aware what an improvement a drop of whale oil will effect to the finish of a thread.)

(*c*) A heavy flow of lubricant helps to wash away the chips and keep the cutting point clear.

Cutting lubricants may consist of a pure oil, a mixture of two or more oils—or a mixture of oil and water. Oils are generally divided into what are termed the " fixed " oils, and the mineral oils. When these are compared it is found that the fixed oils have a greater " oiliness " than the mineral oils, but they are not so stable and tend to become gummy and decompose when heated (see p. 129). The " fixed " oils consist of animal, fish, and vegetable oils, and the chief of these used for cutting are lard oil (animal), sperm and whale oil (fish), and olive, cottonseed and linseed oil (vegetable). Turpentine, which is distilled from vegetable oil, is also used. The mineral oils come from crude petroleum oil pumped at the oilfields, and paraffin is a cutting lubricant belonging to this class.

In order to combine the advantages of the stability of the mineral oils with the good lubricating qualities of the fixed oils they are often mixed, and sometimes sulphur is added to give the property of " wetting " the metal with a highly adhesive oil film. Such oils are known as compounded oils and sulphonated oils.

The most common type of lubricant used for cutting is a soluble oil, which, when mixed with water, forms a white solution known as " suds " or " slurry." This has better cooling properties than oil, but does not lubricate as well. The oil part of it is generally a mineral oil mixed with a soap solution, sometimes with an e.p. agent added. There are many forms of soluble oil on the market and the supplier's instructions should be followed as regards the proportions of oil and water required.

Oils with an Extreme Pressure (e.p.) Additive

The arduous cutting conditions imposed by heat-resistant and stainless steels, nimonic alloys, etc., have led to the introduction of e.p. additives to cutting lubricants. These are based on chlorine and sulphur and under extreme conditions of temperature and pressure form solid films of iron chloride or iron sulphide between the chip and the tool. These films are easily sheared and have high melting points so that they assist in preventing portions of the chip welding themselves to the nose of the tool. (The reader will no doubt be aware of the use of e.p. oils for coping with the severe conditions imposed on the crown wheel and pinion in a car rear axle.)

Application of Cutting Lubricant. The cutting lubricant may be applied to the tool or cutter by hand (using a brush), by means of a small drip tank attached to the machine or by a pump which is driven by the machine and pumps the fluid from a drain sump. For heavy and continuous cutting the pump system is the only one which can be said to effect proper cooling of the tool. Some attention has recently been given to forcing the lubricant upward between the tool and the work for turning operations and it is claimed that this method is more efficient than feeding from above. Generally an overhead flow is used as well to reduce fumes.

Surface Finish

Within recent years a great deal of attention has been given to the investigation of the surface texture produced by various machining and finishing operations, and, although we have not yet reached the stage when surface finish requirements can be specified and produced in the same way that is possible for a given dimension, or fit, information is being built up which may eventually bring this about.

If a machined surface is reproduced to a large enough magnification it will be found to have a wavy profile, the character and shape of the waves varying for different machining methods. Equipment is now

FIG. 129.—Enlarged Profiles of Surface Finishes.

available which will produce an enlarged contour of a surface by traversing a needle-like probe over it, the instrument meanwhile plotting on a chart a greatly magnified reproduction of the up-and-down movement of the probe with its longitudinal traverse. Examples of such profiles are shown at Fig. 129, but in studying them the reader should allow for the fact that the vertical magnification is about 8000 whilst the horizontal enlargement is only about 100, so that in reality the spiky peaks and hollows are quite gentle curves. (If the reader is in doubt as to the reason for such differing scales of magnification he should estimate how long the diagrams would be if the horizontal enlargement were the same as the vertical.)

Measure and Influence of Finish

The present method of expressing a measure of surface finish is to find the average height of the undulations of its contour with reference to a horizontal straight line drawn through the contour in such a position that the loop areas enclosed above the line are equal to those below. When expressed on this basis the surface is said to have a C.L.A. (Centre Line Average) Index of so many micro-inches (micro = 1 millionth). In practice, reasonable standards of attainment are :

Good Average Turning and Smooth Filing—from 32 to 63 C.L.A.
Commercial Grinding   —from 16 to 32 C.L.A.
Lapping and Honing   —from 1 to 8 C.L.A.

In service the texture of surfaces which do not have to fit and mate with other surfaces is not important, and for surfaces which fit together without any relative movement a reasonably smooth finish is good enough to provide the support and alignment necessary. When, however, two surfaces both fit and *run* together their finish is of the utmost importance, since where there are " hills " and " hollows " the first thing that happens in the early periods of their rubbing together is that the " hills " wear down.

When these have become levelled off the surfaces settle down to a comparatively long period of contact without much further wear taking place. Let us suppose that the hills are $\frac{1}{10}$ of a thousandth high on a shaft and in the bearing to which it has been fitted. The initial wear which takes place rapidly removes these, resulting in the shaft wearing to a diameter $\frac{1}{5}$ of $\frac{1}{1000}$ in. less and the hole $\frac{1}{5}$ of $\frac{1}{1000}$ in. more in size, a total difference of nearly $\frac{1}{2}$ a $\frac{1}{1000}$ in. If the reader does not realise what this means let him bore a hole about 1 in. to $1\frac{1}{2}$ in. diameter and turn a plug to be a nice smooth push fit in it (or bore a hole to a standard plug gauge). Now make another plug about $\frac{1}{2}$ a $\frac{1}{1000}$ in. less in diameter and try it in the hole.

It is this problem of the initial wear taking off the hills and hollows which makes workshop engineers so particular in obtaining the smoothest possible finish on motor and aeroplane cylinders and pistons, on high speed bearings, and so on.

CHAPTER 7

THE CHECKING AND MEASUREMENT OF SURFACES

The actual removal of metal is not in itself a very difficult task, but the initial setting for it, and the judgment of the correct point at which to stop it, often call for high skill. If we examine a number of finished articles chosen at random, we shall find that the majority of the finished surfaces on them are either flat or cylindrical in form as shown in Fig. 130. Now the drawings of these parts would give us all the information we required regarding the shape and sizes of the various faces of the components. There are many other things, however, which the drawing would not tell us, but which we should be expected to produce correctly. For example, it would not tell us

F = Flat Surface.   C = Cylindrical Surface.

FIG. 130.—Flat and Cylindrical Surfaces on Components.

that the centre hole in the disc had to be exactly on the same centre as the outside diameter, nor that the edge of the disc had to be square with its face. In the bracket on the right, it would be taken for granted that we should bore the large hole with its centre line parallel to the base, that the centre lines of the two small lug holes were co-axial (i.e. on one and the same centre line), and perpendicular with the sides of the slot, and so on. The aim of the workshop engineer, then, should be to give careful thought to each job and try to fulfil the obligations which have been left unwritten on the drawing, but which are as important as the most accurate size relationship.

Even though we may infer from a drawing that two faces have to be square, or perhaps parallel, it does not follow that we must always spend time in getting the relationship accurate to a thousandth part of an inch. It may be that in some cases the job will be satisfactory if within $\frac{1}{64}$th of an inch, and the reader will be justified in asking, " How am I to know which parts must be very accurate and which not so accurate ? " In reply to this we can only say that, in time, his experience, study and instincts will be his guide, and he should work to acquire the knowledge in the shortest possible time. His ruling principle always should be to so arrange the production of a job that, when finished, it will be *right*. This involves qualities of mind and character which we have already discussed and differentiates the skilled artist from the " just ordinary " worker.

In the light of the above remarks, we will discuss the unwritten accuracy relationships on two simple parts. At Fig. 131 is shown a slotted hexagon nut just as it would appear on the drawing. The outside dimension for the flats of the nut is given as limits with an 8-thousandth tolerance, so its interpretation is clear, but it would be less serious for the flats to be a little less than the minimum size than over the maximum, for in the latter case they might be too large for the spanner to fit over them. The three sets of flats must of course be uniform, although only one set is dimensioned. Nothing is said

FIG. 131.—Slotted Hexagon Nut.

about the angle between the flats, but we know, if the nut is truly hexagonal, this must be 120°. The threaded hole in the nut, stated as ⅝ in. B.S.F., is beyond our control in its dimensions since it would be finished with a tap, but the position of this hole is very much under our control. In the first place, it must be in the centre of the nut ; secondly, the hole should be square with the bottom face of the nut. If it is not so, when the nut is tightened down it will not sit flat on the mating surface and the bolt will be bent in the tightening process. The bottom face should be flat (or very slightly saucer-shaped) and, as just stated, square with the thread ; the top face is unimportant since it does nothing, and the nut thickness is relatively unimportant. The slots across the top of the nut which accommodate the cotter pin will have been dimensioned with sufficient clearance for the pin, so that extreme accuracy is not necessary for their width or depth, but if they do not pass through the centre of the nut it may not be possible to get the cotter through.

We can thus summarise our discussion as follows :

(1) The flats should be uniform and should not be wider than the maximum.

(2) The bottom face should be square with the thread, and should be flat, or slightly saucer-shaped, but not rounded (why ?).

(3) The cotter pin slots should be in the centre of the nut.

As our second example we will take the crank of a bicycle, choosing the type which has arms for attaching the chain wheel (Fig. 132). For the purposes of its application, the only surfaces which need machining are those marked **A**, **B** and **C**, and the holes **D**, **E**, **F** and **G**. Provided the remainder of the surfaces can be forged or pressed to a good smooth finish, and can be made to sizes sufficiently close to bring the crank within the limits set for its weight, then they will only need polishing so as to provide a suitable foundation for the plated or enamelled finish. If the primary forging process is not able to give a sufficiently good finish, it may be necessary to machine these surfaces, but for the purpose of our discussion we will ignore them.

FIG. 132.—Cycle Crank.

When the chain wheel is assembled on the crank, the screws pull it up against the front faces A, and a hole in the wheel fits on the diameter formed by the three portions B. This gives us conditions for the accuracy requirements of A, B and G.

(i) The diameter of which the portions B form a part must be held to close limits so that any chain wheel will fit any crank.

(ii) The above diameter must be true with hole D; if it is not, the chain wheel will not run true.

(iii) Front faces A must run true when the crank is rotated on the hole D. If they are not true, then the chain wheel will wobble out of truth sideways.

(iv) When the chain wheel is assembled, the holes G must correspond with similar holes in the chain wheel; otherwise the screws will not enter. These holes should also be a good fit for the screws which pass through them. The back face of A must be cleared up to provide a seating for the screw heads.

Now for holes D and E.

(i) The diameter of D must be to close limits to ensure a good fit on the axle of the bicycle.

(ii) Hole E must be screwed so as to be a good firm fit for the pedal when it is screwed in.

(iii) The distance between the centres of D and E is not important to $\frac{1}{64}$ in., as no rider would notice such a small variation. He would notice, however, if D and E were not in the centre of the circle of metal containing them.

(iv) The centre lines of D and E must be parallel in all directions. If they are not so, then the pedal will appear as though it has been knocked on one side. The face C, against which the pedal spindle screws, should be faced up true with hole E.

The relation between the cotter pin hole F and hole D is important. Its distance along the crank must be such that the usual form of cotter pin enters for the correct distance, locking up the crank. Its distance from the face of the crank fixes how far the crank goes on to the axle and both these positions should be held to less than $\frac{1}{64}$ in. The diameter of the cotter pin hole must allow a standard cotter pin to a nice sliding fit.

It will be seen that simple though our two examples have been, they contain many problems that must be solved satisfactorily if production is to be successful, and every piece of work that is attempted deserves similar consideration, however simple it may appear.

Tests for the Form and Relationships of Surfaces

We now realise that in checking a piece of work for accuracy, we have not only to verify its dimensional correctness, but also the accuracy and relationships of its surfaces. We will discuss surfaces first.

Flatness

A flat surface is one of the fundamentals of workshop engineering, and although most of the surfaces we produce are flat enough for their purpose, most of them would be far from the precision engineer's standard of flatness.

The methods which are most convenient for verifying flatness are either to test the surface against another surface which is known to

FIG. 133.—A Surface Plate.

be flat or testing with a straightedge. A *surface plate** (Fig. 133) has a surface of proved flatness, and when testing, the top of the plate should first be rubbed with a thin smear of a paste made up of red lead and oil. The face to be tested should be wiped clean, and then placed in contact with the surface plate and moved about. If it is reasonably flat, upon examination after this treatment, spots of the red lead will be visible all over it. Another method using the surface plate is to rest the face to be tested on the plate with a single thickness of cigarette paper under each corner, and if necessary, at other points as well. Pull at each of the papers and if they are all tight the surface is resting on all, and may be assumed flat. This method fails, however, on a surface (e.g. a round one) which is concave, because although the edges would grip the cigarette papers, the centre would not be in contact with the surface plate. If the work is larger than the surface plate, then the plate may be rested on the work, instead of the work on the plate.

* See B.S.S. No. 817.

A *straightedge** may be in the form of a steel strip (Fig. 134 (*a*)), or as a stiff casting with the edge straight, as at (*b*). For lengths greater than 12 in. the ribbed cast-iron pattern is to be recommended. The surface to be tested should be compared with the straightedge

FIG. 134.—Straightedges.

in several directions. Red lead or cigarette papers spaced along it can be used with the cast-iron straightedge which has an edge of appreciable width, but the steel pattern, which has a knife-edge, must be used either with a number of cigarette papers, or by the appearance of " daylight." If an edge is placed against a surface and then held up to the light, any small discrepancy can be detected by the appearance of the light between the two, and our eyes are so sensitive that a gap of $\frac{2}{10,000}$ of an inch can be seen. If we can guarantee our straightedge, this method then gives us a good test for flatness.

Squareness

The *try square* † is the most common tool for testing squareness, and diagrams of the use of this for internal and external testing are shown at Fig. 135. When using the square care should be taken to

FIG. 135.—Using the Try Square.

ensure that its blade is held perpendicular to the surface being tested or errors may occur (see Fig. 135 (*b*)). A good square is valuable, and should be treated with as much care as a watch, but as it is a

* See B.S.S. Nos. 818 and 852. † See B.S.S. No. 939.

I.W.T.   G delusion to put one's confidence in a square which is not accurate, its accuracy should be tested occasionally. One method of doing this is shown at Fig. 136, where a straightedge is clamped to an angle plate, and set so as to correspond accurately with the *outside* of the square blade. The square is reversed, and if it is correct, the *inside* will also check with the straightedge. This assumes, of course, that the blade of the square is parallel; if it is not, the square is useless anyhow.

Fig. 136.—Testing a Square.

The *combination square* consists of a blade which may be used in conjunction with any one of three heads. The various heads enable the tool to be used as a square, a protractor or a gauge for marking lines passing through the centre of round bars (Fig. 137). The complete set forms a very useful workshop accessory, and fulfils many needs, but when a high degree of accuracy is required for squareness, we recommend that an accurate solid try square be used in preference to the square of the combination set.

Centre Finder.

Square.

Protractor.   [*L. S. Starrett Co.*

Fig. 137.—Combination Square.

Parallelism

Depending upon the character of the work, it will be necessary to employ a variety of methods for testing the parallelism of two surfaces. If the dimensions of the part are small enough to be within the capacity

(a) *Parallelism of*   (b) *Test for Bore of Bracket*
  Casting Surface   *being Parallel with Base*

FIG. 138.—Test with Scribing Block.

of calipers, or of a micrometer, its parallelism may be tested by one of these instruments.   For larger work, and for testing the alignment of holes with flat faces, the *surface gauge* or *scribing block* (Fig. 138) used in connexion with a surface table, is useful.   The scriber of the surface gauge has one end bent at right-angles and this may be used as shown at (*a*).   When a hole is being checked as shown at (*b*), the

FIG. 139.—Alignment Tests on a Connecting Rod.

longer the bar that is put through the hole, the more accurate will be the test, but the bar itself must be parallel. Fig. 139 shows how the ends of a motor engine connecting rod may be checked for parallelism in both directions. Before this test is made, the Vee blocks supporting the bottom bar should be checked by trying the scriber along the top of the bar supported in them.

To test parallelism (and distance) between a step and an edge, the **combination** square may be used as in Fig. 140 (*a*). The blade should

Test at Both Ends

(*a*) Combination Square Testing between Step and Edge

Pins guide Block along Edge

(*b*) Using Pins in Scribing Block Base to Set Surface Parallel to Edge of Table

FIG. 140.—Testing for Parallelism.

be adjusted so that when it is slid over one end of the step, with the stock pressed against the other edge, the edge of the step can just be felt. By repeating at the other end of the step, a check on the parallelism is obtained. By this method the square is also being used as a depth gauge to measure the distance between the two faces. Yet another method which is useful for setting up work on machine tables is shown in Fig. 140 (b). This makes use of the little pegs found in the base of a surface gauge which, if pushed through so as to project beyond its base, enable the gauge to move parallel to the edge of the table.

The Dial Gauge.* Two drawbacks to the use of the scribing block for tests of parallelism are : (1) the accuracy depends upon the sensitiveness of our " feel " with the bent end of the scriber on the work. (2) If the heights differ at each of the faces being tested, our test does not give an accurate measure of the difference.

These objections are overcome by the use of a dial gauge, the essential part of which is like a small clock with a plunger projecting

(a) Dial Gauge on Clock Indicator.   (b) Checking for Parallelism.

FIG. 141.

at the bottom (it is often called a " clock indicator "). Very slight upward pressure on the plunger moves it upwards and the movement is indicated by the dial finger which is generally arranged to read in $\frac{1}{1000}$ in. of movement. For very accurate work, gauges reading in $\frac{1}{10,000}$ ths may be obtained. The head is supported on a base and upright very much like that of a scribing block, and for testing parallelism it is used in much the same way. A diagram of the gauge is shown at Fig. 141 (a), and its application for the above purpose at (b).

Use of Dial Gauge for Squareness of Hole Axes. A useful application of the dial gauge is in testing the squareness of two holes or between a hole and a flat face. If a dial gauge is attached to, and rotated with, a shaft which fits into a hole, it rotates on the hole axis and thus may be arranged to indicate the squareness of this axis with

* See B.S.S. No. 907.

a bar in another hole or with a flat face.   An indication of how these
tests may be carried out is shown in Fig. 142 (*a*) and (*b*).   At (*a*)
the position of gauge is adjusted until a reading is shown when it is
in contact with the left-hand end of the bar as shown on the diagram.
It is now swung over until it contacts the other end of the bar and the
two bars are perpendicular if both clock readings are the same.   In

(*a*) Testing Squareness of Bore
Axes *AB* and *CD*

(*b*) Testing Squareness of Face *G*
with Axis *EF* of Centre Hole

Fɪɢ. 142.—Uses of Dial Indicator.

the test shown at (*b*) the reading must remain constant whilst the
gauge and bar are rotated a complete turn.   The reader may, at first,
be rather doubtful as to why this test shows up an error in perpendicu-
larity.   If he is, let him imagine how the clock would swing if there
were a *large* error, and he will then realise that the method is really
very accurate.

Tests for Roundness and Concentricity

Due to faults in machines and tools, distortion and spring in work
and so on, parts which should be round are very often not so.   The
easiest and most obvious way to verify roundness is to use a micrometer
or calipers and test the diameter of the part in several different positions
in the same plane.   If these dimensions vary, the part is not round.
If the test shows the diameter to be the same at every position, the
part can be assumed to be round.   We should like to show, however,
that it is possible to have a shape which, when measured across different
extremities, will appear to be round, although it is not so.   Such a
shape is shown exaggerated in Fig. 143 (*a*), and similar shapes to this
can be and are produced on some classes of machine if conditions are not
correct.   In the shape shown, the diameters d_1, d_2, d_3, etc., are all
equal, so that a micrometer test would give a false impression of roundness, and the only true test is to rotate the figure in a Vee block under

a dial gauge as shown at (b). This will serve to impress the reader
that in the workshop things are not always what they seem.

(a)   (b)

(a) " Constant Diameter " Figure   (b) Test for Roundness with
which would appear to be round if   Vee Block and Clock Indi-
measured across Diameters.   cator.

FIG. 143.

Concentricity. On many turned parts produced on the lathe, it
is important that various diameters shall be true with one another
or have the same centre. This is called concentricity. The clock

(a) Testing Bush for Concentricity

(b) Concentricity Test on Enlarged
Portion of Shaft

FIG. 144.

gauge is again useful for this test, and if the part can be pushed on
to a bar or mandril, it may be tested between centres as shown at
Fig. 144 (a), but the previous precaution of testing the truth of the
mandril itself should be carried out first. This arrangement is also
useful for testing a centred bar for straightness and for concentricity
with its own centres. When it is not convenient to put the article
between centres it may be rotated whilst resting in a Vee block as
shown at (b). For these tests, as well as for certain marking out
operations, a pair of centres mounted on a base-plate, and lined up
to a central slot, form a very useful piece of workshop equipment.
This is indicated in Fig. 144 (a).

Angular Testing

When two surfaces are at any angle other than 90°, the angle between them must be tested with some form of protractor. Instruments for this purpose may have a scale of degrees, enabling the angle to be read off, or they may consist of a gauge which must be set to the angle before use. The *bevel* (Fig. 145) is an example of this second variety of gauge, and must be set to the correct angle before use.

[*L. S. Starrett Co.*

Fig. 145.—Bevel.

The protractor head of the combination square has its own scale of degrees marked on it, and will be found capable of dealing with most of the angular testing encountered. For very accurate work, however, this protractor is not suitable because the scale is very fine, and the degrees are not subdivided. Accurate angular testing should be carried out with the *vernier protractor*. A diagram of this is shown at Fig. 146, together with an enlarged diagram of the vernier scale. The main scale on the protractor is divided up into degrees from 0 to 90 each way. The vernier scale is divided up so that 12 of its divisions occupy the same space as 23° on the main scale (Fig. 146 (b)), so that

$$\text{one vernier division} = \frac{23}{12} = 1\tfrac{11}{12}°, \text{ i.e. } \tfrac{1}{12} \text{ or } 5' \text{ less than } 2°.$$

The instrument therefore allows settings to 5 minutes of angle to be obtained.

Reading the Vernier Protractor

(1) Read off directly from the scale the number of whole degrees between 0 on the main scale and 0 on the vernier scale.

(2) Count *in the same direction* the number of divisions from the 0 on the vernier to the first line on it which is level with a line on the main scale. As each division on the vernier represents 5 minutes, the number of these divisions multiplied by 5 will be the number of minutes to be added to the whole number of degrees. Actually the multiplication is not necessary, as it has been done on the scale.

Thus in Fig. 146 (c), the number of whole degrees is 52, and the mark on the vernier representing 45 minutes is level. The reading is therefore 52°–45'. Diagrams showing some uses of the protractor are shown at Fig. 146 (d).

(a) Protractor.

[L. S. Starrett Co.

Main Scale of Degrees

Vernier Scale

(b) Vernier Scale showing 12 Divisions on Vernier Scale equal to 23° on Main Scale.

(c) Reading 52°—45'. [L. S. Starrett Co.

FIG. 146.—The Vernier Protractor.

[*L. S. Starrett Co.*

(*d*) Applications of Vernier Protractor.

FIG. 146—*contd.*

FIG. 147.—Precaution when using Protractor.

These angles must be =90°
i.e. perpendicular

Hints regarding the Measurement of Angles

(1) *The protractor blade should always be perpendicular to the surface being tested and should lie on a line of greatest slope* (see Fig. 147). The fit between the blade and the surface may be observed by looking for " daylight " or using cigarette papers.

(2) Angles may be dimensioned on drawings in such a way that some doubt exists as to which angle the protractor must be set. Two such cases and the protractor settings for them are shown in Fig. 148.

Fig. 148.—Protractor setting for Obscure Angles.

Although, as a general rule, the distances between lines on a drawing should *never* be measured with a rule, the reader will find that angles shown on drawings are fairly consistent in their accuracy. If, therefore, the reader is in doubt whether he should set the protractor to the angle shown, or to its difference from 90°, he will be fairly safe in putting the protractor up against the drawing.

(3) Always check the reading of the protractor *after* the clamping screw has been locked up, as the setting may have moved.

Measurement

So far we have dealt with checking the accuracy of our work without much regard to its actual sizes. We must now consider the methods employed for the actual measurement of it.

" Line " and " End " Measurement

A length may be expressed as the distance between two lines (line measurement) or as the distance between two faces (end measurement). The most common example of line measurement is the rule with its divisions shown as lines marked on it, whilst we use end measurement when we employ calipers, micrometer, solid length bars, etc., to obtain our size. One of the most difficult problems in precision work is to transfer a dimension from its " line " to its " end " form, and this has probably been brought home to the reader in the setting of his calipers. We can set calipers much more accurately to a given size from the faces of a block than we can from the markings on a rule.

Actually when we set the calipers from our rule we do get an " end " effect on one leg of them if we hold it against the end of the rule.

For this reason, in the shop, we employ end methods as far as possible when we wish to obtain an important dimension ; the process of comparing anything with lines for the purpose of its measurement really requires the assistance of a microscope if any degree of accuracy is to be obtained.

The Rule. When a dimension is given on a drawing as a *fraction*, without any covering note as to a particular type of fit (e.g. press fit, or to suit such and such a part), or without stating any particular method of machining the size (e.g. in the case of a hole, " $\frac{3}{4}$ in. *reamer* "), it may generally be assumed that the dimension may be made with a rule.   If calipers and rule are used it is still a rule dimension.   The degree of accuracy to which work may be produced when measurements are made by a rule depends on the quality of the rule, and on the skill of the user.   The marks on a good-class rule vary from 0·005 in. to 0·007 in. wide, so that we cannot expect to obtain a degree of accuracy much closer than within 0·005 in., but a good workman should be able to work as closely as this.   An important factor is that of possessing a good rule and getting used to it, and the reader is advised to buy the best rule he can obtain and accustom himself to its markings.

Fig. 149.

The most useful and convenient markings are inches on one face of the rule, and metric units on the other.   A good example is the Chesterman No. 1561 D shown in Fig. 149.   On one side this has $\frac{1}{8}$ inches and their subdivisions along one edge and the subdivisions of $\frac{1}{10}$ths along the other.   The reverse side is graduated in millimetres on one edge and $\frac{1}{2}$ millimetres on the other.   The $\frac{1}{2}$ mm. are not much use, as it is generally easier to gauge $\frac{1}{2}$ mm. on the full scale of millimetres than on the half scale.   If the length of the graduation lines for such small divisions were reduced to about $\frac{1}{3}$ of the length they are generally made, the eye would be better able to make use of them. This applies also to the $\frac{1}{64}$-in. rulings on the average rule, and the reader will find it easier to measure, say, $\frac{43}{64}$ in. (i.e. $\frac{11}{16}$ in.–$\frac{1}{64}$ in.) on a scale marked in $\frac{1}{16}$ths and $\frac{1}{32}$nds, than on a full scale of $\frac{1}{64}$ths.   If the reader prefers a 6-in. rule, the Chesterman No. 1561 D/3 is a good example.

Rules marked in $\frac{1}{12}$ths, $\frac{1}{24}$ths, etc., have little use in a workshop and should be avoided.

A good rule is worth looking after and should neither be used as a feeler gauge under shaper tools or milling cutters, nor for scraping Tee slots and machine tables. The end of the rule particularly should be preserved from wear, as it generally forms the basis for one end of the dimension. Rusting of the rule should be avoided by oiling it during week-ends and when it is not in use. The thickness of a rule may often be put to good use, and the rules mentioned above will be found ·040 in. and ·020 in. thick respectively.

When taking measurements with a rule, it should be so held that the graduation lines are as close as possible (preferably touching) to the faces being measured.* The eye which is observing the reading should be as near as possible opposite to the mark being read. This avoids what is called " parallax," and the reader may try for himself the errors which parallax may cause if he reads the large hand of a clock when it is vertical, by looking at it not from the front, but from a very acute side angle.

As far as is possible, the end of the rule should be held flush with one of the faces to be measured, the reading then being taken somewhere along the rule.

Calipers. To measure the diameter of a circular part involves straddling across it to obtain the length of its greatest dimension. Even if the end of the bar is available, a rule alone is not a convenient method of taking its size, so that for round work calipers are used.

(a)
(a) Spring Calipers.   (b) Firm Joint Calipers.   (b)   [L. S. Starrett Co.

FIG. 150.—Calipers.

The shape of calipers varies according to whether they are for external or internal use, and they may be stiff jointed at the hinge of the legs, their opening being maintained by the friction at the joint, or the joint may be free and spring controlled, the opening being adjusted and maintained by a nut working on a screw. Screw-controlled spring calipers are more easily adjusted, but just as good work may be done

* To assist in bringing the graduations close to the work, rules may be obtained with bevelled edges, but great care is necessary that the edges do not get knocked about, as they are easily damaged.

with a good pair of stiff jointed ones which the reader can make for himself.

Examples of calipers are shown at Fig. 150.

When working with outside calipers they should be adjusted by tapping one leg (stiff joint), or by the adjusting screw, until when the work is straddled by the legs, it is just possible to feel the contact between the calipers and the work. The contact should not be too heavy, otherwise the legs may be slightly sprung and a false reading obtained. When a nice feel has been obtained on the job the size should be read on a rule by resting the end of one leg on the end of the rule and taking the reading at the other (Fig. 151 (a)). To set outside calipers to a fairly particular size they should be set from a block or gauge of the given dimension.

(a) Reading the Outside Calipers

(b) From the Rule

(c) From a Micrometer

Reading Inside Calipers

Fig. 151.

Inside calipers are adjusted in the same way, but their manipulation to obtain the size of the hole they are measuring requires a little more skill than with outside conditions. They should be adjusted until they are at the *largest* size at which their legs can just be felt contacting the extremities of a diameter of the hole, and to find this, the joint should be held by the thumb and first finger, one leg held stationary in contact with the inside of the hole and the other leg rocked about in a small circle. After a demonstration by a skilled user, and a little practice, the reader will soon learn the manipulation necessary for the operation. The opening of inside calipers may be checked by a rule or micrometer. If the rule is used, hold the end of the rule and one leg of the calipers pressed against a vertical flat surface (e.g. edge of a lathe bed) and read the other leg (Fig. 151 (*b*)). The micrometer reading may be obtained by holding one leg in contact with the micrometer anvil, and rotating the other leg slightly, at the same time that the micrometer is screwed up, until the " feel " of the top leg against the spindle of the micrometer is eventually obtained (Fig. 151 (*c*)). In this way, with careful use, it is easy to measure a hole to within $\frac{1}{2}$ a thousandth of an inch. As in the case of a rule, the reader should possess his own calipers and look after them.

The Micrometer *

When a part has to be measured to the third place of decimals in the English system, or the second place in the metric, we need a more accurate method of measurement than can be obtained with a rule,

(*a*) Micrometer showing interior Mechanism).

(*b*) Divisions on Micrometer.

FIG. 152.

and the micrometer is commonly used. A micrometer consists of a semi-circular frame having a cylindrical extension (the barrel) at its right end, and a hardened anvil inside, at the left end. The bore of the barrel is screwed 40 T.P.I. and the spindle, to which is attached the thimble, screws through. Adjustment is provided for the longitudinal position of the spindle, and for the tightness of the screw thread. The barrel is graduated in $\frac{1}{10}$ths and $\frac{1}{40}$ths of an inch for a length of 1 in., and the rim of the thimble is divided into 25 equal divisions. See Fig. 152 (*a*) and (*b*). The measurement is taken

* B.S.S. No. 870.

between the face of the anvil and the end of the spindle, and the range of the micrometer is 1 in., so that if we wish to measure up to 6 inches, we must have six micrometers ; 0 to 1 in., 1 in. to 2 in., and so on, with 5 in. to 6 in. as the largest size. There is a model which permits measurements from 0 to 2 in. to be made which has a frame of the size of a 1-in. to 2-in. instrument, with a sliding anvil which has 1 in. of movement. For measuring from 0 to 1 in. the anvil is set to project 1 in. inside the frame and for 1 in. to 2 in. it is slid out, the instrument being set to zero by means of a setting piece 1·000 in. diameter. This micrometer is shown at Fig. 153.

Fig. 153.—0–2 in. Micrometer.

Reading the Micrometer. Since the spindle screw has 40 threads per inch, 1 turn of the thimble opens the jaws $\frac{1}{40}$ of an inch. Now $\frac{1}{40}$ in. corresponds to $\frac{1000}{40} = 25$ thousandths or 0·025 in., and as the rim of the thimble is divided into 25 parts round its circumference, one of these divisions corresponds to $\frac{1}{1000}$ in. (0·001) of movement of the spindle. The barrel is divided into $\frac{1}{10}$ths (numbered 1, 2, 3, etc.), and each tenth is divided into four parts ($\frac{1}{40}$ths.). Each of these small divisions corresponds to the movement caused by one turn of the thimble, so that each time we turn the thimble one of the small divisions is uncovered.

To take a micrometer reading add the tenths, the number of 0·025's showing beyond the last tenth, and the number of odd thousandths on the thimble.

Reading. 0·372″   (a)   (b)   Reading. 0·441.

Fig. 154.

Thus in Fig. 154 (a) the reading is 0·3 + (2 × 0·025) + 0·022
$$= 0.3 + 0.05 + 0.022$$
$$= 0.372 \text{ in.}$$
and in Fig. 154 (b) it is :
$$0.4 + 0.025 + 0.016$$
$$= 0.441 \text{ in.}$$

The Inside Micrometer. For the accurate measurement of the bore of holes an inside micrometer may be used. This consists of a head similar to the barrel and thimble of the ordinary micrometer, and a set of lengthening bars to increase the range. The movement obtained on the head is $\frac{1}{2}$ in. and the bars are inserted up to the size required. The manipulation of this instrument is similar to that

[*L. S. Starrett Co.*

FIG. 155.—Inside Micrometer.

for inside calipers, and the reader should seek the help of an experienced mechanic to show him when using for the first time (Fig. 155).

The Accuracy of the Micrometer. The accuracy with which measurements can be made with a micrometer depends on the skill of the user, the accuracy of the micrometer screw, the number of times the instrument has been dropped and various other factors. The pressure with which it is screwed up to the work will vary the reading and a " heavy " user will obtain a smaller reading than one who uses the instrument lightly. Micrometers can be obtained with a ratchet on the end of the thimble (Fig. 152 (a)), and if the ratchet sleeve instead of the thimble is held when screwing up, the ratchet slips when the pressure on the screw reaches a certain amount. If the ratchet is always used, all the readings will have been obtained under the same measuring pressure and will therefore be consistent.

Some mechanics consider their own " feel " of the micrometer to be superior to that obtained by using the ratchet, and although this may or may not be true, the ratchet does give consistent results for *any* user of the instrument. Results as between different mechanics with their individual " feels " are bound to vary ; in fact the pressure exerted by one individual will not always be the same but will vary with personal factors, e.g. health, temper, tiredness, etc. However, as probably more people use the micrometer without the ratchet than otherwise, the reader should learn a proper conception of micrometer-feel from an experienced mechanic, as it is one of the things he cannot learn from books. There is now a British micrometer constructed with a ratchet connexion between the thimble and the screw, so that readings *have* to be taken through the ratchet.

The accuracy of the micrometer screw will depend on the price paid for the instrument. It cannot be assumed that if the reading is 0 when the jaws are closed, it will be correct when they are open at (say) 0·750 in. for example ; the screw may vary along its length in such a way that at 0·400 the opening is a little *less* than the reading, and when screwed out to 0·800 it might be a fraction of a thousandth *more* than that indicated. The safest way, if a trustworthy reading at any particular size is desired, is to check the instrument against a master gauge at or near the size required. Rough usage and dropping will soon impair the accuracy of any micrometer, and it should be treated with as much care as any other valuable and useful instrument.

The Vernier Calipers *

With a micrometer we take an " end " measurement between two jaws, the opening of which is controlled by a very accurate screw. The vernier also gives an " end " measurement, but the position of the jaws is controlled from a " line " scale, accurate transference being made possible by a vernier scale. A vernier scale is the name given to any scale making use of the difference between two scales which are nearly, but not quite alike, for obtaining small differences. We have already seen how such a scale is applied to a protractor for reading small divisions of a degree ; its principle for length measurement is along similar lines.

English Vernier Scale. The principle of the English length vernier will be gathered from Fig. 156. On the upper (measuring) scale, 1 in. is divided into 10 parts (numbered 1, 2, 3, 4, etc.) and each $\frac{1}{10}$th is divided into 4, giving

$$\tfrac{1}{4} \text{ of } \tfrac{1}{10}\text{th} = \tfrac{1}{40} \text{ in.} = \tfrac{25}{1000} \text{ in.}$$

Top (measuring) scale

Lower (sliding) scale

FIG. 156.

On the lower (sliding) scale, $\frac{6}{10}$ in. is divided into 25 parts. Each of these will have a length of

$$\tfrac{1}{25} \text{ of } \tfrac{6}{10} = \tfrac{6}{250} = \tfrac{24}{1000}$$

and the difference in length between one small division on the measuring scale and one on the sliding scale is

$$\tfrac{25}{1000} - \tfrac{24}{1000} = \tfrac{1}{1000} \text{ in.}$$

If, then, the two zeros are level and the sliding scale is moved until the first small marks are level, the movement will have been $\frac{1}{1000}$ in., or 0·001 in.; if it is moved until the 15th mark on the lower scale is level with a mark on the upper scale, the lower scale has moved 0·015 in., and so on.

FIG. 157.—Vernier Calipers.

* B.S.S. No. 887.

In the vernier calipers the lower scale is part of the sliding jaw and the upper scale forms the body of the instrument which is solid with the fixed jaw (Fig. 157). When the jaws are closed the reading is $\frac{0}{+}$ $\frac{}{0}$ and in order to read the opening when the jaws are at any setting, we count up the total amount on the measuring scale, to the left of the 0 on the sliding scale and add it to the amount indicated on the vernier scale.

Fig. 158 (a) and (b) show two settings of the vernier, the readings being as follows :

(a) To the left of the 0 on the sliding scale the reading is 2·125. The 11 mark on the vernier is level.
    Hence, total reading = 2·125 + 0·011 = 2·136 in.

(b) The reading to the left of the sliding scale zero is 4·850 and the 9 on the vernier is level.
    Hence, total reading = 4·850 + 0·009
                         = 4·859 in.

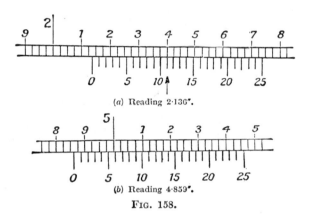

(a) Reading 2·136".

(b) Reading 4·859".

FIG. 158.

Use of the Vernier Calipers. The vernier is made in various sizes from 6 in. upwards, a good size being one capable of working up to 12 in. It is not used for straddling round bars in the same way as a micrometer, but may be employed for measuring large diameters on their ends, or large bores (Fig. 159). When it is used for a bore, or any other inside measurement, the reading will give the *inside* jaw opening, and allowance must be made for the total thickness of the jaw ends. This may be obtained by closing the jaws and finding their combined thickness with a micrometer. For setting the vernier to the work or to a reading, the extra slide shown to the right of the main slide is used. If this is locked, and the main slide left free, turning the knurled finger nut will move the screw, and the main slide attached to it. Without this it would be difficult to obtain a fine movement. When setting the vernier this way, lock up the small slide but do not leave the screw on the main slide quite free, but give it the slightest bit of tension. After adjusting the instrument to the work with the finger nut, clamp up the main slide and check up again on the work.

If the vernier is being set to a particular dimension, check the reading after the main slide has been clamped, and *always clamp the main slide before using.* When using the vernier, balance it lightly in

(a)*External*   (b)*Internal*

Fig. 159.—Use of Vernier to measure Spigot and Recess.

the hands, and *under no circumstances use the slightest force to gauge the work.* The construction of the instrument is such that the jaws are easily sprung open, and the instrument ruined.

As in the case of the micrometer, the reader will be well advised to seek the advice of a skilled mechanic on the manipulation of the vernier.

The Use of Gauges.

The academic distinction between measurement and gauging is that, in measurement, we use some instrument to *measure* the dimension of the part, whilst in gauging we check the accuracy of the work by *comparing* it with a gauge, without being particularly interested in its size.

The variety and scope of the gauges employed in engineering work-shops is so great that it would occupy more than this book to describe them all, but the reader ought to be acquainted with one or two of the more common types.

Hole Gauging.—Plug Gauges. When a mating hole and shaft have to be produced it is always necessary to make some form of fit, depending on the conditions. If the combination is a working bearing, the shaft will have to be a running (easy) fit ; if the shaft has to be a fixture in the hole, such as for a tightly fitting pulley, the connexion between the hole and shaft will have to be such that some force is necessary to assemble them. The pulley might be driven on with a hammer (driving fit) or the shaft forced in under a press (force fit). Naturally, different kinds of fit will require different allowances to be made between the hole and shaft sizes ; for a running fit the shaft will be slightly smaller than the hole, whilst for a force fit it will have to be a little larger. Whatever these variations might be, the hole is always made to the standard (nominal) size and the shaft varied to suit. When boring a hole, therefore, into which another part has to fit, the size of the hole must conform to the exact standard size, and to check this a plug gauge is used. A skilled turner could easily work to the exact bore required by using his inside calipers and a micrometer, but he will always prefer to have the gauge as a final check. A *standard plug gauge* (Fig. 160 (*a*)) has its diameter finished to the standard size (e.g. 1·000 in. for a 1-in. hole) and is used in general engineering workshops, toolrooms, etc., where production quantities are not great, and accuracy is more important. In production workshops, where large

(*a*) Standard Plug Gauge

(*b*) Limit Plug Gauge

(*c*) Plate Gauge

FIG. 160.—Hole Gauges.

quantities have to be produced with lesser skilled operators, a *tolerance* is allowed on the size of the holes which are dimensioned with *limits*. For example, a 1-in. hole might be dimensioned $1\cdot000'' {\substack{+ \ \cdot0012'' \\ - \ \cdot0012''}}$, and provided it measures anything within these sizes, it would be suitable. The 1·000 + ·0012 dimension = 1·0012 in. is the *high limit*, and the 1·000 — ·0012 = 0·9988 in. is the *low limit*. The difference between them (in this case 0·0024 in.), is called the *tolerance*, and represents a safety margin for errors in workmanship, wear of tools, etc. Holes of this type are gauged with *limit plug gauges* which have " GO " and " NOT GO " ends. The " GO " end of the gauge must enter the hole, being made the size of the lower limit, whilst the " NOT GO " end, which is the size of the upper limit, must not enter. Usually the " GO " end is made longer than the " NOT GO " as shown at Fig. 160 (*b*). This is because it is continually being subjected to frictional contact with the sides of the hole and would wear rapidly if short ; also if short it would tend to jamb in the hole. The " NOT GO," which should never enter a hole, need only have sufficient length to carry its size.

For gauging large holes a solid plug gauge would be unduly heavy, and various methods are utilised to reduce weight. The plate gauge (Fig. 160 (*c*)) is such an example and has the extremities of its end plates ground to the required diameter.

Point Gauges. For large holes (more than about 1 ft. dia.),

FIG. 161.—Gauging large Bores with Point Gauge.

plate gauges become unwieldy in use and tend to jamb in the hole. To gauge holes of this type point gauges are commonly used and consist merely of a bar of steel with its ends tapered off and rounded. Gauges of this type are used in much the same way as an inside micrometer, but being of a fixed length, cannot be adjusted to the hole. If one end of the gauge is held stationary in contact with the hole surface, a small amount of sideways rock is possible with the other end between the positions in which it contacts the hole. This is shown in Fig. 161, and the relation between the gauge length (L), the hole diameter (D) and the amount of rock (2w) is approximately as follows : *

$$D = \frac{w^2}{2L} + L$$

Shaft Gauging. Shafts and male components are usually checked with *caliper gauges*, an example of which is shown at Fig. 162 (a). In their smaller sizes, these gauges are generally called *snap gauges*, and are made with the " GO " jaws at one end and the " NOT GO "

(a) Limit Caliper Gauge   (c) Adjustable Caliper Gauge

(b) Snap Gauge   (d) Ring Gauge

FIG. 162.—Gauges for Shafts.

at the other as shown at (b). The use of caliper and snap gauges is almost entirely restricted to production work where large quantities of similar articles are made. In general engineering shops and tool-

* The proof of this is given in the Author's *Senior Workshop Calculations.*

rooms shafts are brought to size by means of the micrometer. In production work, shafts are made to limits in the same way as holes, and these limits are put on the caliper gauges. Caliper gauges may be made with adjustable anvils as shown at (c). These are useful in workshops carrying out the production of medium quantities of different parts, as they may be set to different sizes and limits, thus saving time and expense of making new gauges.

The *ring gauge* (Fig. 162 (d)) would seem to be an obvious method of gauging a shaft, but in practice it is rarely used. This is because a gauge of this type, which entirely envelops the surface being gauged, places an extremely stringent test on its accuracy, and prohibitive time and expense would be incurred in working to ring gauges. Furthermore, a ring gauge can only be used from the shaft end, and must be threaded all along the shaft to test its parallelism. This condition is not always convenient when a shaft is being turned between centres. Lastly, a ring gauge either does, or does not, go on the shaft; it tells us nothing about a shaft which may be slightly too large or too small for it, and we should require two ring gauges for " GO " and " NOT GO " conditions.

Material for Gauges. The gauging surfaces of gauges must be extremely hard and resistant to wear as otherwise they would very soon lose their size. For caliper and snap gauges, the most common material employed is cast steel which is hardened on the gauging faces only. Plug gauges present a more difficult problem because of the distortion and cracking which is liable to occur when cast steel is quenched. If this material is used, extreme care is necessary in hardening to avoid this risk. The heat treatment of gauges is greatly facilitated, and the risk of spoilt gauges eliminated, by using one of the alloy tool steels which harden by oil quenching. Plug gauges of case-hardened mild steel are quite satisfactory as they possess the glass hard skin and tough core necessary for good wear combined with serviceable strength.

The Metric System

The standard of length in the metric system is the *metre*. This is subdivided into 100 *centimetres*, each centimetre being further subdivided into 10 *millimetres*. A metre is equivalent to 39·37 in., so that

$$1 \text{ m.} = 100 \text{ cm.} \qquad 1 \text{ cm.} = 10 \text{ mm.}$$
$$1 \text{ m.} = 1000 \text{ mm.} = 39 \cdot 37 \text{ in.}$$

From this we have that 1 in. = 25·4 mm. and 25·4 is the conversion constant we must use for changing from inches to millimetres and vice versa.

To convert from inches to millimetres *multiply* by 25·4.
,, ,, ,, millimetres to inches *divide* ,, ,,

Some workshops use the metric system entirely, whilst others use both English and metric systems. If the reader happens to be trained where the English system is used, and then moves to a metric shop, he will find that as far as measurement is concerned, he must learn a fresh language, and train his mind afresh. This is because we form a habit of visualising lengths in our minds, and upon seeing a certain dimension on a drawing we mentally picture the length stated. Let us now be presented with a drawing stating lengths in an unfamiliar unit and we are, for a time, like a ship in uncharted waters. It was the writer's experience to be brought up in a shop using both English and metric units, but employing metric for all important dimensions. He therefore cultivated the metric line of thought more strongly than the English, and learned the metric equivalents to all the important inch fractions. Later, when moving to another shop where all English was used, when seeing a dimension, he found himself mentally converting it to millimetres in order to visualise its length, and this habit persisted for some years. At the time of writing, the writer has the unrestricted use of a metric micrometer because all the other possible users are English-minded and will not be bothered to make the conversions !

When drawings are in metric units they are generally dimensioned in millimetres only ; lengths will merely be put down as 260 ; 55 ; 18·63, etc., often without the " mm. " qualification. It is not usual to employ any fractions except the $\frac{1}{2}$ and in the shop it is general to refer to the decimal part of a millimetre as so many hundredths. Thus 0·63 would be referred to as 63 hundredths.

The Metric Micrometer

The screw in this micrometer has a pitch of $\frac{1}{2}$ mm., so that the jaws open $\frac{1}{2}$ mm. for each turn of the thimble. The rim of the thimble is divided into 50 parts, which gives a reading of $\frac{1}{2} \div 50 = \frac{1}{100}$ mm. The barrel is marked in millimetres and $\frac{1}{2}$ mm. divisions, so that to take a reading we add the number of hundredths indicated on the thimble to the millimetre and $\frac{1}{2}$ mm. uncovered on the barrel. In Fig. 163 there are $11\frac{1}{2}$ mm. uncovered, and the thimble reading is

Reading. 11·83 m.m.

FIG. 163.

33 hundredths. The reading, therefore, is 11·5 + 0·33 = 11·83 mm. Metric micrometers range upwards in steps of 25 mm. (0 to 25 ; 25 to 50, etc.) corresponding to the English (0 to 1 in., 1 in. to 2 in., etc.). Had the above reading been on a 25 mm. to 50 mm. instrument the opening would have been 25 + 11·83 = 36·83 mm. When working between metric and English measurement it is useful to remember that $\frac{1}{1000}$ in. $= \dfrac{2\frac{1}{2}}{100}$ mm. approx., and that 1 mm. is about the same as $\frac{40}{1000}$ths in.

The Metric Vernier

An enlarged diagram of the metric vernier scale is shown at Fig. 164. The distance from 0 to 1 on the top scale is 10 mm., and it will be seen that 25 divisions on the sliding vernier scale are equal to 12 mm. on the top measuring scale. The length of the bottom divisions is

Top (measuring) scale

Lower (sliding) scale

Fig. 164.—Metric Vernier Scale.

$\frac{12}{25} = 0.48$ mm., and since the top divisions are $\frac{1}{2}$ (0·5) mm., the difference is $0.5 - 0.48 = 0.02$ mm., which represents the accuracy to which readings may be taken. To read the vernier, count up the total length indicated as far as the 0 on the sliding scale, and note the mark on the sliding scale which is level with a mark on the top scale. This latter amount will represent the number of 0·02 mm. which must be added to the first reading. Hence, opening of jaws = amount indicated up to the 0 + *twice* the indication where the marks are level. Fig. 165 shows metric verniers reading (*a*) 32·32 mm. and (*b*) 18·6 mm.

(*a*) Reading = 32 + 2 × ·16 = 32·32 mm.

(*b*) Reading = 18·5 + 2 × ·05 = 18·60 mm.

Fig. 165.

Another form of metric vernier giving readings to 0·02 mm. is obtained by dividing 49 mm. on the main scale into 50 divisions on the vernier scale. One main scale division is now 1 mm., and a vernier scale division is $\frac{49}{50}$ mm., the difference being $1 - \frac{49}{50} = \frac{1}{50} = 0.02$ mm. This scale avoids the necessity of dividing up the main scale into $\frac{1}{2}$-mm. divisions.

CHAPTER 8

THE BENCH. FLAT SURFACES—FILING, CHIPPING AND SCRAPING

The work carried out at the fitting bench of a workshop will depend upon the class of work for which the shop exists. The benchwork in a toolroom, or general engineering shop working on individual pieces of equipment, will be of a highly skilled nature, calling for extensive knowledge and experience. Here the work will include marking out, and the preparation of work for machining ; the adjustment of details after machining ; the building up of jigs, mechanisms and other assemblies after the machined details have been made ; the making and finishing of tools, gauges and other small details ; the repair and adjustment of machine tools, and so on. A competent fitter at such a bench needs to have a knowledge of the chief methods of machining, with the ability to carry them out himself, a knowledge of materials, measurement and testing. In addition he must be skilled in the various aspects of his own trade as a fitter.

At the other extreme, in a shop working on a mass-produced article, that part of the work called " fitting " might be the mere operation of assembling parts together, a job which, in a simple case, could be learned completely in a few months. We advise the reader to give such an occupation a wide berth, as although he might earn higher wages than if he were learning the trade of a true fitter, he may realise too late that he has been following a " blind alley " occupation and have his whole life ruined thereby.

The Bench and Vise

The work of a fitter will probably take him to various places, but the bench is his headquarters. This should be a rigid structure provided with racks or shelves at the back for storage of articles and tools, so that the bench top may be kept tidy and clear. Lock-up drawers should be available for the reception of each fitter's private tools. A rigid bench is essential, as nothing is more aggravating, and conducive to inaccurate work, than a bench which wobbles about as one applies force to a job supported on it. For holding work whilst operating on it the fitter has a *vise* (or vice) attached to the bench. This consists of an iron or steel cast body into which is fitted a square section slide formed to a jaw at its outer end. The corresponding fixed jaw is incorporated on the body of the vise, and the two jaws are faced with hardened steel jaw-pieces, screwed to the jaws and cut with teeth to help grip the work. The sliding jaw is operated by a screw and nut, and in the quick-operating types the nut only embraces the lower portion of the screw, being capable of disengagement from it by the operation of a trigger at the front of the slide (Fig. 166). The height of the bench should be such that the top of the vise-jaws is at about the same height as the fitter's elbow when he stands normally

(a) Elevation.

[*J. Parkinson & Son.*

(b) Section of quick operating Type.

FIG. 166.—Fitter's Vise.

at the bench with his upper arm hanging vertically, and forearm bent horizontally.

To avoid damage to the surface of finished work by the hardened jaw-pieces, it is usual to employ clamps (or clams) made of copper, brass, lead or soft steel.

The Marking-out Table. This is an essential item of equipment in a fitting shop, and consists of a cast-iron table of fairly substantial dimensions supported horizontally on rigid legs. The top of the table

FIG. 167.—Marking-out Table.

is planed flat, and its edges should be machined square. The smallest practicable size for a marking-out table is about 3 ft. square, and we shall refer later to its uses (Fig. 167).

The Hand-Hammer *

The hammer is probably the most used of all the tools possessed by the fitter, and is an item of his equipment upon which he sets great value. The most common shapes of engineers' hammers are shown at Fig. 168 (a) and they are specified by the shape of the end opposite the striking face, called the *pein*. The ball pein is the most common of the three, the ball end being used mostly for riveting over the ends of pins and rivets. Cross and straight peins are also useful for riveting in awkward places; another use for these ends is that of *peening*. This consists of striking the surface to be peened a number of light,

(1) Ball Pein   (2) Cross Pein   (3) Straight Pein

(a) Fitters Hammers

(b) Rawhide Hammer

Fɪɢ. 168.

sharp blows with the pein of the hammer, the effect being to stretch the metal and elongate it. Thus if the concave side of a bent bar is peened and elongated, it is often possible by this means to straighten the bar.

Hammer heads are made from a plain steel of about 0.6% carbon and are shaped by stamping or forging. The two ends must be hardened and tempered, the centre of the head, with the eye, being left soft. When correctly hardened the face and pein should be able to pass the following tests without showing any perceptible damage or indentation : (a) a blow from the ball pein of a 4-oz. shafted hammer of correct hardness, (b) twelve full blows on the end of a rigidly supported normalised bar of the same material and approximately the same section as the face of the head being tested.

The principal consideration in choosing a hammer for any particular purpose is that of its weight. Engineers' hammers are made in weights varying from $\frac{1}{4}$ lb. to 3 lb., and of this range the most commonly used are hammers ranging from $\frac{1}{2}$ to $1\frac{1}{2}$ or 2 lb. Light hammers are used for lighter and more delicate operations such as light riveting, striking centre punches and small chisels, driving in small pins, etc. Heavy heads are necessary on heavy chipping, driving pulleys and collars on

* B.S.S. No. 876.

to shafts, driving large pins and shafts into holes, etc. To remove an obstinate shaft, pin, pulley or any other detail requiring force, it is useless to employ a light hammer; providing adequate support can be obtained, the hammer will be more effective if it has plenty of weight.

Hammer Shafts. These should be of well-seasoned, straight-grained hickory or ash, free from knots or other defects. They should be of a size and length suited to the size of the head, and after being shaped to suit the eye should be secured with a hardwood wedge.

Blow delivered by a Hammer. The force of the blow delivered by a hammer is a difficult quantity to determine, because of various factors which we cannot measure. If we know, or assume certain things, however, we can form a rough estimate of it.

When a body of weight W is moving at a speed v, its Kinetic Energy is $\dfrac{Wv^2}{2g}$ ft.-lb., where $g = 32 \cdot 2$ if v is in feet per second.

If we can estimate the speed of a hammer head, we can thus calculate the energy it possesses at the moment it strikes its objective, and this energy is available for doing work on the object being struck.

Now Work = Force × Distance moved, so that if we know the distance moved in bringing the hammer to rest we can estimate the *average* force of the blow.

EXAMPLE : A 1-lb. hammer moving at 4 ft. per second strikes a pin and drives it a distance of $\frac{1}{8}$ inch. Estimate the average force of the blow.

$$\text{Kinetic energy of hammer} = \frac{Wv^2}{2g} = \frac{1 \times 4^2}{64 \cdot 4} = \frac{16}{64 \cdot 4} \text{ ft./lb.}$$

This is work stored in the hammer head, and if the head is brought to rest in $\frac{1}{8}$ in. ($\frac{1}{96}$ ft.) we have :
Work = Force × Distance

$$\text{i.e. } \frac{16}{64 \cdot 4} \text{ ft./lb.} = \text{Force (lb.)} \times \frac{1}{96} \text{ ft.}$$

From which Force $= \dfrac{16}{64 \cdot 4} \times 96 = 24$ lb.

Soft Hammers. For hitting finished surfaces which would be bruised or damaged by the hardened face of a hammer some form of soft hammer should be used. The chief soft hammers used have heads of rawhide, copper or lead. The rawhide hammer has a head of cast-iron into which plugs of rawhide are inserted, renewals of these being made when the old ones are worn out (Fig. 168 (*b*)). The lead hammer has a lead head cast on to a length of steel tube, whilst the copper hammer has a copper head fastened in some way to a shaft made of tubing.

Files *
The chief cutting tool used by the fitter is the file. We have already discussed the file tooth, but we must now consider the chief

* See B.S.S. No. 498.

types of file and their uses. The chief files are as follows (see also Fig. 169) :

(1) *Flat File.* This file is parallel for about two-thirds of its length and then tapers in width and thickness. It is cut on both faces (double cut) and both edges (single cut).

Fig. 169.—File Shapes.

(2) *Hand File.* The width of this file is parallel throughout, but its thickness tapers similarly to the flat file. Both faces are double cut, and one edge single cut. The uncut edge is called the " safe " edge and prevents cutting into one face of a square corner whilst the other face is being filed. Both these files are used for general surfacing work, the hand file being used more particularly when filing up to a step which must be straight and square.

(3) *Square File.* This is parallel for two-thirds of its length and then tapers off. It is double cut on all sides and is used for filing corners and slots where the hand file could not be entered.

(4) *Round File.* Tapers similar to square file. Used for opening out holes, producing rounded corners, round-ended slots, etc. Round files are usually double cut on the Rough and Bastard qualities over 6 in. long, whilst the Rough and Bastard under 6 in., together with the Second-cut and Smooth, are single cut.

(5) *Half Round.* The rounded side is not a true half-circle, but only a portion of a circle. This side of the file is useful for many purposes involving the formation of a radius. The flat side of this file

is always double cut. The Second-cut and Smooth are only single cut on the curved side.

(6) *Three Square.* Used for corners less than 90°, and in positions where awkward corners have to be taken out. Double cut on all faces. Other and less common files are as follows :

(7) *Warding File.* Similar to the flat file but thinner and parallel on its thickness. Useful for getting out narrow slots.

(8) *Pillar File.* Nearly the same as the hand file but narrower. Useful in narrow apertures which the hand file would not enter.

Second cut, double cut.

Bastard, double cut.

Rough, double cut.

Bastard, rasp.

Smooth, single cut.

Bastard, single cut.

[*Samuel Osborn & Co., Ltd.*

Fig. 170.—File Cuts (12-in. File).

(9) *Mill File.* Similar to the flat file but parallel on both width and thickness. The *mill saw* file may have one or both edges rounded for forming the radius on saw teeth and in slots.

(10) *The Rasp.* The Horse Rasp is useful for filing soft metals, wood and soft non-metallic materials. The rasp tooth is cut with a pointed punch which gives the tooth form shown (Fig. 170). Generally the faces of a horse rasp are cut partly with rasp teeth, the remainder being ordinary single or cross-cut file teeth.

Grades of Cut. Files may be cut with teeth of the following grades : Rough ; Bastard ; Second Cut ; Smooth and Dead Smooth. The rough grade is not greatly used and the relative tooth sizes for the other grades may be gained from the following table and Fig. 170, which shows a selection of the cuts with which 12-in. files may be obtained.

TABLE 17.   Recommended Practice for Cuts of Files

(*Applying to Flat, Hand, Half Round (Flat Face) and 3 Square.*)

Length of File (in.).		4	6	8	10	12	14	16	18	20
Bastard	Cuts per in. parallel to file length	40	32	26	24	21	19	18	17	16
Second cut		42	38	32	28	26	24	22	20	18
Smooth		60	50	44	42	40	38	36	34	32
Dead smooth		88	84	80	76	72	68	64	60	56

Use of the File.—Cross-filing.   The production of a flat surface by filing is a difficult task.   Whilst we give the following brief description of *cross-filing*, the reader will never learn to file without some advice from a skilled filer, and plenty of practice.   The work should be held firmly in the vise with the minimum amount projecting, and with the surface to be filed truly horizontal.   The file handle is grasped in the right hand as shown at Fig. 171 (*a*), the end of the file-handle pressing against the palm of the hand in line with the wrist-joint.

(a) Cross Filing   (b) Light Filing

Fig. 171.—Holding the File.

The left hand should be used to apply pressure at the end of the blade as shown.   For lighter filing a rather lighter grip is used with the right hand and the end pressure is applied with finger and thumb (Fig. 171 (*b*)). A position should be taken up on the left side of the vise and the feet firmly planted, slightly apart.   A stroke should be made by a slight movement of the right arm from the shoulder, and by a sway of the body towards the work, each of these movements being about equal.   As the file moves over the work it does not move parallel to its length, but in an oblique direction from left to right.   The file must remain horizontal throughout the stroke, which should be long, slow and steady, with pressure only applied on the forward motion.   On the return stroke, although the pressure is relieved from it, the file remains in contact with the work.

Success in filing flat is dependent on keeping the file horizontal throughout its stroke, and this is controlled by the distribution of pressure as between the two hands.   The fault with beginners is to apply too much downward pressure with the right hand at the beginning, and with the left hand at the end of the stroke, causing the file to rock, and produce a round instead of a flat surface.   Careful practice in gradually shifting the pressure from the left to the right hand will ultimately bring success in the production of a flat surface.   But even with the best regulated filing there is always a tendency to rock the file slightly, and the curved surface of a tapered file tends to make a hollow surface, thus counteracting any slight rocking.

To test the surface of work during filing a straightedge should be placed on it occasionally, and the line of contact viewed for "daylight." When any considerable amount of metal has to be removed, the bulk of it should be removed by a rough or bastard-cut file and the surface progressively brought to a finish by second-cut and smooth files.

Draw Filing. File marks may be removed and a good finish imparted by draw-filing (Fig. 172). For this purpose a fine-cut file with a flat face should be used (e.g. a mill file).

FIG. 172.—Draw Filing.   FIG. 173.—File-holder for working on large surfaces.

Filing Broad Surfaces. When a surface is so wide that the handle would prevent the full stroke of the file, a surface file-holder must be used. This clamps on the tang of the file (Fig. 173). Surfaces produced in this way are generally finished flat by scraping (see later), so that small errors in flatness may be corrected during that process.

The Pinning of Files. Soft metals when filed tend to clog the file teeth with minute lumps of metal (" pins "), and if the file is not cleared this accumulation will not only stop the efficient cutting action, but also scratch the work. If the pins are not too firmly wedged they may be removed with a *file card*, which is a brush made from a strip of webbing having thin, hard wire bristles, and nailed on to a piece of wood. Tightly-wedged pins must be scraped out with the point of a scriber. Pinning may be partly prevented by chalking the file or applying turpentine, but these methods should not be used when filing cast iron or brass as they are only applicable to ductile metals and cause the surfaces of brittle metals to glaze under the file.

The Care of Files. The teeth of files are very brittle and easily broken. For this reason files should never be heaped together, nor mixed carelessly with other tools, but should always be kept each in its separate rack. For similar reasons a new file should not be used on a surface of unknown hardness such as the surface of a casting or welded joint. Brittle metals such as cast iron and brass are not readily filed with a worn file, so that new files should be started on these metals, later being transferred to working on mild steel which can easily be cut with a file having teeth slightly worn. When filing a cast-iron surface with edges in the black, scaly condition, the edges should be chamfered slightly with the *edge* of the file to prevent damage to the file teeth on the hard scale.

Chisels and Chipping

The cold chisel is an important cutting tool used by the fitter, and engineers' chisels are distinguished from other chisels by the fact of their not having a wooden handle. The four most important types of chisel are the flat, the cross-cut, the half-round and the diamond chisel. Chisels are made from cast tool steel of octagonal cross-section,

Fig. 174.—A Flat Chisel.

the heaviest being made from about $\frac{3}{4}$-in. material and the smaller sizes from lighter section steel down to about $\frac{3}{8}$ in. Alloy tool steels may also be used for chisels, with improved results (see p. 57). *Centre punches* and *drifts* are modifications of the chisel.

The Flat Chisel. This is the general-purpose chisel of the fitter and in its heaviest form is made about 8 in. long when new, the lighter sizes being proportionately shorter. It is tapered and flattened for about one-third of its length to the cutting edge, which should be

Fig. 175.—Cutting with the Flat Chisel.

about $\frac{3}{32}$ in. thick on the large chisel, and less in proportion for smaller chisels.

The cutting edge is ground to an angle suited to the material being worked upon, as we have already discussed on page 137, and it should not be exactly straight, but given a slight curvature, as shown in Fig. 174. After forging to shape and roughly grinding, the chisel edge should be hardened and tempered, as explained on pages 36–9. Consequent grinding after finishing should be carried out with care, as otherwise the edge will be overheated and softened. If this occurs it will be necessary to harden and temper the chisel all over again. On no account should the head of the chisel be hard where it is struck by the hammer.

The flat chisel is used for cutting sheet and plate material, as shown at Fig. 175 (*a*) and (*b*), for cutting out slots after their outline has been previously drilled, as shown at (*c*), for surfacing work as explained later, and for miscellaneous cutting jobs as they arise.

The Cross-cut Chisel. The cutting end of this chisel is forged to the shape shown at Fig. 176, the cutting edge AB being $\frac{1}{4}$ in. to $\frac{3}{8}$ in. wide. From the edge, the metal thickness tapers off slightly, being slightly thinner at CD. This is to permit the body of the chisel to clear when a groove is being cut.

FIG. 176.—Point of Cross-cut Chisel.

FIG. 177.—Grooves cut by Cross-cut Chisel.

The original use of this chisel, and from which it derived its name, was for cutting grooves across the faces of surfaces which required to be finished off flat, the grooves being the preliminary to the removal of the main metal, with a flat chisel. This is shown in Fig. 177, where the face A B C D in the rough state must be finished flat down to the line marked. Grooves are first cut with the cross-cut chisel as shown, the width of metal between them being slightly less than that of the flat chisel. This metal is then removed with the flat chisel, and the surface finally finished by filing and scraping. With the extension of the use of shaping, planing and milling machines, however, this method of surface production is only employed in cases where it would not be convenient to use a machine. The chief uses of the cross-cut chisel now are for cutting keyways, slots, and in entering places where the flat chisel is not a convenient tool.

The *half-round* and *diamond* chisels are shown at Fig. 178. **The** half-round pattern is useful for cutting grooves such as oil grooves in bearings and similar work. The diamond chisel is often used for

(a) Half-Round Chisel   (b) Diamond Pointed Chisel

FIG. 178.

cutting holes in plates such as boiler plates, and for grooving the start of a drilled hole to correct for an error in the starting of the drill.

General Points on Chipping. The chisel should be held about midway between the head and edge and at the correct inclination, as if it is at too great an angle the edge will cut too deep, whilst if the angle is not enough the chisel will cease to cut. Within these limitations, the smaller the angle the more effective are the hammer blows, and hence the greater the efficiency. The edge should be kept well up against the shoulder formed by the cut and chip, and particles of metal should be kept away. When the chisel approaches the edge of a surface, particularly if the metal is cast iron, it should be reversed, or the cut taken at right angles to the previous one. If this precaution is neglected the edge of the metal is likely to be broken away.

Chipping Ribs. When a surface, such as the base of a bracket, has to be bedded on and screwed to the surface of a rough casting, it would be a difficult and tedious operation to mate the two surfaces together if the surface to be fitted consisted of solid and continuous metal. The bedding together is greatly facilitated, however, by cast-

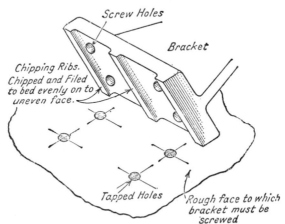

FIG. 179.—Chipping Ribs.

ing the bracket with its base in the form of a ribbed pattern, and this is bedded on to the rough surface by chipping and filing these ribs until they contact at all points with the surface to which their faces must be fastened. Such ribs are called chipping ribs, and their use facilitates the attachment of extra brackets to the body or legs of machine tools (Fig. 179).

The Centre Punch

This tool, which is shown at Fig. 180, is used when circular dot marks are required. When a job has been marked out it is usual to follow along the lines with small dot marks in case the lines themselves

FIG. 180.—Centre Punch.

become obliterated. The surface which is so marked is then finished to the centre of the dot mark. Centre punches are also used for marking the centre point of drilled holes for the purpose of giving a start to the drill ; marking the centre of circles to provide a point for placing one leg of the dividers to scribe the circle, and so on. Punches are usually made of cast steel, being hardened and tempered in the same way as a chisel.

Drifts

A drift is a tool used to finish off small non-circular holes to shape. Holes which are square, hexagonal, rectangular, etc., in shape, particularly if their dimensions are small, constitute very difficult problems in finishing to size. They are generally finished very near to size and shape with chisel, file or any other convenient method, and then a drift is made with its end to the exact size and shape of the finished hole, all metal behind this being filed away for clearance. After hardening and tempering, the drift is hammered, or pressed through the hole, and if the previous work has been done properly the drift will just clean up the sides of the hole to size and shape. A simple drift is shown at Fig. 181 (a) and a more elaborate one made with a number

FIG. 181.—Drifts.

of cutting edges at (*b*). On the drift shown at (*b*) each tooth removes a little bit more metal than the one in front of it, the final two or three teeth being made to the finished size and shape of the hole. Drifts of this type are generally forced through under steady pressure as from an *Arbor press* (Fig. 182). A *Key-drift* (Fig. 181 (*c*)) is a tool for driving out keys from pulleys and gears (keys such as that in Fig. 187). The *Pin-drift* is a round tapering punch for drawing out pins such as are used to hold crank handles, levers, etc., on to shafts. This is similar to a centre punch except that it has a flat point

[*Jones & Shipman, Ltd.*

FIG. 182.—Arbor Press.

and a longer taper (Fig. 181 (*d*)). Neither the key-drift nor the pin-drift do any cutting, but merely act as connexions between the hammer and the object to be moved.

Scrapers and Scraping

The shaper, planer and milling machine have robbed the file and chisel of a large amount of the metal removing they did in the past and the use of surface grinding methods has supplanted a great deal of scraping for the finishing of machine surfaces and slides. It is not likely, however, that scraping will ever be completely replaced as there are still many occasions where the type of work renders grinding impossible (e.g. Fig. 184) or where its quality demands the individual attention associated with the scraping process.

It will be appreciated that a surface produced by chipping and filing cannot be finished accurately flat by these methods. Furthermore a machined surface, although being nearer to flatness than one that has been filed, will probably still need slight correction due to warping and distortion taking place after machining.

The Flat Scraper. The flat scraper is a tool for working up the surface of a flat face for the purpose of removing errors in flatness, and leaving a smooth finish. From Fig. 183 (*a*) it will be seen that the flat scraper resembles a file, and in many cases flat scrapers are made from old files by flattening out the end, grinding and re-hardening. A good scraper should be made from the best steel procurable and its edge kept in good condition. As the cutting force on a scraper is comparatively light and without shock, its edge need only be given a slight degree of temper, a fact which is favourable to its successful working since the fine scraping cut which it takes tends to dull the edge rapidly. After the edge has had a preliminary grinding, taking care not to draw the temper, it should be finished off by rubbing on an oilstone, by holding the scraper close to the end and rubbing the end on the

(a) Flat Scraper

(b) Half-Round Scraper

Fig. 183.—Scrapers.

stone with a rocking motion in a plane containing the edge of the tool (see diagram). This should be repeated, in addition to stoning the sides of the cutting edges, until the edges are dead sharp. During use, it will be necessary to bring up the edge from time to time by end rubbing on the oilstone as just explained.

Using the Scraper. The purpose of the scraper is to correct slight irregularities from flatness, and if these are very great, the surface should be brought nearer to perfection by some method other than scraping, as the process is rather laborious, and not intended for the removal of much metal We will assume that a surface has been

[Heenan & Froude, Ltd.

Fig. 184.—Using the Flat Scraper.

planed reasonably flat, and is to be scraped up to a flat finish.   The
first thing necessary is a standard of flatness with which to compare
the surface being scraped, and for this a surface plate (Fig. 133) is
necessary.   If the surface to be worked on is smaller than the surface
plate it can be rubbed on the plate, otherwise the surface plate will
have to be reversed and rubbed on the surface.

After thoroughly cleaning the plate and surface, the plate should
be smeared with a thin layer of prussian blue, or red lead in oil, the
other surface then placed on it and rubbed about slightly.   If there
is any deviation from flatness, the high parts will be smeared with some
of the marking substance from off the surface plate.   These portions
must now be reduced in height by scraping, and this is done by holding
the scraper as shown at Fig. 184, pressing on with the left hand, and
making short strokes $\frac{1}{2}$ in. to 1 in. long.   The scraper is left in contact with the surface for the return stroke but no pressure is applied
to it.   Having gone over the surface with strokes in one direction, the
next set of strokes should be made at right-angles to the first, and
this changing round procedure repeated until sufficient metal has been
removed.   From time to time, of course, a trial should be made by
rubbing the work on the surface plate, then working at the parts where
the marking compound shows contact to be taking place.   Gradually
the surface will be brought to such a condition that its whole area is
covered by small areas of contact and it may be considered sufficiently
accurate for average requirements when these spots are $\frac{1}{8}$ in. to $\frac{3}{16}$ in.
apart.   Much patience and practice is necessary for scraping, and when
the reader has become proficient at producing a flat surface he may
then try producing the handsome frosted effects seen on the beds and
slides of machine tools.   For successful cutting keep the scraper sharp,
and do not hold it too high.

The Half-round Scraper.   This scraper (Fig. 183 b) is used for
working up internal cylindrical surfaces and is also a very useful
tool in the kit of a centre lathe turner.   It is often made from
an old half-round file.   Our remarks regarding the condition and
finish of the cutting edge of flat scrapers applies to this tool.   The
half-round scraper is useful for finishing the surfaces of cylindrical
bearings for the purpose of bedding in the shaft.   This operation is
carried out as follows :   We will assume that the bearings are in two
halves, and that they have been bored as near as possible for the shaft
to be a running fit ;   also that the shaft has been ground or otherwise
smoothed on the parts where it takes its bearing, and any " out of
roundness " corrected.

The bottom halves of the bearings are fitted into position in the
casting which supports them, and the bearing portions of the shaft
are smeared with a thin layer of red lead paste or prussian blue.   The
shaft is placed in position, rotated for a few turns and then taken out,
when the high spots on the bearing liners will be shown up by traces
of the marking agent adhering to them.   These areas must be scraped
with the half-round scraper, and the operations of trying in the shaft
and removing the high spots repeated until the whole area of both
bearings shows a covering of contact points $\frac{1}{8}$ in. to $\frac{3}{16}$ in. apart.   When
the bottom liners have been completed the shaft may remain in position,

the caps and top liners put on and the nuts pulled up until the shaft can just be rotated. Upon removal of the top liners the high places will again be visible and these must be scraped until contact over the whole area is obtained and the shaft is a good running fit with the bearing cap nuts tight. It may be necessary to file some metal off the flat joining faces of the two bearing halves or, alternatively, thin pieces of sheet copper or brass (shims) may have to be placed between them to open them out slightly. Subsequent wear up to a limited amount may later be taken up by removing the shims and re-bedding the shaft, or filing metal off the joint faces and re-bedding. If the shaft is not re-bedded after such an operation it may only be making contact with the bearing liner at top and bottom.

The Hacksaw. The hacksaw is the chief tool used by the fitter for cutting-off, and for making thin cuts preparatory to other chipping and filing operations. There are many sizes and types of hacksaw blades on the market with special recommendations for particular classes of work and in view of the variable factors governing the selection of a blade it is advisable to keep a stock of different blades to meet the different sawing conditions. A diagram of a hand-saw frame is shown at Fig. 185, and the blade fits over two pegs which project

[*James Neill & Co., Ltd.*

FIG. 185.—Hacksaw Frame.

from the pins sliding in the ends of the frame. The wing nut at the front end of the frame on some types, and the screwed handle on others, is for tensioning the blade, and adjustment is provided in the construction of the frame for blades of different lengths. The length of the blade is that between the outside edges of the holes which fit over the pins, and the most usual blade for hand work is one measuring 10 in. long by $\frac{1}{2}$ in. wide. Blades may be of carbon or high-speed steel, and may be finished either with the cutting edge only hardened, or they may be hard right through. The soft-backed blades are tougher and less liable to snap than the all-hard blades, but are not as efficient. High-speed steel blades, although more expensive than those of carbon steel, will generally be found cheaper, if the cost is reckoned in terms of useful life.

Hacksaw teeth are specified by the number of teeth per inch, the *pitch* of the teeth being the reciprocal of this number (e.g. a blade with 16 teeth per inch has a pitch of $\frac{1}{16}$ in.) (Fig. 186 (*a*)). If the reader examines the teeth of a hacksaw blade he will notice that the teeth have a *set* to the sides. This causes the blade to cut a slit wider than itself, and prevents the body of the blade from rubbing or jamming in the saw-cut. Often alternate teeth are set to right and left, every third or fifth tooth being left straight to break up the chips and help the teeth clear themselves (Fig. 186 (*b*)). Fine-toothed blades,

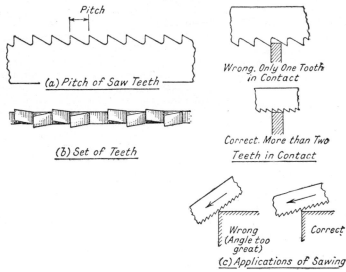

FIG. 186.—Hacksaw Teeth.

for cutting thin metal, are sometimes made with a wavy set to minimise stripping of the teeth from the blade.

The choice of a blade for any particular class of work is largely governed according to the pitch of the teeth ; these should be as large as possible to give maximum clearance for the chips and avoid clogging, but at the same time at least two or three teeth should be in contact with the surface being sawn.   If this is not attained the teeth will be stripped from the blade ; sawing too sharply over a corner will also result in teeth being torn off (see Fig. 186 (c)).

The best all-round blade for hand use is one with 16–18 teeth per inch.   For other and special classes of sawing the following blades should be used :

(a) Solid brass, copper and cast iron—14 teeth per inch.

(b) Silver steel and thin cast steel rods ; thin structural sections 22 or 24 teeth per inch.

(c) Sheet metal and tubing (e.g. steel, copper and conduit tubing) 32 teeth per inch.

Blades must be strained tightly in the frame and slow, firm and steady strokes (50 per minute) should be used, lifting the blade slightly on the return stroke.   Breakage of blades may be caused by the following : (a) rapid and erratic strokes, (b) too much pressure, (c) blade held too loosely in the frame, (d) binding of the blade from uneven cutting, (e) work not held firmly in the vise.   Solid metals should be cut with a good pressure and thin sheets and tubes with light pressure. Insufficient pressure at the start of a cut may cause the teeth to glaze the work, and so rub their edges away.

Work on Flat Surfaces

We have now discussed the characteristics and operation of the tools used for cutting and finishing flat surfaces on the bench and we might, with advantage, discuss one or two cases in which the use of these tools will be necessary.

The fitter is the agent whose responsibility it is to finish and adjust the machined surfaces of parts so that the parts assemble together correctly and with satisfactory results. In the course of this work he may have to make certain small details for which it would not be worth setting up a machine.

EXAMPLE 1. *Fitting a key.*

Let us consider the job of fitting and keying a detail such as a lever on to the end of a shaft, with a taper gib-headed key (Fig. 187). When the details arrive at the bench for fitting, the shaft will have had the key-way cut on a milling machine, the boss will have had its keyway cut by slotting or key-seating if such a machine is available and the key may have been roughly shaped up with metal left on all over for the fitter.

FIG. 187.—Lever fitted to Shaft with Taper Gib Key.

The shaft will have been turned so as to be the correct type of fit in the hole of the boss so that this aspect will not concern the fitter. If no machining method is available for the keyway in the boss, the fitter will have to cut it with hand tools, and even if it has been cut he may have to file the taper on its bottom face. In this, and any other keying job, it is important that a good fit is obtained between the *sides* of the key and the keyways in shaft and boss. In this particular case of a taper key, the top tapered face of the key must also fit all along the bottom of the boss keyway, since this fit, when the key is driven home, secures the boss on to the shaft. The order in which the work must be done and the precautions necessary may be summarised as follows :

(1) The width of the keyways in the shaft and in the boss must be exactly the same, and if they are not already so, the narrowest must be filed on its sides. They can be tested for similarity and parallelism with a block gauge or inside calipers.

(2) If the key has been roughly shaped to size, it must now be filed up on its width so as to be parallel, and a nice push fit in the two keyways. If it is in the rough material form, it must be marked out and cut to shape by a combination of sawing, chiselling and filing according to circumstances. This preliminary shaping should leave about $\frac{1}{32}$ in. on the width and thickness, after which the sides may be finished as above.

(3) The bottom of the keyway in the boss should now be inspected

for taper. As this is $\frac{1}{8}$ in. per foot, the measurement between the far side of the hole and the bottom of the keyway should be more at the front end of the boss than at the other. If the boss is 2 in. long, the difference will be $\dfrac{2 \text{ in.}}{12 \text{ in.}} \times \frac{1}{8} = \frac{1}{48}$ inch. This is not particular to a few thousandths but should not vary too much from its correct amount. If the taper is not correct, or if none has been put on, it must be filed. At the same time check the depth of the keyways as being to the drawing.

(4) The boss must now be assembled on the shaft and the key finished by filing its top and bottom faces flat, and with the correct taper on the top. To do this, file the bottom of the key flat and square with the sides, and then file the top to approximately the correct taper, until it can be entered a little way. A smear of red lead paste or prussian blue on the bottom faces of the boss keyway will now show whether the key taper conforms to that on the keyway. If adjustment is necessary, take the least possible amount of metal off in doing it as the key may enter too far. When the taper is correct, file the top down to it until the key enters with the head end about $\frac{1}{2}$ in. from the boss face. Drive the key in fairly tight and drive it out again, examining its surface for polish where contact has taken place. Finally touch up to get perfect contact and until, when driven home hard, the underside of the head is $\frac{1}{8}$ to $\frac{1}{4}$ in. from the boss face. Cut off any surplus length from the tail end of the key, and finish the head by smoothing up and chamfering all edges and corners.

If the boss keyway has to be cut on the bench, this should be made the first operation. Mark off the keyway at each end, and if possible, run two sawcuts with their outer edges about $\frac{1}{32}$ in. from the sides of the keyway and their depth $\frac{1}{32}$ in. less than the depth of the keyway. Remove the intervening metal with a cross-cut chisel and finish the keyway by filing with a parallel file, taking care that whilst you are watching for the size at one end, the other end of the file does not wander and overstep the mark, and test for parallelism with inside calipers from time to time.

EXAMPLE 2. *Squaring the head of a screw, and preparing a suitable hole in the end of a key.*

The finished screw and key are shown at Fig. 188 (*a*), and the screw, when it comes from turning, will have a solid head $\frac{23}{32}$ in. diameter, with a line turned on it to mark the end of the squared portion. We will assume that the key has been forged to shape, with the end left blank.

(i) Using a safe-edge file, commence to file the screw for one of the flats of the square, terminating the flat about $\frac{1}{64}$ in. short of the scribed line. When the filing is about $\frac{3}{32}$ in. deep, test for flatness, and with micrometer or calipers test for parallelism from the opposite turned edge (Fig. 188 (*b*)). Correct for any errors in flatness or parallelism, and complete the filing of the flat until it measures $\frac{39}{64}$ in. from the opposite side of the bolt head (i.e. one half head dia. ($\frac{23}{64}$ in.) $+$ one half the square ($\frac{1}{4}$ in.)).

(ii) Turn over and file the opposite side of the square until it is flat, and parallel with the first one, finishing it off to a width of $\frac{1}{2}$ in. (Fig. 188 (*c*)).

(iii) Commence filing the third flat of the head and get it flat, square with one of the other faces, and parallel with the turned surface opposite to it. Continue to file it down, maintaining the above relationships, until it measures $\frac{39}{64}$ in. from the opposite side.

(iv) Finish off by filing the fourth flat of the square, making it parallel with the opposite one and finishing to $\frac{1}{2}$ in. thick. Finish the end shoulders of the flats uniformly to the scribed line and file about a $\frac{1}{32}$ in. chamfer on the front edges and corners of the square.

(v) With odd-legs find centre of key-boss, and scribe its centre lines

(a) *Finished Screw Head and Key*

(b) *First Flat Finished*

(c) *Second Flat Finished*

(d) *Marking-off the Key Boss*

FIG. 188.—Filing a Square-head Screw and Key.

AB and CD. With dividers, scribe and dot punch a $\frac{1}{2}$-in. diameter circle. Set dividers to one half the diagonal of a $\frac{1}{2}$-in. square (approx. $\frac{23}{64}$ in.) and, from the centre, mark this distance off on each centre line. Scribe and dot punch the $\frac{1}{2}$-in. square (Fig. 188 (d)).

(vi) Enlarge the punch mark in the centre, and drill out with a drill about $\frac{15}{32}$ in. diameter.

(vii) Use a square file to open out the drilled hole to within about $\frac{1}{64}$ in. of the marking out for the square hole. (Be careful that the file does not cut on its sides and bite in beyond the marking out.) Check the filing for being square with the face of the forging.

(viii) With a smooth file complete the filing of the squared hole. During this finishing, the work should be constantly tried with the square on the screw head and the hole carefully filed until the square will enter with a nice sliding fit in any of its four possible positions. Finish the key by taking off all rough corners and edges. The screw and key heads will be improved by giving them a final potash surface-hardening treatment.

EXAMPLE 3. *To fit the sliding block shown at Fig. 189 (a).*

When they come to the bench, the slot in the casting, the cast-iron block and the two steel retaining plates will have been shaped or milled, with a few thousandths left on for adjustment when fitting. The block has now to be let into its groove, and the retaining plates set and secured with screws. As the block is required to slide it will be advisable to finish scrape its bearing surfaces, i.e. top, bottom and sides.

(i) With a vernier, measure the width of the block and the sides of the slot to see how much material has been left on. At the same time check them for parallelism. There should not be much metal to remove, suitable conditions being such that the width of the block at its corners may just be forced a little way into the slot. The thickness of the block should be about the same as the depth of the slot.

(ii) If much material remains on the width it is advisable to remove most of it by filing. Verify from which part to remove it to bring the size to the drawing dimension and set to work. When filing, maintain flatness, parallelism and squareness as near as possible. Continue removing metal with the file until a corner of the block may just be forced into the slot.

(iii) Now set to work on the base of the block and scrape it up flat to a surface plate (see p. 160). When this is finished, scrape up the two sides flat, parallel and square with the base. Check occasionally with the slot to ensure that you are not removing too much metal (Fig. 189 (*b*)).

(iv) The sides of the slot may now be scraped until the block will enter, and as soon as this occurs feel which are the tight places and scrape them down. When the block can be moved about, put a thin smear of red lead paste on it and find the high spots on the sides of the slot by pulling the block backwards and forwards. Continue scraping down the

(a) Sliding Block Assembled

(b) Finished Block showing where Accuracy is necessary (ii & iii)

About ·001″

(d) Conditions before Fitting Strips (vi)

(c) Letting Block into Slot (iv & v)

Fig. 189.—Fitting Sliding Block.

high spots until the block is a nice sliding fit. Chamfer its bottom edges if necessary to let it down to the bottom of the slot (Fig. 189 (*c*)).

(v) When the sides are fitting satisfactorily, smear some marking paste on the bottom of the block and *without forcing it down* rub it along the bottom of the slot. Scrape down the high portions and continue the process until contact is taking place over the whole area of the base.

(vi) The conditions between the top faces where the retaining strips go may now be checked. With a micrometer measure the block to see if its top faces are parallel with the base, and the thicknesses equal at both sides ; if not, file up until they are correct. When the block is now placed in the slot its top faces must be adjusted so that they are about 0·001 in. *below* the top faces of the slot (Fig. 189 (*d*)). This will probably entail adjustment to one pair of faces, and when doing it, take care to preserve flatness and parallelism. (If material has to be taken off the slot faces, test across the top with a straightedge.) The above clearance should be obtained with the top faces of the block finished by scraping.

(vii) Now pick up the retaining strips and file or scrape their bottom surfaces perfectly flat. Polish the other faces (for appearance) and remove all sharp edges and corners having a near chamfer.

(viii) Mark out and drill these strips for the screws, then clamp them in position and spot the casting for the tapping holes. Drill and tap the casting, finally screwing on the plates to complete the job (see next Chapter for drilling, tapping, etc.).

CHAPTER 9

THE BENCH (cont.). MARKING OUT, DRILLING, SCREWING

Unless work is of such a simple nature that its surfaces can be machined without any guidance other than the measuring facilities at the disposal of the machine operator, or unless the machine operator himself is very skilled and may be relied upon to obtain the correct surface relationships without any help, it is usual to indicate the position of finished surfaces by lines scribed on the component. These lines assist the machinist in setting up the work in his machine, and indicate to him the limit to which he may allow the cutting to proceed. The process of marking out is one of the shop activities for which the fitter is generally responsible, and is employed when the number of similar parts to be made is not great. For large quantities, marking out would be unduly wasteful of time and expense; in such cases it is eliminated by holding the component, whilst machining, in a jig or fixture, which locates it in the correct position, and provides some means for guiding the tool or cutter in the proper path.

Tools Used for Marking Out

Before going on to the discussion of actual marking out examples, we must take note of a number of workshop tools and appliances used in connexion with marking out as well as for other purposes, and with which we have not yet had occasion to deal. We have mentioned the *marking out table* which is an essential part of the equipment.

The **Angle Plate** (Fig. 190 (*a*)) is for supporting a surface at right-angles to the surface of the table. It is provided with plenty of holes and slots for accommodating the bolts necessary to secure articles to it. An *adjustable* angle plate is useful for angular work.

Vee Blocks (*b*) are used for supporting shafts and bushes and are generally made in pairs. It is important that a shaft, when resting in the blocks, shall be parallel with the surface table. This may be checked by trying a dial indicator over the shaft at each end. A shaft, clamped in a long vee block, may be supported perpendicular to the table if the end of the shaft is square with the vee surfaces (*e*). Vee blocks may be of cast iron, or of mild steel hardened and ground, the latter generally being used for the smaller sizes.

Parallel Strips (*c*). These are useful for supporting work on the marking-off table, and may be of cast iron smoothly machined, scraped or ground, or of steel which, when hardened and ground, makes very durable strips. The corresponding widths of a pair of strips must be of exactly similar dimensions, the strips must be perfectly parallel, and all their faces square; their lengths are relatively unimportant. Several sets of strips of varying sizes should be available.

Spirit Level (*f*). If the top of the marking-off table is level, as it should be, the spirit level is useful for setting surfaces parallel to it. The level is also necessary for levelling up machine beds and tables.

Toolmaker's Clamps (*d*) are an essential item of a fitter's kit, and two or three pairs should be available. They are handy for clamping work as shown, in addition to many other uses.

FIG. 190.—Bench and Marking-out Accessories.

Dividers and Trammels (Fig. 191 (*a* and *b*)) are used for scribing circles, marking off lengths, etc. Trammels are made to extend beyond the range of dividers, and those shown at (*b*) have a bar 14 in. long, but two or more of these bars may be joined together with sleeves of the form shown. The bent legs enable the trammels to be used in the same way as inside calipers.

Hermaphrodite Calipers (*d*). In spite of its name, this is a useful tool, being half calipers and half dividers. When a line has to be scribed parallel to an edge, or an arc parallel to the rim of a circular disc or bar, the caliper end is moved along in contact with the edge and the line scribed with the point of the instrument. A better name to give this instrument in the workshop is *jennies* or *odd-legs*.

Feeler Gauges (*c*). These form a useful accessory not only on the bench, but also in connexion with many other jobs in the shop. They consist of a series of blades or leaves, having thicknesses ranging from about $1\frac{1}{2}$ to 25 thousandths. Feelers may be used to gauge small distances (e.g. in flatness tests) and may be used in conjunction with other gauges. For example : the width of a slot $1\frac{1}{64}$ in. (1·016) could be measured by using a 1·000 in. standard plug gauge together with a feeler of 0·016 in. thickness.

The scribing block, square, protractor, etc., which we have already described, will also be needed for marking off. In addition, a number of thin steel wedges, packings, jacks (Fig. 191 (e)) and other oddments

(a) Dividers.   (b) Trammels, with Joining Sleeve above.   [L. S. Starrett Co.
(c) Feeler Gauges.

Finding the Centre   Scribing a Parallel   Jack
of a Bar   Line   Wedge
(d)   (e)
FIG. 191.—Marking Out and General Accessories.

will be useful. These are gradually collected as different needs arise, and they should be kept in a box along with an assortment of bolts and nuts, clamps, etc.

Examples of Marking Out

We will now discuss the marking out of a few typical components, first of all reminding the reader that for a scribed line to be visible, it is first necessary to prepare the surface which is to receive it. The rough faces of castings which have to be marked should be brushed over with a little whitewash which, when dry, will show up a line scribed on it. Machined surfaces may be prepared by brushing them over with copper sulphate solution which leaves a thin film of copper on the surface. This shows up a scribed line very clearly.

The second point we should like to stress is that marking out does not dispense with the use of measuring instruments for the control of machining. However exact a component is marked out, the marking line may be up to 0·010 in. wide. For the simple fractional dimensions on a drawing, which may generally be finished to within $\pm \frac{1}{64}$ in., or 0·010 in., it is quite in order to work to the scribed line, but for particular dimensions the line must only be used as a guide, the final finishing being done to micrometer, vernier or some other exact measuring method.

EXAMPLE 1. *To mark out the vee'd plate shown at Fig. 192* (a).

Here the plate may first be shaped to its finished rectangular dimensions, viz. $3\frac{1}{2}$ in. × 2 in. × $\frac{3}{8}$ in. thick.

(1) Cover one side with copper sulphate solution, set the odd-legs to $\frac{3}{8}$ in. and mark lines $\frac{3}{8}$ in. from each edge and $\frac{3}{8}$ in. from one end. Open odd-legs and test from each side, adjusting odd-legs until the point marks

FIG. 192.—Marking off Vee'd Plate.

the centre of plate. Scribe a line down the centre (Fig. 192 (*b*)) and make small dots at (i) and (ii).

(2) Set dividers to an opening of $2\frac{1}{4}$ in., and mark (iii) and (iv) from (i) and (ii). Scribe $\frac{1}{4}$-in. and $\frac{13}{32}$-in. circles and dot punch round them (Fig. 192 (*c*)).

(3) Set odd-legs to centre line, increase the opening by $\frac{13}{16}$ in., and scribe a short line each side at the vee end. Set protractor to 45° and scribe lines for sides of vee (*d*).

(4) Open odd-legs to $\frac{1}{8}$ in. more than centre setting and scribe short lines to meet vee lines. With small square from edge of plate, scribe line for bottom of $\frac{1}{4}$ in. slot, $\frac{1}{8}$ in. from where side line cuts vee. Centre dot shape of vee (Fig. 192 (*e*)).

EXAMPLE 2 (Fig. 193 (*a*)).

This plate will come for marking out already turned to 6 in. diameter, bored $1\frac{1}{4}$ in. and faced up to $\frac{1}{2}$ in. thick.

(1) Brush one side over with copper sulphate solution and drive a piece of lead, brass or hardwood into the hole. With the odd-legs find the centre and dot punch it lightly. Set the dividers to $1\frac{15}{16}$ in. and scribe the $3\frac{7}{8}$ in. diameter hole circle (Fig. 193 (b)).

(a) Plate to be Marked Out

(b) Centre Found. Hole Circle Scribed

(c) Flats and Centre Line Marked

(d) Hole Centres Marked

FIG. 193.—Marking out a Plate.

(2) Clamp the disc to an angle plate with fitter's clamps. Set the scribing block point to the centre dot, and from a rule held vertically against the angle plate read off the height of the scriber point. Raise the point $2\frac{1}{2}$ in. and scribe a line for the top flat on the disc. Lower the scriber point by $4\frac{3}{4}$ in. and scribe a line for the bottom flat. Adjust the edge of a square to intersect the centre dot and scribe a vertical line on the disc, using the square blade as a guide. The plate is now as shown at Fig. 193 (c).

(3) The angle between any pair of 5 equally spaced holes is $\frac{360}{5} = 72°$. Hence the two upper outside holes will have their radial centre lines inclined at $90 - 72 = 18°$ with the horizontal centre line, and the line joining the centre of the plate to each of the lower holes will be inclined at $\frac{72}{2} = 36°$ with the vertical centre line. Set a protractor or bevel gauge so that its blade is inclined at $18°$ with the base and adjust it up to the work (using a parallel strip for packing if necessary) so that the edge of the blade intersects the centre dot of the disc. In this way mark the radial centre lines for each of the upper outer holes. Set the protractor so that its blade is inclined at $36°$ with the vertical ($54°$ with horizontal) and in the same way as before, scribe the radial centre lines for the two lower holes (Fig. 193 (d)). The work may now be removed from the angle plate.

(4) Dot punch the hole centres very lightly, and starting at the top hole set the dividers to the next hole and run round to check that the hole centre distances are all equal. If there is any slight discrepancy it

must be corrected, but in doing this the centre position of the top hole must not be moved. The operation is completed by scribing circles for the $\frac{17}{32}$ in. holes, and dot punching the surfaces to be machined with small punch marks about $\frac{1}{4}$ in. apart, at the same time making larger punch marks at the centres of the holes.

EXAMPLE 3. *To mark out the bracket shown at Fig. 194 (a) which has to be machined on the surfaces marked " " ".*

(1) Whiten the edges and upper surface of the base, the edges, front and rear faces of the top machined portion. Set the bracket on wedges and packings as shown at (b), and adjust its position until the rough face of the base is approximately square and the other faces of the bracket parallel with the table. If the base and the other faces of the bracket are not quite square, it will be necessary to effect a compromise and split the error when setting it up.

(a) Bracket to be Marked Out. Machined where shown ✎ ✎ ✎

(b) Marking Vertical Lines

(c) Marking Horizontal Lines

FIG. 194.—Marking out a Bracket.

(2) Set the scriber point level with the back face of upper portion of the bracket, raise its height by 1 in. and scribe line, (i) all round, lower it $\frac{1}{2}$ in. (·502) and scribe line, (ii) on both sides, lower it a further $\frac{5}{8}$ in. (1·125—·502) and scribe the machining line for the front edge of the base (line iii). Inspect to see that the markings allow a reasonable amount of machining, and that when machined, the base will be approximately 3 in. deep. Set the scriber point $1\frac{3}{8}$ in. above the bottom edge of the base and scribe line (iv) for the hole centres.

(3) Set an angle plate square with the sides of the bracket (Fig. 194 (c)), and with a scribing block on the angle plate set the point of the scriber level with the centre of the un-machined sides of the 1·500 in. slot. Mark this centre line (v) on the sides and rear face of this portion of the bracket.

Increase, and decrease this setting of the scriber point by $\frac{3}{4}$ in. (0·750), and scribe lines (vi) for the slot sides.   Reset point of scriber to slot centre, reduce it by $3\frac{1}{4}$ in. (3·250) and mark the machining line round the edge of the base (line vii).

(4) From the sides of the bracket, with odd-legs set at $\frac{3}{8}$ in., mark the other centre line required for each of the four $\frac{13}{32}$ in. holes.   Dot punch hole centres, scribe hole circles, and dot punch the remainder of the marking out to complete.

EXAMPLE 4.   *To mark out the bracket shown at Fig. 195* (a) *which is to be machined on the base, boss faces and bores.*

(The holes in the casting will be cored about $\frac{1}{4}$ in. less than their finished diameters.)

Before we proceed to a consideration of the marking-out methods to be used, it will be well for us to discuss the machining of the bracket, as

FIG. 195.—Marking out a Bracket.

the method chosen for machining will influence the scheme to be adopted for marking it out.   We will summarise the points in connexion with the machining :

(1) The boss faces may be faced on the planer or shaper, at the same time that the base is being machined or they may be machined at the time of boring.

(2) The holes may be bored on a lathe faceplate (the bracket revolving), or they may be done on lathe saddle, milling machine, boring machine, etc. (bracket stationary and tool revolving).

(3) It will be easier to get the 2·125 dimension correct by facing the top boss face, and measuring its distance from a plug in the already bored

$1\frac{1}{4}$-in. hole, than it will be to bore the hole 2·125 in. from the already faced boss.

(4) If the height of the base boss is made $4·125 - 2·625 = 1·500$ in. from the base, when the top hole is bored 4·125 in. from the base, the 2·625 in. dimension will come correct automatically.

(5) As we have stated before, the marking out for the holes and for the dimensions given in decimals is only intended as a guide for setting up and machining ; the actual surface dimensions will have to be measured and finished to gauges and/or measuring instruments.

We will assume, therefore, that the bracket is machined as follows :
(1) Set up and machine the base on a planer or shaping machine.
(2) Bore the $1\frac{1}{4}$-in. hole, and face the $2\frac{1}{4}$-in. boss, with the bracket bolted to a lathe face-plate.
(3) Bore the $1\frac{1}{2}$-in. hole and face the *outer* end of the $2\frac{3}{4}$-in. boss with the work secured to an angle plate on the lathe face-plate.
(4) Face the inside end of the $2\frac{3}{4}$-in. boss on a shaping machine.

Now for the marking-out operations :
(1) Plug the holes, whiten the casting round the edges of the base and bosses, and on the faces of the bosses. Pack up on wedges or packing and adjust until top face of base is parallel with marking-out table when tested with the bent end of the scriber (Fig. 195 (*b*)).

(2) Using the odd-legs, find the centre of the $2\frac{3}{4}$-in. boss, and by measuring from a square blade held in contact with a long edge of the base, check that this is about in the centre of the base. If it is not, re-position it, striking a compromise between the centre of the base and the centre of its own boss. Set the point of the scribing block level with this centre, re-set it $4\frac{1}{8}$ in. (4·125) lower and mark the machining line round the base (i). This should show at least $\frac{1}{8}$ in. of machining allowance, and indicate the base as coming about $\frac{3}{4}$ in. thick when finished, otherwise a compromise must be effected, but the $4\frac{1}{8}$ in. must not be varied (i.e. the top hole would have to be thrown slightly off the centre of its boss). After marking the base, raise the scriber $1\frac{1}{2}$ in. (4·125 − 2·625) and mark round the edge of the $2\frac{1}{4}$-in. boss (ii). At this setting the centre line of the $2\frac{3}{4}$-in. boss may be marked round it (see diagram).

(3) Set up the bracket with a jack under the boss as shown at Fig. 195 (*c*), and adjust until the smoothest long edge of the base and the machining mark on it are both square with the face of the marking-out table. This involves setting and testing in two planes at right angles. Set the scriber point level with the centre of the $2\frac{1}{4}$-in. boss, raise it $2\frac{1}{8}$ in. (2·125) and mark round the edge of the $2\frac{3}{4}$-in. boss. Raise the scriber a further $1\frac{3}{8}$ in. and mark the upper face of the boss in the same way (lines iii and iv) These should show about $\frac{1}{8}$ in. of machining on each face, and if there is insufficient on one or the other a compromise must be made by throwing the centre of the $2\frac{1}{4}$-in. boss to one side or the other.

(4) Set the bracket on the smoothest long edge of its base (the one used for squareness in (3)), pack up the boss and set the base machining mark square with the table. Pick up the centre of the $2\frac{3}{4}$-in. boss and mark it all round the bracket (Fig. 195 (*d*), line v).

Finish off by scribing the circles for the bores and dot punching all the lines with punch marks about $\frac{1}{4}$ in. apart.

Referring back to our discussion of the possible machining methods for this bracket the reader will see that if the boss faces are planed or shaped before boring, the marking out for boring must be done *after* the faces have been machined as the facing would remove any previous marking put on them. This procedure must be adopted for any case when a hole is to be bored in a face which has to be previously cleaned up on some other machine.

(a) Taper Shank Drill.

(b) Parallel Shank Drill.

(c) Jobber's Drill.   [*Samuel Osborn & Co., Ltd.*]

FIG. 196.—Twist Drills.

Drilling Operations on the Bench

The fitter, during the course of his work, will have much occasion to make use of various drilling operations. We have already discussed the twist drill as a cutting tool (p. 139), so that we may now consider drills themselves, and the drilling processes likely to be encountered on the bench.

The drill is a tool for originating a round hole. We say " originating " to distinguish between cutting a round hole from the solid metal, and enlarging a hole that has already been cut such as is carried out by reamers, counterbores, etc.

The **twist drill** is the most commonly used variety of drill, and twist drills are specified according to the end by which they are held, called the *shank*. Drills may be *taper shank, parallel shank* or *jobber's* drills, and are shown at Fig. 196. Jobber's drills are shorter than the other varieties and are usually confined to sizes up to $\frac{1}{2}$ in. diameter. Above about $\frac{1}{2}$ in. diameter, the sizes of drills advance by $\frac{1}{64}$ths in. and metric sizes are obtainable in full and $\frac{1}{2}$ mm. sizes. Below $\frac{1}{2}$ in. there is a wide range of letter and number drills, particulars of which are given in the Appendix. These drills are held in the machine by special chucks, an example being shown on the electric drill at Fig. 203. Very often, due to slipping in the drill chuck, the shanks of jobber's drills become scored, and the size markings obliterated. The **drill gauge** (Fig. 197) enables any drill to be readily selected by

[*L. S. Starrett Co.*]

FIG. 197.—Drill Gauge.

trying in the holes of the gauge. The gauge shown is for drills rising by $\frac{1}{64}$ in. steps to $\frac{1}{2}$ in. diameter. Similar gauges may be obtained for number and letter drills, and for tapping drills for screwed holes.

An additional aid for the storage and selection of drills up to $\frac{1}{2}$ in. is a base having a series of holes the exact size of each drill in the series. The sizes are marked on the base so that any drill can be readily selected.

Taper shank drills have a taper called the Morse taper, and particulars of Morse tapers are also given at the end of the book. The size of taper incorporated on any particular drill will depend on the drill diameter, and the following table shows approximately how these vary.

TABLE 19. Morse Taper Shanks on Drills

Morse Taper No.	1	2	3	4	5
Range of drill sizes included	Up to $\frac{9}{16}$ in.	$\frac{9}{16}$ in.– $\frac{15}{16}$ in.	$\frac{15}{16}$ in.– $1\frac{1}{4}$ in.	$1\frac{1}{4}$ in.– 2 in.	Over 2 in.

At the end of the taper shank of a drill is a tongue called the *tang*, and when the taper shank is fitted into the socket or machine spindle, this tang engages in a slot. If the taper itself is in good condition the frictional grip between this and the surface of the taper hole should

Blow

Drift

Machine Spindle

Tang on Drill

be almost, if not entirely, sufficient to drive the drill, but if the taper becomes damaged, more load will be thrown on the tang in driving the drill, and if the drill seizes in the hole, the tang may be twisted off. For this reason, taper shanks should be given every consideration in use and always extracted with the proper taper drift (Fig. 198).

Fig. 198.—Extracting Drill with Taper Drift.

The number of the Morse taper hole in a machine spindle will depend on the size of the machine, varying from No. 1 in small machines, to No. 4 or No. 5 in large ones, and when a drill has to be accommodated in a spindle with a larger taper than its shank, taper sockets must be used (Fig. 199). These should also be cared for, as if they become damaged the drill fitted into them will no longer run true.

Drills may be made of either carbon steel or high-speed steel. The carbon steel drills are much cheaper, but suffer from the disadvantage that their temper is easily drawn and the edge rendered too soft for further work. When this happens the blued portion should be ground right off and a fresh point made higher up the drill. For

(a) Sleeve.

[Samuel Osborn & Co., Ltd.]

(b) Taper Shank Socket.

FIG. 199.—Taper Sleeve and Socket for Drills.

high-speed drilling, and cutting hard steel with well-supported drills, the high-speed variety are cheaper in the long run, but for slow speed work, and in cases where the drill is more likely to be spoiled by being broken than from any other cause, it is doubtful whether the use of high-speed drills is a paying proposition.

The flutes of a twist drill are always made with a right-hand helix. This, combined with the right-hand rotation of the drill, forces the chips up the flutes and away from the cutting edges. The direction of slope of this helix also puts cutting rake on the lips, as we have previously discussed.

The **flat drill**, which was the forerunner of the twist drill, is shown at Fig. 200. This drill is easily forged and ground to any required size, but the results it gives are not comparable with those obtained

FIG. 200.—A Flat Drill.

from a twist drill ; this is mainly because the twist-drill point is backed up and kept true by the body of the drill following behind, whilst the point of the flat drill has no such influence to guide it. The principal present-day use of the flat drill is for boring very long holes, in which process a cutter in the form of a flat drill is carried at the end of a long bar. The arrangement gives the best results when the work revolves, the drill and bar being held stationary and fed into the hole (e.g. on a lathe). Generally the bar which carries the flat cutter has tubes sunk into it for conveying cutting lubricant to flush away the swarf and avoid choking up of the drill.

Drilling Machines and Appliances

The three principal types of power machine used for drilling are :

(a) The *sensitive* machine. A light form of machine used for holes up to about $\frac{1}{2}$ in. diameter.

(b) The *upright* or *pillar* machine, in sizes up to that which can drill holes up to 2–3 in. diameter.

(c) The *radial* drill, where the drill head is on an arm and may be swung or moved over the area of the machine table or base.

Radials may be of the sensitive, or heavy types. A diagram of a medium upright machine is shown at Fig. 201. This machine is provided with four direct speeds (470–1465 r.p.m.), given by electrical pole changing in the driving motor shown on top of the spindle. By providing an alternative geared head four additional lower speeds may be obtained. In its ungeared form the machine will drill holes up to $\frac{3}{4}$ in. diameter in mild steel, this being increased to 1 in. on the geared machine. The drill spindle is hand fed by the lever shown on its right-hand side and has vertical movement of 5 in.

[*Frederick Pollard Ltd.*

FIG. 201.—Medium upright Drilling Machine.

The fitter will have occasion to use various of the hand-drilling appliances for holes where it is not possible to bring the work up to a machine. The **breast drill** (Fig. 202 (a)) may be used for holes up to about $\frac{1}{2}$ in. diameter. Pressure is applied to the drill by pressing the body on the shaped end plate, whilst the drill is rotated by the handle. The hand drill for drills up to $\frac{1}{4}$ in. is similar to the breast drill except that it is smaller, and has a handle instead of a breast-plate. Both breast and hand drills are fitted with a chuck for holding straight-shank jobber's drills.

The **ratchet brace** (Fig. 202 (b)) is a hand-drilling appliance, and although slower than the breast drill, is capable of dealing with larger holes. The length of the operating-lever varies from 12 in. to 24 in., depending on the size of brace, and this rotates the drill during its forward stroke, the pawl slipping over the ratchet as it is taken back for the next stroke. To feed the drill it is necessary to have some form of back plate to take the pressure which is then applied by turning the hexagon feed nut a small amount each time the drill makes a working stroke. The pointed end of the feed nut centres itself on the pressure plate and maintains the alignment of the drill as well as transmitting the feeding pressure necessary. The length of feed that may be given to the drill varies from about $2\frac{1}{2}$ in. on the small sizes to $3\frac{1}{2}$ in. on the large, and some braces take a taper shank drill whilst others require a square shank. The brace is a slow way of drilling, because only about half a turn may be given to the drill for each stroke, but in awkward situations it is a valuable means of overcoming difficulties.

FIG. 202 (a).—Breast Drill.   FIG. 202 (b).—Ratchet Brace.

Electric Hand Drills. For quickness of operation, the electric drill has a great advantage over the breast drill, for not only does it leave both hands free to guide and feed the drill, but also rotates the drill with more uniformity, and possesses that extra amount of weight necessary to give improved balance and manipulation. A switch is incorporated convenient for the hand so that the drill may be positioned before it is started up. Electric drills of the breast type may be obtained to take drills up to about $\frac{5}{8}$ in. diameter, and an example of one is shown at Fig. 203. For small drills up to $\frac{1}{4}$ in., a lighter, higher speed type may be obtained rather similar in shape to a pistol, and operated with one hand. Where extremely high speeds are necessary, small hand drills driven by a compressed air motor may be used.

Holding and Locating Work for Drilling

Unless work is so large and heavy that there is no danger of its moving, or being rotated with the drill, it should always be clamped

[*Wolf Electric Tools Ltd.*

FIG. 203.—Electric Drill.

or held by some method, and too much attention cannot be given to clamping because unclamped or insecurely clamped work is not only a danger to the operator, but also a cause of inaccurate work and broken drills. The chief danger in drilling occurs just as the drill point breaks through at the underside of the part being drilled. Whilst the point is being resisted by solid metal, the feeding pressure causes some spring to take place in the machine and the work, putting them into a similar condition to a strong spring which is compressed slightly under a load. As soon as the drill point breaks through, most of the resistance against it suddenly vanishes and the stress in the machine releases itself by imparting a sudden downward push to the drill, just as a sudden relieving of the load from a spring would allow the end of it to jump up. The sudden downward push on the drill generally causes one or both of the lips to dig in, often with disastrous results. When feeding the drill by hand the pressure should be eased off when the point is felt to be breaking through, and for this reason small drills should always be fed by hand. Special care is necessary when drilling thin plate as the drill point often breaks through before the drill is cutting on its full diameter.

The Vise. A great deal of drilling work may be held in a vise and a good example of a vise suitable for this is shown at Fig. 204. Care should be exercised to ensure that when the drill passes through the work it does not drill into the bottom of the vise.

[*J. Parkinson & Son.*

FIG. 204.—Vise for holding Work on Drilling Machine.

Clamps and Bolts. The tables of most drilling machines are provided either with Tee slots to accommodate bolt heads, or with long slots running through. Whichever be the case the slots enable bolts and clamps to be used as shown at Fig. 205. When using this

Fig. 205.—Clamping Work on to Drilling Machine Table.

method of holding, the packing for the outer end of the clamp should be as near as possible the same height as the work, and the bolt should be either in the centre or nearer to the work, as shown in the diagram.

Vee Blocks. Cylindrical work which has to be drilled perpendicular to its axis is best supported on one or more vee blocks. When the hole has to pass through the centre of the work, the centre line should be scribed across the end of the bar or bush with a scribing block, the line being continued along the curved surface of the cylinder as far as to where the hole must be. A centre dot may then be punched on this line for the hole centre and the circle scribed with dividers. The work is now adjusted so that the centre mark on the end of the cylinder is vertical when tested with a square from the machine table at the same time that the hole centre is under the point of the drill. This is shown at Fig. 206, where is also indicated a U clamp which holds the work and permits the drill to pass through it. When clamping work on to vee blocks or tables always apply the clamp at a point where its pressure is supported directly underneath. (*Note.*—If a bar or bush has a hole in its end so that the odd-legs cannot be used to

Fig. 206.—Setting and Clamping for Drilling a Shaft.

find its centre, this may be found as follows : (1) Scribe a line across the end as near central as can be judged. (2) Turn the bar half a turn, and try the scribing point along the line. If they are at the same height when the line is level it is on centre ; if not, scribe another

First Line
Scribed

Centre Line
midway between

Line Scribed,
after turning
Shaft ½ turn

FIG. 207.—Finding Shaft Centre with Vee
Blocks and Scribing Block.

line parallel with the first one, set the scriber midway between the two and scribe a line which will be the centre line (Fig. 207)).

Angle Plate. When a hole has to be drilled parallel to a face, an angle plate provides a convenient method of support, and such a set up is shown at Fig. 208.

Locating Drilled Holes. We have already discussed the marking out of drilled holes and might add that a hole should never be started without some form of location even if only a punch mark to indicate the hole centre, and provide assistance for the initial starting of the drill point. When a hole is being drilled to marking out, a careful watch must be maintained at the commencement, to ensure that the

FIG. 208.—Drilling with Work Clamped to Angle Plate.

full diameter of the hole will coincide with the marking, and the drill point should be lifted once or twice before the point impression reaches the full diameter. If it is seen that the drill has wandered from the centre it must be " pulled " over by cutting a groove down that side of the impression to which it is desired the drill shall travel. This is shown at Fig. 209, and the groove may be cut with diamond chisel, half-round chisel or centre punch. The correction of the drilling must be accomplished before the drilled hole has reached its full diameter, as after that very little may be done to pull the drill over. It is

FIG. 209.—Correcting for Drill starting off Centre.

easier to start a reasonably small drill on a given centre than a large one ; also the point and web of a large drill being relatively thick, considerable pressure is required to feed a large drill through the work. For these reasons, when a hole to be drilled is greater than $\frac{7}{8}$-in.–1 in., it is generally advantageous to drill through first with a drill about $\frac{5}{16}$ in. If this is centred correctly the larger hole will be correct, as the second drill will follow the axis of the smaller one.

Accuracy through Method. Most workshop jobs may be completed satisfactorily and with no apparent difficulty if only they are done by the proper method. Tackle them any other way, and the most aggravating hitches occur, with everything seeming to go wrong. Drilling is no exception to this rule, and the most simple job is worth a little thought before commencing to drill.

Many drilling jobs are concerned with two plates which have to be bolted together, a plate which has to be screwed on to another face, a bracket base which has to be secured to another casting, and so on. The fastening is effected by bolts passing right through (Fig. 210 (a)), or by some form of screw which passes through one plate and screws into the other. To locate one plate in an accurate position relative to the other, *dowels* are often used. These are pins made of *silver steel* (about 1% carbon) accurately ground to size, and driven into well-fitting holes in both plates. With such an arrangement, however many times the plates may be dismantled, they can always be put together in the same position. The bolts or screws are not expected to provide this location, because they are clearance in their holes.

Now in cases such as these, the actual positions of the holes are relatively unimportant, but unless the holes in both plates are exactly coincident (in line), the bolts, screws or dowels will not pass through to enable the fastening to be made.

To ensure that the holes shall be in alignment, various methods may be adopted.

(1) If bolts are being used, requiring similar holes in both plates, one plate may be marked out, and then clamped in the correct position on top of the other, using fitter's clamps. Both plates are then drilled together. As a precaution against the plates moving during the process of drilling a number of holes the end ones may be drilled first, and a drill or fitting bolt passed through to lock the plates whilst the remainder of the drilling is completed.

(b) Fastening by Screws

Screwed Hole in Bottom Plate

Holes Slightly Larger than Bolt

Dowel, a Good Fit in Both Plates

(a) Fastening by Bolts Passing Right Through

Dowel

(c) Enlarged Section Through Bolt and Dowel

Fig. 210.—Fastening by Bolts and Screws.

(2) When a plate is screwed to another (Fig. 210 (b)), the holes in the upper plate must be clearance for the bolts, whilst those in the lower one must be drilled smaller to allow for tapping the thread. This may be carried out as follows : (a) drill through both plates with the smaller drill as above and then, after taking them apart, open out the holes in the upper plate, or (b) mark out and clamp together, drill upper plate and allow the drill point to penetrate the surface of the lower plate until it just about reaches its full diameter. Take the plates apart and use the drill-point indentations as a guide for drilling the smaller holes in the lower plate. If this second method is employed and there are dowel holes to be put in, these should be drilled in both plates at the same time and not spotted through for subsequent drilling as in the case of the bolt holes.

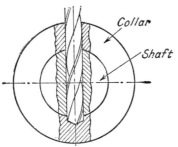

Collar

Shaft

Fig. 211.—Drilling assembled Collar and Shaft.

Collars on Shafts. The above principle must be followed when a collar and shaft have to be drilled for the purpose of pinning the collar in position with a pin running right through (Fig. 211). In theory, if a hole is drilled dead central in the shaft, and a similar one in the collar, they may be assembled, and the pin driven home. In practice, it is extremely difficult to get a hole dead central, and as the pin in the above case must be a good fit in both parts, drilling the parts separately would inevitably lead to failure in entering the pin. If the collar is assembled on the shaft and the two drilled at once, a slight error will not affect the job and there will be no doubt about fitting the pin through.

Location of Faces.—Clearance for Bolts and Screws. It is only in rare cases that the shank of a bolt is made a dead fit in its hole for the purpose of positioning the part, and when this is done the bolt is called a *fitting bolt*. Generally, it is easier and just as effective to use dowels, or a *tenon* and *tenon slot*. A tenon-slot location is shown at Fig. 212, but it should be noted that if a location parallel

One Dowel for
Endwise Location

Tenon
Slot

Tenon

Fig. 212.—Locating with Tenon and Slot.

to the slot is required an additional dowel is necessary. When two dowels are used for locating they should be as far apart as is reasonably possible because in that way they are more efficient in their function of locating (Fig. 210). Any necessary location having been provided by dowels or other means, the clamping bolts or screws are made slightly clearance in their holes, and this clearance provides for slight variations in bolt and hole, mis-alignment of thread, etc. The following table may be used as a guide for the allowance necessary for clearance.

TABLE 20.   Bolt and Screw Hole Clearances

Diameter of bolt or screw .	Up to $\frac{5}{16}$ in.	$\frac{5}{16}$ in. to $\frac{3}{4}$ in.	Over $\frac{3}{4}$ in.
Clearance on diameter of hole	$\frac{1}{64}$ in.	$\frac{1}{32}$ in.	$\frac{3}{64}$ in. or $\frac{1}{16}$ in.

Reaming

A drill cannot be relied upon to produce a hole having sufficiently good qualities of finish and accuracy for many purposes, and when accurate holes are required a *reamer* must be used for finishing to size. The reamer does not originate the hole in the same way as the drill, but merely imparts to the previously drilled hole the necessary smoothness, parallelism, roundness and accuracy in size. Reaming, however, will not correct any errors which may be in the hole with regard to its position, or direction, because the reamer merely follows the previously drilled hole, and if this hole were drilled out of square, or incorrectly positioned, then the reamed hole will have the same defect.

Hand reamers are operated by hand with a tap wrench fitted on the square end of the reamer, with the work held in the vise. Sometimes the square end of the reamer is held in the vise and the work fed on to the reamer by hand. These reamers cut on the flutes which may be straight, or helical, and are tapered at the end for about $\frac{1}{4}$ of their length, the extreme front end diameter being about 0·010 in. less than the reamer size. The shank is a few thousandths of an inch less than the diameter of the flutes. A straight fluted hand reamer is shown at Fig. 213 (a). The minimum amount of metal should be

(a) Straight Fluted Hand Reamer.

(b) Machine Reamer (Spiral Fluted).

[*Samuel Osborn & Co., Ltd.*]

(c) Chucking Reamer.

(d) A Floating Holder.

Fig. 213.—Reamers.

left for removal by hand reaming, from 0·002 in. to 0·005 in. being sufficient, as this class of reaming must be regarded essentially as a corrective rather than a metal-cutting operation, and if too much is allowed, not only will the edges of the reamer rapidly wear and lose their size, but also the finished hole may be oversize and inaccurate. Since the problem of high speed in cutting does not enter into hand-reaming operations, these reamers may be made of cast steel, and on the larger sizes case-hardened mild steel gives satisfactory results.

Machine Reamers. The solid fluted machine reamer is similar to the hand reamer except that it has a taper shank. These reamers may have straight flutes, but more often they are cut with a left-hand helix as shown at Fig. 213 (*b*), the angle made by the flute, with the length of the reamer, varying from 4° to 8°. The helix is made left-hand to counteract the tendency the reamer would have to screw itself into the hole if the flutes were right-hand, and even straight-fluted reamers have a slight tendency to draw in. Machine reamers may be of carbon or high-speed steel.

Chucking reamers are machine reamers with shorter flutes as shown at Fig. 213 (*c*), and may be either of the type known as *rose* reamers, or *fluted* reamers. The rose reamer does not cut on the diameter of its flutes but is bevelled off and clearanced to cut on its end, the diameter of the flutes being about 0·0002 in. per in. of length less at the back than at the cutting end (body clearance). Reamers of this type will remove greater amounts of metal than fluted reamers, but when doing so do not give such accurate holes, and should be followed by a fluted reamer when accuracy is desired. They are useful for enlarging cored holes, and other work of a rougher nature. The fluted reamer cuts on the flutes in the same way as an ordinary solid reamer.

Floating Reamers. Reamers generally give better holes when they are used with a *floating* holder, to permit the reamer to follow the previous hole naturally and without restraint. The end of a drill or reamer fitted into a machine is normally rigid, but when a floating holder is used it is free, and within limits may " float " about and follow the previous hole. A diagram of such a holder is shown at Fig. 213 (*d*), from which it will be seen that whilst the cross-pin drives the socket round, it does not prevent it from floating or wobbling about.

Expanding Reamers. All cutting tools are liable to wear, and to the reduction of their dimensions by the grinding necessary to keep them sharp. This does not matter in the case of many tools, but it is important in a reamer, because we rely on its size to impart accuracy to the hole it produces. When a solid reamer becomes worn, therefore, it must either be ground down to the next size smaller, or the teeth slightly enlarged by softening the teeth, expanding them slightly by hammering their fronts with a punch, re-hardening and

[*Buck & Hickman, Ltd.*

Fig. 214.—Expansion Reamer.

grinding up again to size. To avoid this, expanding reamers are made. These are of various types, a common one being shown at Fig. 214. When the reamer has lost its size the diameter of the flutes is increased slightly by springing them open with a tapered pin operated by the screw, after which they are re-ground to the correct size. The amount of expansion possible varies from 5 to 10 thousandths of an inch on the diameter.

Taper Reamers.—Taper Pins. Collars, pulleys, etc., are often secured to shafts by a taper pin as shown at Fig. 215 (*a*) and the fitting of these is a bench job. Taper pins may be bought as a standard article, and have a taper of 1 in 48 on the diameter and are specified

(*a*) Collar fixed to Shaft with Taper Pin.

[*Samuel Osborn & Co., Ltd.*]

(*b*) Taper Pin Reamer.

Fig. 215.

according to their large end diameter. In fitting such a pin, the collar and shaft to be fitted must be assembled together whilst the taper pin-hole is drilled and reamed to suit the pin. First of all a drill is put through which is slightly smaller than the small diameter of the pin and then the hole is reamed out with the taper reamer (Fig. 215 (*b*)) until the pin fits. The diameter of the drill to put through first may be calculated from the large diameter and length of the pin; for example, on a $\frac{5}{16}$ in. diameter taper pin 2 in. long the taper would be

$$\tfrac{1}{48} \times 2 = \tfrac{1}{24} = 0.042 \text{ in.}$$

The small end of the pin would, therefore, be

$$\tfrac{5}{16} \text{ in.} - 0.042 \text{ in.} = 0.3125 - 0.042 = 0.2705 \text{ in. dia.,}$$

and the nearest drill to put through preliminary to reaming would be $\frac{17}{64}$ in. dia. (0.266 in.).

Cutting with Reamers. Because it must hold its size as long as possible, the tooth of a reamer is usually made with a reasonable amount of *land* on its top and is not brought to a sharp edge as is the tooth in other tools. This land may be up to $\frac{1}{32}$ in. wide and is sometimes eased off very slightly with an oilstone. The reamer is sharpened by grinding the *front* of the tooth as shown at Fig. 216.

Reamer Sharpened by Grinding this Face

Land

Fig. 216.—Reamer Tooth.

In general, a reamer should be run at about one-half of the speed that would be used for a drill of the same size, and the feed may be from two to five times that for a drill, the lower feed applying to rose reamers. Except when cutting cast iron, a cutting lubricant should always be used for reaming. The amount of metal that should be left in the hole for reaming should not be more than ·010 in., and may with advantage be less, but due to the impossibility of obtaining drills except in steps of $\frac{1}{64}$ in., it is often necessary to ream out $\frac{1}{64}$ in.

If trouble is experienced due to this being too much, it may be necessary to rose ream the hole after drilling and before flute reaming.

Counterboring. The preparation of holes for certain purposes involves increasing the diameter of the hole for a certain distance down. This is called counterboring, and is done with a cutter of the type shown at Fig. 217 (*a*) which cuts on its end as shown at (*b*). The

(*a*) Counterboring Cutter.

(*b*) Counterboring

(*c*) Counterbore for Head of Cheese Head Screw

FIG. 217.

projection at the end of the cutter may be incorporated solid with it, or screwed in as a peg, and by piloting in the hole, serves to steady the cutter, keeping it concentric. The screwed peg type permits a cutter to be used on different holes by having a set of pegs of various sizes. These are often called *peg cutters*, and a common use for them is in cutting the counterbore for the head of a cheese-head screw as at (*c*). Another use for cutters of this type is in *spot-facing*, an operation often performed round holes drilled in the rough surfaces of castings to provide a flat seating for the surfaces of nuts and washers (Fig. 218).

(*a*) Spotfacing

(*b*) Application of Spotfacing

FIG. 218.

Countersinking. Countersunk head screws and wood-screws require a 90° chamfer cut round their hole as a seating for the under-side of the head. This is cut by means of a countersinking cutter as shown at Fig. 219. More often than not, countersinking is carried out with the point of a drill after it has been ground to an included angle of 90°. This is unavoidable if a countersinking cutter is not

(a) Countersunk Screw. (b) Countersinking Cutter

Fig. 219.—Countersinking.

available, but involves some drill wastage because the drill has to be ground to 90° to do the countersinking and then reground to 120° for its normal work.

Screw Threads.—Thread-cutting at the Bench

The cutting of internal and external threads with hand tools is an important part of the work of a fitter. When a line is marked round a cylindrical bar so that it advances in the form of a screw, the effect is equivalent to that of wrapping a triangle, or inclined plane, round the bar. This is shown at Fig. 220 (a), and for ordinary threads, the

Triangle ABC wrapped round bar
by bringing C towards you.
(C wraps round to B)

Helix Angle (α)

Pitch of thread for single thread.
Lead for multi-start thread

Circumference of Bar = πd

(b) Thread Cut as a Groove to enable Nut to Engage

(a) Screw as Inclined Plane (Wedge) Wrapped round Cylinder

Fig. 220.—Development of Screw Thread.

distance the line advances whilst it makes one complete turn round the bar is called the *pitch* of the thread. When viewed from the side of the bar the thread is not perpendicular but slopes at an angle α. This angle is called the *helix angle* of the thread. If we regard the thread as a sloping plane wrapped round the cylinder, we see that an object resting on this plane and moved round it, will be caused to move along the bar because of its rising up the plane, and the distance that the object moves parallel to the bar in one turn will be the pitch. In order to put this into practical effect, our thread line must be made into a groove, Fig. 220 (b), so that engagement may be effected with corresponding grooves in the inside bore of the nut, which fits the screw. Thus, when a nut is turned on a screw, for every turn it makes it moves along a distance equal to the pitch.

Locking Power of a Thread. If we pursue our consideration of a screw as an inclined plane, a wedge is an inclined plane, so that the principle of the screw is identical with that of the wedge. Let us consider the clamping of a plate to a surface as shown at Fig. 221, where the bolt and nut method is shown at the left, and the wedge

Fig. 221.—Diagram to show a Screw Thread and its Equivalent Wedge clamping a Plate.

at the right. (The wedge will require an upper surface to balance the pressure it exerts on the plate, and allow it to be " wedged " in. In the bolt this pressure acts through the threads and is transmitted to the bolt head which presses against the under surface as shown.) A very sharp wedge as at (a) will have a small angle and, if the reader refers to Fig. 221, will be equivalent to a fine pitch thread. At (*b*) is shown a blunter wedge, and its equivalent thread which is of coarser pitch than at (*a*). The wedge at (*c*) is of larger angle still, with a corresponding thread of very coarse pitch.

Now the reader probably knows from experience, that when a wedge of very slow taper is driven in, much more pressure may be exerted between two surfaces than when the wedge is more blunt; at (*a*) for example, the pressure of the wedge would be greater than at (*b*), which in turn would exceed that at (*c*). We thus see, then, that fine threads are capable of giving greater locking effects than coarse ones.

Now let us consider the force required to knock the wedge out, which is equivalent to loosening off the nut. The reader will know from experience that the narrow wedge requires more force to free it than the coarse one. Such being the case, a fine thread requires more force to unscrew the nut, and this means that the nuts of fine threads are much less likely to work loose than coarse ones. The wedge shown at (*c*) is so blunt that probably it would fall out itself and would not require pressure to release it! This means that the nut would not tighten, but would release as soon as the pressure were taken off the spanner.

Fig. 222.

Before passing to actual threads there is one further point. A fine thread, because of its fineness, is thinner and more delicate than a coarse one. This fine thread, however, may be subjected to an enormous force when the nut is tightened, and this may lead to *stripping* the threads from the bolt or nut. The danger is greatest when the bolt or nut is made of a soft, weak metal, and very often, if one end of a stud is screwed into a soft metal such as aluminium, whilst the other end takes a steel nut, the end screwed into the aluminium has a coarser thread than the other (Fig. 222).

The Whitworth Screw. This screw thread is named after Sir Joseph Whitworth, a pioneer of workshop engineering, whose life no student should fail to read. In his time Whitworth found that the work of engineers was greatly impeded by the lack of standard practice in the use of screw threads, and in 1841 he instituted a standard system. The value of Whitworth's work may easily be appreciated if the reader imagines what the position would be like now, as it was then, if every different engineering concern adopted their own fancy with regard to the form and pitch of the threads they put on screwed parts. The Whitworth thread form and its application on Whitworth bolts, screws and nuts is given in the Appendix, Table 2.

British Standard Fine (B.S.F.) Thread. Whitworth thread pitches are too coarse for many purposes and in such cases the B.S.F. thread is used. This thread is of Whitworth shape, but for corresponding diameters, the thread is finer than Whitworth's standard (Appendix, 3).

American Standard (Sellers) Thread. This is the American equivalent of our Whitworth thread (Appendix 4).

International (Metric) Thread. The standard thread used on the Continent. The thread form proportions are the same as the American standard (Appendix 4).

The Unified Thread. During the 1939–45 War a great deal of confusion was caused by different thread systems in use on equipment, and after the war a number of conferences were held with the object of standardising this and other aspects of engineering practice. The Ottawa conference of 1945 between America, Canada and Britain achieved much in this field and as a result the Unified thread standard was published in 1949. There are two types of this thread: the Unified Coarse (UNC) and the Unified Fine (UNF) (Appendix 5).

British Association (B.A.) Thread. This thread is used for instrument work (Appendix 6).

British Standard Pipe (B.S.P.) Thread (often called " Gas " Thread). The chief use of this thread is for gas- and water-pipes, but it is used for other purposes where a large diameter with a relatively fine thread is required. The thread shape is Whitworth. The B.S.P. size is specified according to the *bore* of the tubing upon which it is cut, and this is apt to be misleading. For example, a $\frac{1}{2}$-in. B.S.P. thread is the thread that would be put on the *outside* of a tube of $\frac{1}{2}$-in. bore, and has a top diameter of 0·825 in. (Appendix 7).

(a) Taper Tap.

(b) Second Tap.

(c) Plug Tap.

Grinding Wheel

(e)

(d) Adjustable Tap Wrench.

[*John Hall (Tools), Ltd.*]

Fig. 223.—Taps and Wrench.

Cutting Internal Threads—Taps

A tap may be regarded as a bolt with a perfect thread cut on it, which has been provided with cutting edges and hardened, so that when it is screwed into a hole it cuts an internal thread which will fit an external thread of the same size. Taps are made of high-carbon or high-speed steel by turning a screw, and then cutting flutes along it so as to provide cutting edges, as shown at Fig. 223 (*e*). The shank of the tap is left plain and the end is squared to accommodate the *tap wrench* (*d*), which is used to screw it into the hole. After hardening and tempering, the flute at the front of the threads is ground up to provide the necessary sharpness on the threads for cutting (Fig. 223 (*e*)).

Taps are usually made in sets of three to cut any particular size. These are called taper, intermediate and bottoming; or taper, 2nd and plug. The taper tap has its leading end tapered off for a length of 8 to 10 threads, and this is the first tap to use, the tapered end permitting the tap to enter the hole and cut to the full thread gradually. The second tap has only two or three threads chamfered, and follows the taper tap; if a hole is open at both ends this tap is suitable for finishing the thread in it. The thread on the plug or bottoming tap runs to its extreme end and this tap should be used as the final tap when a full thread must be cut to the bottom of a blind hole.

Drilling and Tapping a Hole. For tapping, a hole must first be drilled to a diameter approximately equal to the bottom of the thread, and these *core* diameters are given in the tables of screw threads in the Appendix. The core diameter may be found by subtracting twice the depth of thread from the top diameter, and for the Whitworth shape the depth of thread is $0.64 \times \text{pitch} = \dfrac{0.64}{\text{No. of t.p.i.}}$. Thus for (say) a screw of $\frac{3}{4}$ in. diameter with 11 t.p.i. Whitworth form, the double depth of thread would be $\dfrac{2 \times 0.64}{11} = \dfrac{1.28}{11} = 0.116$ in., and the core diameter: $0.75 - 0.116 = 0.634$ in. The tapping drill must be chosen as the nearest size larger than this, which is

$$\tfrac{5}{8} \text{ in. } (0.625) + \tfrac{1}{64} \text{ in., i.e. } \tfrac{41}{64} \text{ in. } (0.641).$$

When the hole to be tapped is " blind " (i.e only open at one end) it should be drilled one or two threads deeper than is required for the finished depth of the tapped hole

[For ordinary purposes, tapping holes are often drilled larger than the theoretical core diameter shown above, as this facilitates the tapping process without prejudicing the thread unduly. Recommended practice for this is to drill a hole, which when tapped will result in a thread about 88.5% of the full form and for Whitworth threads such tapping drill sizes are found from the formula $T = D - 1.1328p$ (D = top dia. of thread, p = pitch).]

Having drilled the tapping hole, the taper tap is fixed in the tap wrench and started in the hole, but before commencing to screw it round for cutting the thread, its position must be adjusted until it stands *square with the top surface* of the work, and it must be maintained square. This may be assisted by setting the tap vertical with a small square or, better still, after drilling the tapping hole, leave the work in the same position, replace the drill by a small centre like a lathe centre. Enter the tap and keep it straight for the first few turns by keeping the centre in contact with the centre hole in the tap. For all materials except cast iron a little Russian fat or whale oil on the tap will lubricate its action and improve the finish of the threads. When the taper tap is felt to have started its work and its squareness has been checked, the cutting of the thread may proceed, but the tap should not be turned continuously, but after about every half-turn it should be reversed slightly to clear the threads. At the same time, the facility or otherwise with which it is doing its work may be felt from the resistance encountered at the wrench, and if any stiffness develops, no force whatever should be used, but the tap carefully wriggled backwards to clear it. When a blind hole is being tapped the tap should be withdrawn from time to time and the metal cleared from the bottom of the hole. Ultimately, if the hole is straight through, the reduction of resistance will indicate that the taper tap is cutting a full thread and it may be removed from the hole which may be finished with the second tap. When a blind hole is being tapped resistance will be felt when the end of the tap reaches the bottom of the hole, and no force must be used at this point, as the tap may be broken or the thread stripped. Remove the taper tap and take the second one down as far as it will go, finally cutting the threads at the bottom of the hole with the plug tap. Great care should be exercised when using small taps, particularly in blind holes, but in spite of his care the reader will occasionally have the misfortune to break a tap in the hole. When this happens he may be able to get it out with a punch, but if it resists all other means it must be softened by heating, and drilled out, the hole afterwards being re-tapped.

Tapping by Machine. When large numbers of holes have to be tapped, hand-tapping is a slow process, and the work is expedited by driving the tap with the drilling machine, running on a slow speed. The main precaution to be observed is to provide some means whereby the tap drive from the machine is not solid, but incorporates a slipping device which will come in to operation when the tap sticks in the hole, or reaches the bottom, and so avoid breaking the tap. One type of machine tapping attachment is shown at Fig. 224 in which it will be seen that the tap is driven through the dogs (notches) which are kept

[*Herbert Hunt & Sons.*

Fig. 224.—The Pearn Tapper.

in engagement by the spring. If the tap sticks, the resistance causes the dogs to ride over one another and compress the spring. With the attachment shown, the machine must be reversed to screw the tap from a blind hole. Other attachments are made with a reversing arrangement incorporated.

Ground Thread Taps. The ordinary tap suffers from the disadvantage that any hardening, distortion and scaling which may have occurred to the thread is detrimental to its shape, and for accurate work the thread may not fulfil requirements. To overcome this, the threads of ground taps are form ground to their exact shape after hardening, thus allowing a perfect thread to be produced.

Cutting External Threads—Dies

The tool used for cutting external threads on bars or tubes is called a *die*, and in principle consists of a nut having portions of its thread circumference cut away and shaped to provide cutting edges to the remaining portions of the thread. After hardening and sharpening up on the cutting edges, this is screwed on to the bar upon which the thread is to be cut. In order to hold and manipulate the die it is carried in the centre of a pair of operating handles called *stocks*. There are various forms of dies, and some of the most usual are shown at Fig. 225. At (*a*) is shown a solid die, whilst at (*b*) is a split die together with its stocks. The split permits of a certain amount of adjustment in the size the die will cut by springing it a small amount open, or closed, by means of the screws in the stocks. The solid die nut is not usually employed for cutting threads from the solid, but for rectifying damage and knocks to existing screws. The dies shown at (*c*) consist of a pair of dies or jaws which fit into the stocks and are clamped by a screwed ring. These dies slide and may be adjusted by screws which bear against their outer faces. This permits the dies to be set a small amount open whilst the first cut is taken down a bar and closed in to the correct size for the final finishing cut. A rather similar arrangement is shown at (*d*), but in this case the dies may be opened sufficiently to admit the unscrewed bar between them. By this means a thread may be cut by threading the dies over the bar, clamping them tightly to the bar and rotating, then passing backwards and forwards over the portion that has to be screwed and gradually closing the dies until the proper diameter is reached. For cutting fine threads on large diameters this method is better than starting from the end, as by clamping the dies on to the bar first, the problem of maintaining the thread square with the axis is facilitated.

The action of dieing a thread is very similar to that of tapping, except that it is more difficult to start the die square. Generally, only one or two of the die threads are chamfered, and this does not give as much assistance as the long taper on the taper tap. In starting the die, great care is necessary, therefore, to maintain its face as near as possible square with the bar, at the same time that the die is pressed on to the end of the bar to help the commencement of cutting. The action is assisted by chamfering off the end of the bar for a distance equal to about two threads. When the cut is under way the die should be worked backwards and forwards similar to the method explained for tapping, and the threads should be supplied with some form of cutting oil. Certain designs of stocks and dies incorporate a bush for guiding the bar or tube being screwed so that the thread is cut square. This method is shown at Fig. 225 (*e*), and is greatly superior to a plain die, particularly for screwing B.S.P. threads, where a fairly fine thread has to be cut on a large diameter.

(a) Solid Die Nut.

(b) Split Die and Stock.

(c) Stock with Loose Dies.

(d) Stock and Dies suitable for Fine Threads.

Dies

Adjusting Screws

Bush Screwed into
Stocks for Clamping
Dies

Guide Bush
to suit Tube
being Screwed

(e) Pipe Dies with Guide Bush.

[Lehmann Archer & Lane, Ltd.
[John Hall (Tools), Ltd.

FIG. 225.—Stocks and Dies.

CHAPTER 10

INTRODUCTION TO THE LATHE

The lathe is the father of all machine tools and is recorded in the early history of many races, when, equipped with a fixed tool-rest, it was used for wood turning. For its development to the form in which we now know it, we owe much to Henry Maudsley, who developed the sliding carriage, and in 1800 built a screw-cutting lathe on which he turned screws having from 16 to 100 threads per inch, and which were the best screws that had been made up to that time. About 1830 Maudsley constructed a lathe with a 9-ft. face-plate, which was used to bore large cylinders and turn flywheels.

In its operation the lathe holds a piece of material between two rigid supports called *centres*, or by some other device such as a *chuck* or *face-plate*, screwed or secured to the nose or end of the *spindle*. The spindle carrying the work is rotated whilst a cutting tool supported in a *tool-post* is caused to travel in a certain direction, depending upon the form of the surface required. If the tool moves parallel to the axis of rotation of the work a cylindrical surface is produced (Fig. 226 (*a*)),

(*a*) Production of a Cylindrical Form.   (*b*) Production of a Flat Surface.

Fig. 226.—Surface Formation on the Lathe.

whilst if it moves perpendicular to this axis it produces a flat surface as at (*b*). The tool-post is supported on a *cross-slide* which moves perpendicular to the spindle axis, whilst the cross-slide is integral with a *carriage* which slides along the *bed* of the lathe. The spindle axis is parallel with the slideways of the bed, so that movement of the carriage along the bed causes the tool to move parallel with the spindle axis. The above-mentioned parts of the lathe are all indicated on the diagram shown at Fig. 227.

The Size of a Lathe. In this country, lathes are specified according to the height of the centres above the bed, and the bed length. Thus a 6-in. × 6-ft. lathe would have a bed 6 ft. long, with the centre of the spindle 6 in. above the bed, and would accommodate work 12 in. diameter *over the bed*. The diameter of work which would clear the

[Colchester Lathe Co., Ltd.

A, Headstock (all gear type); *B*, Tailstock; *C*, Bed; *D*, Bed slideways; *E*, Carriage; *F*, Apron; *G*, Cross-slide; *H*, Compound slide; *I*, Tool-post (square type shown); *J*, Driving pulley cover; *K*, Starting handle; *L*, Leadscrew; *M*, Feed-shaft; *N*, Tray; *O*, Nut for retaining chuck and face plate; *P*, Change speed levers; *Q*, Change levers for feed and screw-cutting; *R*, Reversing lever for feedshaft and leadscrew; *S*, Chasing dial; *T*, Gap bed; *U*, Cover for feedshaft and leadscrew driving gears; *V*, Lever for screw-cutting nut; *W*, Lever for engaging feed; *X*, Main switch panel.

Fig. 227.—A Centre Lathe.

carriage would, of course, be less than 12 in. The length of bed is no indication of the longest job that could be supported between the centres, because it includes the length of headstock and tailstock. Probably a 6-ft. bed would accommodate a job about 3 ft. 6 in. long between the centres. In America, the " swing " of the lathe, and not the height of centres, is specified, and they would call our 6-in. lathe a 12-in. swing.

The Bed. The bed of the lathe forms its body structure and is supported at a convenient height on legs. It is cast with a box-like cross-section to give the necessary stiffness for resisting the twisting and other stresses which occur in practice and which, if they strained the bed unduly, would destroy the accuracy of the lathe. The top of the bed is planed to form guides or ways for the carriage and tailstock. The shape and disposition of these ways varies amongst different makers, but two common forms are shown at Fig. 228. The reader should observe, and make note of other lathe beds.

Fig. 228.—Examples of Lathe Bed Sections.

Gap Bed. To accommodate short jobs requiring a larger swing than could be accommodated over the bed, many lathes are made with a gap in the bed, extending for a short distance in front of the headstock. This gap enables a face-plate larger than the normal swing to be used, and widens the range of work for which the lathe may be used (see Fig. 227, at T).

The Carriage or Saddle. This is a flat-shaped casting, planed on its underside to fit the ways of the bed so that it may slide along. The guides, on which the cross-slide takes its bearing, are planed on the top surface of the carriage, and are perpendicular to the grooves with which the carriage bears on the bed.

To the front of the carriage is attached the *apron* (see p. 245), and the combined carriage and apron is often called the *saddle*.

The Headstock is situated at the left-hand end of the bed and serves to support the spindle and driving arrangements. It is constructed of cast iron, and incorporates bearings for the spindle at each end. The steel spindle is hollow so that bars may be passed through it if necessary, and has a Morse taper hole at the nose end for accommodating the centre. On some lathes the spindle-nose is threaded to enable chucks and face-plates to be screwed on (Fig. 231), but this practice is giving way to other methods. One of these is the flanged spindle (Fig. 232), whilst another, as employed on the machine at Fig. 227, is the American long taper type nose where the chuck or plate is secured by a draw nut and driven by a key. The considerations for abandoning the screwed nose are (1) the liability of the thread to wear or become damaged and thus lose its centralising accuracy, (2) to guard against the chuck screwing off when the machine is provided with a stopping brake, (3) that the enlarged end of a flanged spindle contributes to its strength and stiffness.

The Driving Plate screws on to the spindle-nose and carries a projecting pin which drives work held between centres by engaging with a *dog* or *carrier* (Fig. 229) clamped to the work.

FIG. 229.—Lathe Carrier.

Chucks may be of the 4-jaw independent, or 3-jaw self-centring patterns. Each jaw of the 4-jaw chuck is operated by a separate square-threaded screw, whilst in the 3-jaw type all the jaws close in together, actuated by the *scroll*, which is a spiral groove cut on the face of a flat disc. The principle is similar to the movement of a nut by

[*F. Pratt and Co., Ltd.*

(a) Independent 4-jaw Chuck. (Jaws are reversible.)

[*Richard Lloyd & Co., Ltd.*

(b) 3-jaw Self-centring Chuck (showing Scroll).

FIG. 230.—Lathe Chucks.

a screw except that the " screw " is cut on the face of a disc. The 3-jaw chuck is easier to operate, but its gripping efficiency is much

FIG. 231.—Method of carrying Chuck on Screwed Spindle-nose.

less than that of the 4-jaw (Fig. 230). The chuck is adapted to a screwed nose spindle by using a *back-plate* as shown at Fig. 231, whilst on the flanged spindle it is bolted direct (Fig. 232). To ensure true running the recess in the chuck is a good fit on the diameter of the plate or spindle flange and is bolted hard on the face (generally the back-plate is finish turned in position). This is a common method of locating two large circular plates together so that they register accurately, and is called *spigoting*, the projection on the one plate, which fits into the recess in the other, being called a *spigot*.

The Face-plate is used to hold work which can neither be turned on centres nor held in a chuck. It has bolt slots for accommodating the necessary clamping bolts (Figs. 256-8).

[*John Lang and Sons, Ltd.*]

FIG. 232.—Flanged Spindle.

The Tailstock is the counterpart of the headstock, and carries the right-hand centre for supporting work when turning on centres. It is also used for supporting and feeding drills, reamers, etc., when it is necessary to use these for drilling work held in the chuck. The body of the tailstock is a casting, planed on its base to fit the ways of the bed, and when in its normal position, the barrel which carries

(a) Section through Barrel

(b) Lower Half in Section on AB to
show Method of Setting Over

Fig. 233.—Arrangement of Tailstock.

the centre is in line with the spindle. An adjustment is provided for setting the tailstock centre to one side for taper turning (see later). The barrel of the tailstock is moved by the wheel or handle at its far end and is bored with a Morse taper hole at the end nearest the headstock. A section through a tailstock is shown at Fig. 233 (*a*) and an end view at (*b*); to move the tailstock over, one screw is loosened and the other tightened.

The Compound (Top) Slide. On most lathes a compound slide is interposed between the tool-post and the cross-slide. This slide may be swivelled to any angle and its use enables the tool to be moved in directions other than those permitted by the carriage and cross-slide.

Fig. 234.—Compound Slide.

The length of such movement is limited to the travel of the compound slide, but generally the type of work for which it is used does not require a long travel. The compound slide is useful for turning and boring short tapers, chamfers, and other jobs requiring an angular movement of the tool (Fig. 234).

The Feed Motion. Besides holding and rotating the work, and supporting and guiding the tool which operates on it, a lathe must be capable of *feeding* the tool along or across at a predetermined rate. If power feed were not available for the tool, the usefulness of the machine would be greatly curtailed because all the movements would have to be made by operating the wheels or levers by hand. This would lead to irregularity in the turning, and no operator could give his attention to the work at the same time as operating the handles without getting tired very quickly. For screw-cutting, accurate mechanical feed of the tool is necessary to produce threads of correct pitch (see later).

The feed motion is transmitted to the carriage and cross-slide by the *feed-shaft*, a long, plain shaft with a keyway, which runs along the front of the bed. On some lathes, a separate feed-shaft is dispensed with, and the motion transmitted by a keyway cut along the *leadscrew*, the screwed shaft running along the bed of screw-cutting lathes. The feed-shaft is driven by gearing from the main spindle, and means are provided for varying the ratio of the drive to give different rates of feed. This may take the form of a gear-box (Fig. 271) with one or more levers for moving the gears, or the speed ratio may be altered by fitting different gears. To reverse the direction of rotation of the feed-shaft a tumbler gear arrangement is generally fitted. A diagram showing one arrangement of the drive to the feed-shaft and lead-screw is shown at Fig. 235, which also shows details of the tumbler gear reversing mechanism. On some of the simpler lathes the feed-shaft is driven by a belt, and whilst this method restricts the number of feeds that may be obtained, it provides a factor of safety because if trouble occurs anywhere the belt slips off and avoids what often proves to be an expensive smash-up. Whatever may be the form of drive to the feed-shaft, however, the lead-screw must be gear-driven in order

Fig. 235.—Diagram showing Drive from Spindle to Headscrew or Gear-box. (Upper Portion in Section in left-hand View.)

that the correct speed ratio may be maintained (see later discussion on screw-cutting).

From the feed-shaft (or the keyway in the lead-screw), the feed motion is transmitted to the carriage and cross-slide by mechanism contained in the *apron*, the front part of the carriage to which is attached the hand wheels, knobs and levers for operating the carriage and cross-slide. The apron mechanism of the lathe at Fig. 227 is shown at Fig. 236 and operates as follows : The feed-shaft, which is shown out of position, is normally located on the line indicated and carries a worm-box which can be swung up under the action of lever N (W on Fig. 227). This box houses gear K, driven by a sliding key, driving gear L and worm M as a unit, so that these are always rotating whilst the feed-shaft is in motion. To engage the longitudinal feed, N is raised into slot P, thus lifting the worm box and meshing M with B. This drives the shaft carrying B and A which, being in mesh with the rack under the bed front, causes the saddle to traverse along. The cross-feed is engaged by raising N into slot Q and meshing M with wheel C. This drives gear D through an intermediary (not shown), and D is in mesh with and drives a gear on the cross-slide lead-screw. For screw-cutting the half-nut E is lowered by the cam on H into engagement

[*Colchester Lathe Co., Ltd.*

Fig. 236.—Lathe Apron Mechanism.

with the lead-screw by raising lever G. The operation of raising G swings down the locking piece J and this prevents the feed worm-box from being raised to engage the feed whilst screw-cutting is taking place. F is the gear of the chasing dial and R the traverse handwheel connected to B by a pinion not shown.

The Centres. These are worthy of attention, as the accuracy of centre work is greatly influenced by their condition. The shanks of centres are usually finished with a Morse taper and the point which fits the centre hole in the work is generally made to an angle of 60° (sometimes, for heavy work, the centre angle may be 75° or 90°). The headstock centre is accommodated to the taper hole in the spindle by means of a taper reduction sleeve (Fig. 237 (*a*)), and as this centre rotates with the spindle it is often called the " live " centre, as opposed to the tailstock centre which is stationary, and called the " dead " centre. The fact that the live centre rotates with the work imposes the need for special precautions because, if it is not running true, the turned surface of the work will not be concentric with the centre hole when the tool approaches the headstock. Now, when the tool is turning near the tailstock centre, the turned surface there is bound to be true with the centre hole because the centre is stationary, and the work revolves on it. If, then, we are turning with the live centre untrue, the surface will be concentric at one end, gradually becoming out of truth with the centres and increasing as the tool approaches the headstock. When the work is reversed in the machine to finish the portion previously covered by the driving dog, we shall be turning it up to a similar diameter but on a slightly different centre, and instead of the two turned surfaces matching up, a step will be left, the effect being as shown exaggerated at Fig. 237 (*b*). Great care should be taken to ensure that the headstock centre is perfectly true, and the following precautions should bring this about without difficulty (the truth of the live centre may be tested with a dial indicator). The shank of the centre should be perfectly round and straight, and a perfect fit in the bore of the reduction sleeve which should also fit

Fig. 237.

perfectly in the taper hole in the spindle. These surfaces should not be allowed to become knocked about and should always be cleaned before fitting together. A punch mark or scribed line should be put on them so that they may always be fitted in the same relative position.

Lathe centres are usually made of carbon tool steel and should be hardened with little or no temper. Extreme hardness is not as necessary for the live centre because it is not subject to wear, but if the tailstock centre is not very hard it will soon seize up. When the centre points need renovating the operation is best performed by putting each one in turn in the spindle, running the lathe, and grinding them with a *tool-post grinder* held in the tool-post and fed with the compound slide set at 30° with the spindle axis. The tool-post grinder is a small electric grinder rather like the breast drill shown at Fig. 201, but with a shank to clamp it in the place of the tool, and a high-speed grinding wheel instead of the drill chuck.

A *half-centre* is a centre which is cut away almost to its point and is used in the tailstock for facing up the ends of work (Fig. 237 (c)).

Steadies. For supporting long, slender work against the pressure of the cut, a steady is used. The fixed or 3-jaw steady (Fig. 238 (a)) is clamped to the bed of the lathe and supports the bar, being turned by means of three jaws set at 120° with each other. Usually, before this steady is put on, the bar is skimmed up true for a length of about an inch at the point where it is desired that the jaws shall be placed. Due to the fact that this steady clamps to the lathe-bed, the carriage cannot pass it, and a bar being supported by it must be turned up in

(a) 3-Jaw Fixed Steady

Clamp for Holding Down

(b) Use of Fixed Steady for Work on the End of a Long Bar

Hole Axis

Bar Axis

(c) Error in Hole Bored in End of Bar not Running True behind Chuck

Jaws   Adjusting Screws

(d) Travelling Steady

FIG. 238.—Lathe Steadies.

two parts by being reversed end for end after half its length has been machined.

A very useful application of the 3-jaw steady is for centring, or for turning, drilling or boring operations at the end of bars, and the set up is shown at Fig. 238 (b). The advantage of using the steady, even although the bar might have been held in the chuck and pushed up the hollow spindle, is that accuracy is ensured, because if the other end is true in the chuck, then the whole bar is running true and the operation being done is sure to be co-axial with the bar. Imagine, for example, a hole is to be bored in the end of a bar which, for the purpose, is pushed into the hollow spindle and held in the chuck. We can true up the short length protruding from the chuck jaws, but we cannot see whether the whole length *inside* the spindle is true, and if it does not run true, then the hole we bore will have an error which is shown exaggerated at Fig. 238 (*c*).

The *travelling steady* (Fig. 238 (*d*)) is fixed to the carriage and travels along with the tool, supporting the bar against the thrust of the cut by means of jaws which are opposite the tool and slightly behind it, so that the bearing is taken on the round portion which the tool has just finished. This steady is used in cases where it would not be convenient to turn half-way and reverse the bar to complete the turning as is necessary when using a fixed steady. The reader should observe with regard to this steady that when the tool and jaws are set and clamped, the diameter turned is invariable, being that diameter which will just pass through the three points made up of the tool and the steady jaws. The turned bar, then, should be *parallel*, but there is no assurance that it will be *straight*.

Graduated Sleeves. The compound and cross-slides are moved by means of a screw which engages with a nut attached to the slide, the screw generally being cut with a square, or acme thread. The hand lever, wheel or knob is pinned or keyed to the end of this screw, and in addition there is a graduated sleeve which has a number of divisions shown on it, with a zero (0) mark scribed level with its edge on some stationary face (Fig. 239). This is for obtaining an accurate measure of the slide movement and the maximum use should be made of it, but it is first necessary to calculate the value of its divisions. This is easily done by dividing the number of divisions into the movement given to the slide by one turn of the screw. For example, if one turn of the screw moves the slide 0·200 inch ($\frac{1}{5}$), and

FIG. 239.—Indicating Sleeve for Movement of Slide.

there are 100 divisions round the sleeve, 1 division will represent $\frac{0\cdot200}{100} = \frac{2}{1000}$ in. of slide movement. The movement of the slide for one turn of the handle is easily checked with a rule, as it is almost sure to be an even fraction of an inch (e.g. $\frac{1}{2}$, $\frac{1}{3}$, $\frac{1}{4}$, $\frac{1}{5}$, $\frac{1}{6}$, etc.), corresponding to a whole number of threads per inch on the screw.

Stops. Many lathes are provided with stops for the carriage and cross-slide, which permit the slide to be brought to the same position every time. They are useful when a number of similar articles have to be machined, as they save the time of constant checking, and free the mind of the anxiety of machining undersize. Fig. 240 shows a carriage-stop being used for facing blanks in a 3-jaw chuck. The previously machined face of the blank is always set against the inner face of the jaws, and the stop set so that when the carriage is against it, the blank will be the required thickness. When working against a stop, care should be exercised to use the same pressure against it each time or slight variations may occur. We shall refer to cross-slide stops again when discussing screw-cutting.

FIG. 240.—Use of Stop.

Turning on Centres

The first stage in turning work between centres is that of drilling the ends of the work to accommodate the lathe centres. The correct form of centre hole is shown at Fig. 241 (*a*), and this is best produced

(*a*) Centre Hole.

(*b*) Combination Centre Drill.

FIG. 241.

by the *combination centre drill* (*b*). The hole could be produced by first drilling with a small drill followed by countersinking to the 60° angle, but this is a roundabout method and should only be used if a centre drill is not available. The small hole at the bottom is important as it ensures that the lathe centre bears on the angular part and not at its extreme point. A common fault is to make the centre hole too large, and nothing looks worse than huge unsightly centre holes in the ends of nicely finished work. Centre drills may be obtained in all sizes, and if the lathe centres are looked after (i.e. with good points) there is no reason for having centre holes larger than necessary.

If the centre holes are to be drilled on a drilling machine, the centre of the bar should first be found and centre-punched at each end. To find the centre, odd-legs, vee blocks and scribing block (pp. 209, 162), or the centre-finding square of the combination set may be used. The holes may then be drilled by supporting the bar vertically under the spindle of a sensitive drill, care being exercised to hold the bar rigidly and feed the centre drill carefully, as these are rather delicate and soon break. Another method of centring is to use the 3-jaw chuck of the lathe to hold the bar, whilst the drill is held in a Jacob chuck in the tailstock. If the bar is too large to go up the hollow spindle, the 3-jaw steady may be used as shown at Fig. 238 (*b*). The lathe method is convenient, because the end of the bar can be faced to length at the same time. When a large amount of centring has to be done a special centring machine is a more convenient method than any other. This generally consists of a short bed with a self-centring chuck mounted at one end. A drill spindle is mounted on the bed so that its axis is central with the chuck.

After the bar has been centred, a driving dog must be clamped to it, and the lathe prepared by attaching the driving plate, fitting the centres and setting the machine to a suitable speed for the size of the bar to be turned. If the ends of the work were not faced to length with the centring operation, the half centre should be fitted to the tailstock first, and the end facing carried out before any other turning is done (Fig. 237 (*c*)). If this facing is left until later, and the ends of the bar are not square with the axis, one side of the centre hole will have less bearing surface than the other, and the centre, in bedding itself in, will wear more off that side than the other, causing the centre hole to become slightly eccentric with the turned diameter.

Before fitting the bar between the lathe centres a little Russian fat or other suitable lubricant should be put in the tailstock centre hole, and then the tailstock centre adjusted, until when the bar is held and turned, it can just be felt that the centres are gripping it. The feel must be neither too easy nor too tight, and the adjustment should be felt from time to time as it may get tight due to the bar expanding with the heat of the cutting or loose due to wear of the tailstock centre hole. When adjusting the tailstock do not loosen the clamping screw right off, but have it so that it grips the barrel very slightly. It should be clamped up tightly after the proper adjustment has been obtained. When the ends of the bar have been faced, the facing tool should be taken out and a straight rougher, with cutting angles suitable for the material being turned, set in the tool-post. The nose of the tool should be adjusted to be level with the centre, and its overhang from the tool-post support as small as possible. At the same time it should be possible for the tool to be brought to the end of the bar without the necessity for a large projection of the tailstock barrel to avoid the tool or carriage fouling the tailstock body.

Everything is now ready for taking a cut along the bar, and after calipering the rough bar, and determining from the drawing, or pattern, how much material there is to be removed, a roughing cut may be put on and the carriage feed engaged. The depth of the roughing cut will depend on how much metal there is to remove, on the size and strength of the machine and on the rigidity of the work. If there is not much metal to come off, a small cut should be taken, and as soon as possible a trial made of the diameter being turned. On the other hand, with plenty of material to be removed, the cut should be as large as the machine will take, and if all the precautions regarding the clamping of the tool, tailstock and driving dog, lubricating the tailstock centre, etc., have been taken, there is nothing to be feared about taking a reasonable cut. The length for which the cut may be allowed to proceed along the bar will depend on the job. If it has to be turned parallel for its whole length, the cut may proceed until the tool, or some part of the carriage, approaches close to the driving dog, when the traverse must be stopped. If work is being turned up to a shoulder a rule must be held on the job, and the cut stopped when within $\frac{1}{16}$ to $\frac{1}{32}$ in. of the finished dimension. This process may be repeated until the portions that may be turned with the dog on the far end are within about $\frac{1}{16}$–$\frac{1}{32}$ in. of their finished sizes, when the work must be reversed, and the other end roughed out.

Finishing. When the roughing out has been completed it will be advisable to touch up the tool for finishing, or change it for another. Also, it may be necessary to look out other tools for such purposes as facing and cornering shoulders, etc. At this point also, if the bar has been turned a fair amount smaller than when starting, the speed may be increased to the next step, and to obtain a good finish, the feed reduced. The same general procedure as for roughing may now be followed for finishing, except that more attention must be paid to finish, and to the measurement of the diameters and lengths. Important sizes should be turned using a micrometer for measurement and less important ones measured carefully with calipers. If lengths are required to closer limits than may be obtained with a rule, the micrometer, vernier, depth gauge or some other suitable instrument must be used.

The reader should cultivate the habit of finishing his work with the *tool* and not with a file or emery cloth. A limited use of emery cloth is permissible to obtain a good finish, but a file should *never* be used to finish a cylindrical surface. First-class turners regard the use of a file with the contempt it deserves, and the reader should not consider himself in the higher grades of the trade until he is able to share the same opinion. An old file may be kept handy for removing the very sharp corners from the edges of shoulders and ends of diameters, but this should be its only application. Plenty of practice in using the calibrated sleeve on the cross-slide will eventually train the reader to finish work to dead size with the tool.

Correcting for Non-parallel Turning

We have not yet mentioned the possibility of the lathe turning out of parallel. If the head and tailstock centres are not exactly on a line parallel with the travel of the carriage, when a cut is taken along a bar held between them the bar will not be parallel. The error may be rectified by moving the body of the tailstock a small amount to one side or the other, by means of the adjustment shown on Fig. 233 (*b*), and we leave it as an exercise to the reader to ascertain from the error on his work whether the tailstock must be moved towards or away from him. What we do advise him is, to find out, and remember, which way the tailstock moves when the adjusting screws are turned in a certain direction, so that when he wishes to move it away from him, he does not do the reverse.   This is because the movements generally required for correction are so small that no check (e.g. sight or feel) is possible, and the process of trial and error necessary to bring the job parallel is often a trial of one's patience.   If the work is not parallel, and there is not much material on it with which to make the necessary experimental cuts, adjust the tailstock a little and then feed in the tool until it just skims the work at the smaller end.   Take the reading on the graduated dial, move the tool to the other end and feed it in until it cleans up the diameter to the same as that at the smaller end. Observe the reading on the graduated dial which, if the setting is correct, should be the same as before.   If, to bring the two ends the same, the tool has been moved *beyond* the previous reading, then *more* movement of the tailstock is needed, whilst if the previous reading is not reached, the tailstock movement has been too much.   Do not try to remember these rules but use the method, and reason out the correct solution.

We will now discuss one or two typical centre turning jobs, but must impress on the reader that for every job there is generally more than one method of approach.   We will endeavour to give what we consider to be good standard practice, leaving any improved modifications for adoption by the more expert of our readers.

EXAMPLE 1.   *To turn up the mandril shown at Fig. 242* (a) *from mild steel* 1⅜ *in. diameter*, 9⅜ *in. long.*

Mandrils are used on the lathe, as will be explained later, for finishing work on centres which has been partly finished in the chuck.   They should be hardened and ground on the top diameter (as is called for in this case), and the centre holes are recessed as shown to prevent any damage to them when pressing, or driving the mandril into the work.   We must leave a grinding allowance of 0·020 in. on the top diameter.   The lengths on the mandril are unimportant, and the reduced diameters at the ends, which are for accommodating the driving dog, need not be worried about as to accurate measurement.

(i*a*) Hold the bar in the 3-jaw chuck, face one end, centre drill and recess centre hole.   Reverse in chuck and treat the other end the same way (Fig. 242 (*b*)).

Or

(i*b*) Mark out centres with odd-legs, centre punch and drill centre holes on sensitive drilling machine.

If (i*b*) is adopted, before proceeding to the turning, face the ends and recess the centre holes, using the half centre to support the work at the tailstock end (Fig. 237 (*c*)).   As metal is faced away from the centre hole, it will probably be necessary to go back to the drilling machine and deepen it somewhat.

(ii) To allow 0·020 in. grinding, the top diameter of the mandril must be turned to 1·253 + ·020 = 1·273 in. approximately.   If it is brought to between 1·270 and 1·276 and reasonably parallel, it will be satisfactory.

Fit a driving dog at one end, place between centres and using a straight roughing tool, turn the bar to 1$\frac{9}{32}$ in. diameter as far as the dog will allow. Two cuts along should be sufficient and at this stage a check may be made for turning reasonably parallel (Fig. 242 (*c*)).

(iii) Change the dog to the other end of the bar, clean off the unturned portion, then turn down to 1 in. diameter for a length of 1⅛ in. (*d*).

(iv) Swing the tool round in the post, or fit another tool with a straight face, set at 45° and chamfer the end (*e*).

(v) Clamp the driving dog on the 1-in. diameter portion, using a piece of sheet copper or brass under it to avoid damage to the turned surface. Place between centres, reduce and chamfer the other end as at (iii) and (iv).

(vi) Finish off by turning the top of the mandril to 1·270/1·276 in. diameter. Do not worry unduly about the taper as the grinder will set his machine to give it correctly.

FIG. 242.—Operations in Turning a Mandril.

(vii) Remove sharp edges from all corners with an old file. Inspect centre holes, and if any burrs have been thrown up round them fit the half centre and take a small cut with the side tool to remove them. Clean out the centre holes with a centre drill if they are at all rough. If the mandril had not been finished by grinding, much more accuracy would have been required in finishing its top diameter. It would have been necessary to finish this to drawing sizes after making sure that the live centre was running dead true (the reader should realise the reason for this, also the necessity for good, smooth centre holes).

EXAMPLE 2. *To turn the pin shown at Fig. 243 (a), from a piece of mild steel* 1¼ *in. diameter,* 7⅛ *in. long.*

(ia) Hold the bar in a 3-jaw chuck, face one end and drill the centre. Reverse in chuck, face other end to length and centre drill (Fig. 243 (*b*)).

Or

(*ib*) Mark out centres with odd-legs, centre punch, and drill centres on sensitive drilling machine.

If method (*ib*) is adopted, before proceeding to the turning, face ends to length with the half centre and deepen the centre holes slightly if facing removes most of the countersunk portion.

(ii) Fit dog or carrier to one end, place between centres and turn top of bar to $1\frac{5}{32}$ in. diameter up to carrier, using a straight roughing tool. Two cuts should be sufficient, and at this stage a check may be made for parallelism, the tailstock being adjusted if necessary.

(iii) Change the dog to the other end of the bar, clean off the unturned

(a) Pin

(b) Face Ends and Centre   (c) Turn Top and Reduce

(d) Finish Shank and Shoulder

Fig. 243.—Turning a Pin.

portion and commence to turn down for the 0·750 in. diameter portion, stopping the tool when the turned length is $4\frac{3}{32}$ in. Continue this until the reduced diameter is about $\frac{25}{32}$ in. (= ·750 + $\frac{1}{32}$), and level up the shoulder as near as possible with the same tool (Fig. 243 (*c*)).

(iv) Grind a tool to a $\frac{1}{16}$ in. nose radius, and set it so that the shoulder may be faced, and the shank turned at the same setting (Fig. 243 (*d*)). Square up the shoulder as far in as the turned diameter, and to barely $4\frac{1}{8}$ in. from the end. Use the micrometer to turn the shank to about 0·760 in. diameter, disengage the feed when the tool is about $\frac{1}{16}$ in. from the shoulder and continue by hand (do not let the carriage pause) almost to the shoulder. Return the tool and set it to cut the shank to 0·750 in. diameter (not more), by turning a length of about $\frac{1}{8}$ in., and " mic'ing," until the correct size is reached. Engage the feed, and when the tool approaches to within about $\frac{1}{16}$ in. of the shoulder, disengage the feed with the right hand, allowing the left hand to continue the rotation of the traverse wheel so that the carriage movement is at the same rate as before. Transfer the right hand to the cross-slide handle, and as soon as the tool touches the shoulder, press it in sufficiently to ensure that the shoulder will skim up, then, without any pause, commence to feed the cross-slide slowly outwards with the right hand. This will complete the shank and the shoulder, and by working this way a clean-looking joint between the two surfaces is obtained.

(v) Set any tool having a straight portion at 45° and turn the chamfer on the end.

(vi) Remove the work, take off the carrier and put a carrier on the smaller diameter, first wrapping a piece of sheet copper or brass round to prevent damage. Put in the lathe and finish the top diameter to $1\frac{1}{8}$ in. With a file remove the sharp edges from each end of the $1\frac{1}{8}$ in. portion. If, during the process of turning, burrs have been thrown up round the centre holes, these may be removed by replacing the half centre and using the ending tool again, or they may be taken off with a half-round scraper.

. EXAMPLE 3. *To turn the pin shown at Fig. 244* (a) *from steel* 2 *in. diameter*, $5\frac{1}{2}$ *in. long.*

(i) Centre, and face the ends to length as explained in (i*a*) and (i*b*) for Example 1.

(ii) Attach driving dog and turn down to $1\frac{25}{32}$ in. diameter as far as the dog (3 cuts along should be sufficient for this).

(iii) Reverse end for end, and turn the top down to the previously turned portion. Now rough down the $\frac{7}{8}$ in. diameter portion until it is about $\frac{29}{32}$ in. diameter, with the shoulder roughly squared up to $2\frac{5}{32}$ in. from the end of the bar (Fig. 244 (*b*)).

(iv) Reverse, and put a dog on the reduced portion. Rough down to $1\frac{9}{32}$ in. (= 1·250 + $\frac{1}{32}$) diameter, leaving the collar roughly squared up, and $\frac{13}{16}$ in. wide (= ·750 + $\frac{1}{16}$). Rough the end to $\frac{25}{32}$ in. diameter, leaving $1\frac{1}{2}$ in. (1·500) between the two shoulders (Fig. 244 (*c*)).

(v) Reverse with dog on the small end, and finish the $\frac{7}{8}$ in. diameter as explained in Example 2 (iv). This diameter may be finished to calipers as the fractional dimension means that it may be finished to within 0·010 in. of size. The collar will now be $\frac{1}{32}$ in. over its finished size. With file, remove sharp edges from end corner of bar.

(vi) Reverse, put dog on $\frac{7}{8}$ in. portion with brass to prevent damage. Finish the large diameter to 1·250 in. (micrometer) and face collar (if necessary) to $\frac{1}{32}$ in. over $\frac{3}{4}$ in. Finish the small diameter to $\frac{3}{4}$ in. (calipers) and face collar to leave a *full* $1\frac{1}{2}$ in. between them. Finish the top to $1\frac{3}{4}$ in. diameter (calipers).

(vii) Check that the work is nice and firm between the centres, grind up a side tool to $\frac{1}{32}$ nose radius, and face the collar to 0·750 in. wide. For this operation lock the carriage so that it cannot move along the bed ; on most lathes a screw or handle is provided for this purpose. Feed the tool towards the shoulder with the compound slide set parallel to the bed, taking small cuts down the shoulder and testing with a micrometer until the 0·750 in. is reached. Leave the corner with a $\frac{1}{32}$ in. radius blending in to the 1·250 in. diameter (Fig. 244 (*d*)).

(viii) File a piece of material to 1·508 in. (micrometer or vernier) for setting the tool. Loosen the carriage and with the same tool as in (vii) clean out the corner radius at the $\frac{3}{4}$ in. diameter, noting the reading on the cross-slide indicating sleeve when the tool just skims the $\frac{3}{4}$ in. diameter. Lock the carriage again, check the work for firmness between centres, and set the tool from the other shoulder with the setting piece. With the tool thus set, face down the shoulder (Fig. 244 (*d*)), stopping when the $\frac{3}{4}$ in. diameter is reached (as noted on the sleeve).

(ix) Grind up a thin tool $\frac{1}{16}$ in. wide, rounded on its end. Lock the

FIG. 244.—Operations in Turning a Pin.

carriage and using the graduations on the cross and compound slide sleeves feed the tool in $\frac{1}{32}$ in. each way, to give the undercut (Fig. 244 (*e*)).

(x) Remove all sharp edges with a file, remove burrs from centre holes and polish diameters with fine emery cloth and oil, if a nice finish is required.

EXAMPLE 4. *To turn the limit gauge shown at Fig. 245* (a) *from cast steel.* The gauge is to be hardened, and ground on its end, gauging diameters.

The English equivalent of 30 mm. is 1·181 in., and of 130 mm. it is 5·18 in. We shall therefore require a piece of material $1\frac{3}{8}$ in. diameter by $5\frac{1}{4}$ in. long to make the gauge. To finish the knurled handle a knurling tool will be required. This is shown at Fig. 245 (c) and consists of a holder carrying two hardened wheels with their faces milled at an angle, so that when they are pressed against a round surface the surface is marked with the crossed knurling.

(i) Centre, and face the ends of the bar.

(ii) Fit a dog to one end, clamp between centres and rough turn to 31 mm., up to the dog.

(a) Gauge to be Turned

(b) Turn Centre

(c) Knurl Handle

(d) Relieve Ends of Knurling

Fig. 245.—Turning a Limit Gauge.

(iii) Reverse end for end, and complete the turning of the top diameter.

(iv) With a tool sink in (and rough to $22\frac{1}{2}$ mm.) leaving the end about $32\frac{1}{2}$ mm. long. Swing over the tool and turn to the other end, leaving it about $18\frac{1}{2}$ mm. long (Fig. 245 (b)).

(v) Touch up the tool, grinding about a $\frac{1}{16}$-in. radius on the nose, finish turning the centre to 22 mm. diameter and face the end shoulders to leave the gauging portions 18 mm. and 32 mm. long. Be careful to match up the cut where meeting in the centre.

(vi) Set the knurling tool in the tool-post and adjust so that it is square with the work. Press the rollers *hard* on to the handle portion of the gauge until the markings are seen to form ; engage the feed and allow the tool to traverse to the other end.   If, after the first attempt, the markings are not deep enough, repeat the process (Fig. 245 (c)).

(vii) Remove the knurling tool and with the tool used in (iv) and (v) relieve the ends of the knurling (Fig. 245 (d)).

(viii) Finish the top of the gauging diameters to 30·5 mm. diameter (i.e. 30 mm. + ½ mm. (0·020 in.) grinding allowance).

(ix) Remove sharp edges with an old file, and any burrs thrown up at the centre holes.   Inspect the centre holes and remove any roughness on the countersunk portion.

Chuck Work on the Lathe

If the reader studies the full possibilities of the chuck, he will find that its technique opens up a wide field of interesting work, and offers much greater scope for the development of the higher grades of skill in lathe work than does turning on centres.   Unfortunately, many turners are too prone to the use of centres and many jobs are machined in this way which could be turned much more accurately and efficiently by using a chuck.   If the reader, therefore, wishes to make himself master of the full technique of the lathe, he should give sufficient attention to chuck work, and allow himself to be guided by those of his turner advisors whom he knows to make full use of their

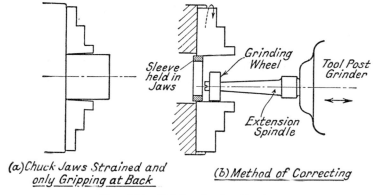

(a) Chuck Jaws Strained and only Gripping at Back

(b) Method of Correcting

Fig. 246.—Holding in the Chuck.

4-jaw chuck, rather than by those who always incline to the use of centres, or to the 3-jaw chuck.   A chuck may often be used in conjunction with the tailstock centre and the combination forms a very rigid and satisfactory method of holding, particularly for heavy cuts (see Fig. 254).

To be properly equipped, a centre lathe should be supplied with both 3-jaw self-centring and 4-jaw independent chucks, the 3-jaw having two sets of jaws for the purposes shown at Figs. 240 and 242 (b). This is not necessary on the 4-jaw because the same jaws may be reversed.   The 3-jaw chuck is quick, and easy to use, because the work is automatically self-centred (or at least it should be, but never is for the greater part of the life of such a chuck).   For this reason many turners, and particularly the impatient young ones, use a 3-jaw chuck, when in the interests of accuracy and efficiency they should be using the 4-jaw pattern, and, consequently, never master the art of quickly setting up a job in the 4-jaw, and never become sufficiently skilled in chuck work to realise the superiority of the one over the other.

The self-centring chuck is very useful for light turning jobs, but the chucks of this pattern usually supplied with centre lathes cannot be relied upon to grip sufficiently well for heavy cuts, or when a job requires holding on a short length. Their " self-centring " character-istic is not to be relied upon after the newness has worn off, and if this is counted as an important property, the gripping portions of the jaws should be ground from time to time with a tool-post grinder. This grinding also corrects the distortion which occurs to the jaws due to holding work near their fronts, causing their gripping faces to depart from squareness with the chuck face and only gripping with their back portions on work extending for their whole length (Fig. 246 (a)). To grind the jaws they should first be gripped on to a piece of material of a size representing the average opening of the jaws when in use. This should be pushed as far to the back of the jaws as possible, so that all but the short length gripping it may be ground. An extension spindle will be required for the tool-post grinder which should be clamped with its spindle parallel to the lathe bed. With both the lathe and the grinder running, the grinding wheel is traversed by hand back-wards and forwards, and the cut applied by the cross-slide in amounts to suit the capacity of the wheel to take it. When the whole length of the jaws has been cleaned up they should be taken out and the small unground portion finished off by hand (Fig. 246 (b)).

Setting Work in the 4-Jaw Chuck. Many turners fail to appreciate the 4-jaw chuck because, apparently, the setting up of a round bar is laborious. Actually, with a little practice, this becomes the work of a few minutes, and the superior gripping power means added safety, greater peace of mind and less possibility of the work moving during an operation.

Marked on the front of the chuck will be found a number of rings about $\frac{3}{8}$ in. apart, which should be used as a guide for the preliminary setting of the jaws, and which will enable the work to be set to within about $\frac{1}{16}$ in. of centre. From that point, take a piece of chalk in the right hand, rest the hand on a block so that the chalk is about at centre height, and grip the right wrist with the left hand for additional steadiness. Run the lathe and hold the chalk until the high side of the work is marked by it. Loosen slightly the jaw (or jaws) opposite the chalk mark, and tighten the side of the chalk mark. Repeat this process until the work runs true and a continuous chalk line is made round it. With diligent practice the reader will soon master this, and when proficient, he should be able to set up to a few thousandths of an inch very quickly.

When work has to be set true both on the diameter and on the face, set the diameter true without tightening too much, and then set the face true by tapping with a spanner or hammer ; finally tighten all jaws equally. Often, when one side of a disc has been faced up, it must be reversed in the chuck for facing the other side parallel. A good method of setting this is to use inside calipers from the face of the chuck to the machined face of the disc, tapping the disc until its inner machined face is parallel with the chuck face.

His approach to chuck work will bring the reader into contact with two aspects of lathe operation which we have not yet discussed. These are : boring and the use of mandrils.

Boring

To form the surface of a hole truly, it must be bored with a single-point tool. A hole which has been drilled and reamed may be cylindrical, parallel and accurate to size, but there is no guarantee that its centre line will be true with the rotational axis of the work because the drill may have run out a little, and the reamer will have followed the drilled hole. Such a hole, therefore, may not be true with other surfaces which have been turned on the work.

A hole may be finished to size by reaming, after boring, with confidence, because if only one or two thousandths are left for the reamer

(a) Set-up for Boring

(b) Boring Bar

Fig. 247.—Boring.

to remove it will follow the bored hole, and the accuracy will be preserved. This method, in fact, is often a quicker and better way of finishing a hole to size than by boring it right out, because when boring, the fear of overshooting the mark and making the hole oversize, tends to make progress very slow on the last one or two cuts.

The set up for boring is as shown at Fig. 247 (a) and the tool used should be as large as will conveniently pass clear through the hole. A good and easily made tool is one forged up from round material, and supported on a small vee block as shown. For large holes a *boring bar* should be used, as this gives greater rigidity, and the tool may be renewed cheaply and easily. Boring bars may be obtained in numerous forms, an example being shown at Fig. 247 (*b*).

Lathe " Boring Taper." If the headstock has been accurately located on the bed, so that the axis of rotation of the spindle is exactly parallel with the bed ways, when a job is held in the chuck, and bored with a single-point tool, it will be parallel. At some time in his career, however, the reader will encounter a lathe which does not bore parallel. The conditions causing this are shown exaggerated at Fig. 248, where SS is the axis of rotation of the spindle and work, and BB the axis of the bed, parallel to which the tool moves. In the diagram, the spindle axis is inclined to the front of the lathe and the hole bored will be

(*a*) Spindle Out of Line with Bed

(*b*) Effect on Boring Work in the Chuck

FIG. 248.—Showing Cause of Lathe Boring Taper.

large at the back end ; if the error is the other way, the hole will be large at the front.

The fault may only be corrected by adjusting the headstock until the spindle axis is set parallel with the bed, and on flat bed lathes there is often a screw adjustment underneath the head for the purpose. When the headstock fits on the inverted vees of a vee bed, however, the correction can only be made by scraping up the vee grooves in the headstock, a difficult and tedious operation. If, therefore, a vee bed lathe is boring taper, and it is verified that the fault is not caused by tool wear, or tool off centre, the user will have to make the best of it. In any case the error will be very small and may generally be corrected by removing the excess metal with a half-round scraper. Small holes may be corrected by finishing them with a reamer.

The Mandril

For completing work which has been bored and partly turned in the chuck a mandril is used. This is a straight bar with its ends reduced to accommodate the driving dog, its top diameter being ground to a good finish, and accurately true with the centre holes. The centre holes are recessed so that they may not be damaged when the mandril is being driven in the work. A taper of about ·010 in. per foot is put on the top diameter, the small end being small enough to enter the size of hole for which the mandril is made, and the other end large enough so that the mandril will not pass right through the hole. To cause sufficient frictional contact for the work to be driven against the cut the mandril is forced into the hole on a *mandril press* (Fig. 182). Mandrils are usually made of mild steel, and case-hardened.

A mandril should not be used if, by using a little extra forethought in setting up in the chuck, a surface may be finished that way. Although mandrils are true when new, they tend to become damaged, bent or worn on their centre holes, and in using a worn mandril the reader may be putting his confidence in something which is worthless.

Examples of Chuck Work. We will now discuss the production methods for a few chuck jobs, adding the proviso, as before, that alternatives are possible, but the methods we give represent good standard practice. As guiding rules in chuck work, as well as in many other machining operations, the reader should observe the following :

(a) Always do as many operations as possible *at the same setting*. This ensures accurate results automatically. As a simple example, consider the turning and boring of a bush. If turning and boring are both carried out at the same setting in the chuck, the bore is sure to be true with the outside diameter. Any other method, using separate settings, always opens up the possibility of error.

(b) Rough out all surfaces to within $\frac{1}{32}$–$\frac{1}{16}$ in. of size before commencing to finish. Taking the bush again ; if the top diameter is finished before the hole is started, the heavy drilling and boring to get the hole out may distort the bush with heat, or move it in the chuck. Both faults would be fatal.

EXAMPLE 5. *To turn the bush shown at Fig. 249* (a) *from mild steel* $2\frac{1}{4}$ *in. diameter,* $2\frac{5}{8}$ *in. long.*

First Setting

(i) Set up the material in the 4-jaw chuck, holding on a length of about $\frac{3}{8}$ in. Set the lathe speed to turn $1\frac{3}{4}$ in. diameter (i.e. about 160 R.P.M.).

(ii) Face the end until it cleans up. Put a drill, about $\frac{1}{2}$ in. diameter, in the tailstock, and drill through the work. If the drill tends to wobble about when it is pressed against the work, press the tool against it to hold it still. This may be taken away when the drill has started.

When the $\frac{1}{2}$-in. drill has been taken through, replace it by a $\frac{7}{8}$-in. drill and enlarge the hole (Fig. 249 (b)).

(iii) Turn the top of the bush to $1\frac{25}{32}$ in. ($1\cdot750 + \frac{1}{32}$) diameter, for a length of 2 in. (Fig. 249 (c)).

(iv) Set a boring tool so that its point is on centre, and its body clears the hole when passed through. Commence to bore the hole by putting on a cut $\frac{1}{64}$–$\frac{1}{32}$ in. deep. Obtain inside calipers, micrometer and 1-in. plug gauge. After taking one cut through, measure the bore, than proceed with the boring until the finished size is reached (Fig. 249 (d)). At this stage the reader may finish bore to the plug gauge, or he may bore to within about 0·002 in. of size, and finish with a reamer. If he feels confident enough to finish the hole by boring, that may be done now ; but if he decides to use the reamer, that operation should be postponed until the work is otherwise finished, and ready to be taken from the chuck. If *boring* to the plug gauge, bore to the inside calipers and micrometer, until only a few thousandths remain in the hole. Put on the cut estimated to bring the hole to size, and traverse it in for about ⅛ in., run back the carriage and try the plug gauge. If it enters easily, take off some of the cut, run the remainder of the cut slightly further in, and try again with the plug, which should, this time, either fit or be too large. If the plug is too large at the first trial put on a little more cut and try again. Eventually, the end of the plug may just be entered, and then the cut should be

Fig. 249.—Turning a Bush.

fed through. When this has been taken through, the plug may still not enter the hole beyond the first trial length, because the tool has sprung slightly, and if it is fed through again, *without putting on any more cut*, the gauge may be entered.

(v) Finish turn the top of the bush to 1·750/1·752 in. diameter, using a finishing tool with about a $\frac{1}{16}$-in. nose radius.

(vi) With a knife tool face the end, square out the corner of the shoulder, and face up to the 2-in. dimension (Fig. 249 (e)).

(vii) Finish ream the hole if this has been left for reaming.

(viii) With an old file remove sharp edge from bottom corner of bush, with a half-round scraper do the same on the inside bottom corner. (A half-round scraper is an essential item in the kit of turner's tools.)

Second Setting

Either 1 (*a*). Set up in chuck, holding fairly gently. Turn top to 2⅛ in. diameter and face to length (Fig. 249 (*f*)). Remove sharp edges with file outside, and half-round scraper from bore.

Or 1 (*b*). Press on to a mandril. Turn top to 2⅛ in. diameter and face end to length. Remove sharp edges with file. Hold lightly in chuck. Remove sharp edge left from not being able to face right up to the mandril.

Parting-off

The reader will find that his work will be facilitated by being able to cut off a job after he has turned it up. This is called parting-off, and is carried out with the parting-off tool as shown at Fig. 250.

In theory, the process of parting-off in the lathe is simple. The tool is clamped in position and carefully fed to the work which it proceeds to part off without difficulty. In practice, particularly on a lathe which is beginning to show signs of wear, the process is far from easy, and when the reader has experienced the tool digging in and breaking, he will realise that theory and practice require considerable manipulation to make them agree. However, in spite of any difficulties, let him not descend to the humiliation of cutting off in the lathe with a hacksaw, but persevere until he has overcome the difficulties which confront him.

FIG. 250.—Parting-off.

The parting tool should have less rake than a turning tool for the same material, and should be narrower at the back than at the cutting edge, with clearance all round. The edge may be slightly tapered so that it cuts deeper at the side away from the chuck. The width of the tool will vary according to the size of work, but should be between ⅛ in. and 5/16 in. It should be set slightly *below* centre and clamped tightly, with the minimum of overhang. Before parting-off, the carriage should be locked against lengthwise movement, and the compound slide set in line with the bed. Reduce the speed to about one-half that for ordinary turning and feed in the tool slowly by hand. When it has penetrated to about the depth of its width, withdraw it, and move it a few thousandths sideways with the compound slide ; feed in again, and after a further similar penetration into the solid metal, bring it out and move it sideways a slight amount to the other side of its original position, and so on. This minimises the tendency of the tool to dig in and cause trouble. With these precautions and care in feeding, the tool should do its work without trouble, but if there is end play (lengthwise slackness) in the lathe spindle the tool may still dig in, and the thrust arrangements on the spindle should be adjusted. Often, difficulties in the operation of parting-off may be overcome by working with the tool supide down, and running the lathe reversed. The tool should always be as near as possible to the chuck, and the cranked parting tool (as shown at Fig. 125 (*d*)) helps to attain this.

EXAMPLE 6.　*To turn the pin shown at Fig. 251* (a) *from* 1-*in. diameter bar.*

First Setting

(i) Obtain a piece of 1-in. diameter bar and grip it tightly in the 3- or 4-jaw chuck with about $1\frac{1}{2}$ in. protruding.

(ii) Turn down the top to $\frac{29}{32}$ in. diameter for a length of about $1\frac{5}{8}$ in. Face end.

(iii) Reduce to 0·625/0·626 in. diameter for a length of 1 in. (Fig. 251 (*b*)). Finish top to $\frac{7}{8}$ in. diameter.

(iv) Set straight tool edge to 45° and chamfer end of pin.

(v) With tool $\frac{1}{16}$ in. wide, clean out corner, turn undercut and skim underface of head.

(vi) Part off, leaving head $\frac{9}{32}$ in. thick.

Note.—The head of the pin could be chamfered before parting off, and after the parting tool has penetrated a distance of about $\frac{1}{8}$ in. If done at this stage the end of the chamfer should be measured $\frac{3}{16}$ in. from the underside of the head.

Second Setting

(i) Hold on shank in chuck, push underside of head against chuck jaws and set true.

(ii) Face top of head and chamfer (Fig. 251 (*c*)).

(*a*) *Pin to be Turned*

(*b*) *Turn, Chamfer, Undercut and Part-off*

(*c*) *Face and Chamfer Head*

FIG. 251.—Turning a Pin.

CHAPTER 11

THE CHUCK (*cont.*)—THE FACE-PLATE—TAPER TURNING—
SCREW-CUTTING

The production of more complicated parts often requires several settings to obtain the desired accuracy and, in addition, resort must be made to various other methods and aids. The following example will serve to illustrate this, and it will be observed that although the bush does not greatly differ from the one we have already discussed, the shoulder at the bottom of the larger bore makes considerable changes necessary in the method of turning.

EXAMPLE 1. *To make the bush shown at Fig. 252* (a) *from material* $2\frac{3}{8}$ *in. diameter,* $2\frac{3}{4}$ *in. long.*

1st Setting

(i) Set up in the 4-jaw chuck holding on a length of about $\frac{3}{8}$ in. Face end.

(ii) Drill through, about $\frac{1}{2}$ in. diameter, and open out the hole with a $\frac{13}{16}$ in. drill.

(iii) Turn shank to $1\frac{13}{16}$ in. diameter ($1\cdot750 + \frac{1}{16}$) for a length of $2\frac{1}{4}$ in. (Fig. 252 (*b*)).

2nd Setting

(i) Hold on shank in 3- or 4-jaw chuck and set reasonably true.

(ii) Rough face end, leaving about $\frac{1}{16}$ in. on the total length ; rough turn head to $2\frac{5}{16}$ in. diameter and open out the hole to $2\frac{1}{4}$ in. deep with a $1\frac{1}{4}$-in. drill (Fig. 252 (*c*)).

(iii) Rough bore hole to $1\frac{15}{64}$ in. ($\frac{1}{64}$ in. less than size), to depth of drilling.

(iv) With specially ground boring tool, square out the bottom of the hole to a depth of $2\frac{1}{4}$ in. $+ \frac{1}{64}$ in. If a bed stop for the carriage is available set this to the carriage when the tool face is the correct distance from the end of the bush as shown at Fig. 252 (*d*). Feed the tool by hand, controlling the point at which to stop winding the cross-slide, by the graduated sleeve. Take a preliminary note of the reading when the tool just skims the surface of the bored hole, and when winding in to cut away the metal, stop at the observed mark.

(v) With the same tool as (iv), finish boring the hole to the plug gauge. The bed stop will look after the depth, and use the power feed until the carriage is about $1\frac{1}{8}$ in. from it, when the travel should be completed by hand. If no stop is available, feed the last $\frac{1}{8}$ in. by hand, stopping when the tool is felt to contact the shoulder.

(vi) Finish face bush end to a distance of $2\frac{1}{4}$ in. from bottom of hole ; finish turn head to $2\frac{1}{4}$ in. diameter. Remove sharp edges from end of hole and head.

3rd Setting

(i) Obtain a piece of scrap material about $1\frac{1}{2}$ in. diameter, 3 in. long, and set it in the chuck with about 2 in. protruding. Turn this down up to the chuck until its diameter is such that the $1\cdot250$ in. bore of the bush will be a tight press fit. This is to be used as a peg upon which the bush is to be supported for its final turning (Fig. 252 (*e*)).

(ii) Press the bush on to the peg by winding the tailstock barrel against it (take care to keep the axes of the bush and peg in line).

(a) Bush to be Turned

(b) Face End, Rough Top and Drill

(c) Open-out Hole, Rough Turn Head

(d) Square-out Bottom of Hole, Finish Bore, Face and Turn

(e) Peg for Last Operation.

(f) Finish Turn Top, Finish Bore End

FIG. 252.—Turning a Bush.

(iii) Turn the shank of the bush to 1·748/1·750 in. diameter, face the head to thickness and face the end to length (Fig. 252 (f)).

(iv) Bore the end of the bush to 0·875 in. ($\frac{7}{8}$) plug gauge.

(v) With old file and half round scraper, remove sharp edges from all corners. Remove from chuck, and press peg out of bush.

EXAMPLE 2. *To turn the ring shown at Fig. 253* (a) *from a casting having* $\frac{1}{8}$ *in. of machining all over.*

1st Setting

(i) Set up in 4-jaw chuck holding *inside* the bore on the *outside* of the chuck jaws.

(ii) Rough face and rough turn top⎫Fig. 253 (b).
(iii) Finish face and top diameter ⎭

(iv) Turn radius with a radius tool.

2nd Setting

(i) Clamp in 4-jaw chuck holding on top diameter. Press machined face back against jaws and set top diameter true with clock indicator.

(ii) Rough face and bore⎫Fig. 253 (c).
(iii) Finish face and bore ⎭

(iv) Remove all sharp edges from corners.

(a) *Ring to be Turned*

Radius Tool

(b) *Face and Turn Top. Turn Radius*

(c) *Face and Bore*

FIG. 253.—Turning a Ring.

Combined Use of Chuck and Tailstock Centre

When a bar is held in the lathe and subjected to a heavy roughing cut, a considerable deflection is likely to take place under the pressure of the tool. It should be our object to support the work in such a manner that it is as stiff as possible in order that the deflection may be reduced to a minimum. When a bar is held between centres, the centres merely provide supports but do not contribute to the stiffness of the shaft, and its ability to remain straight under pressure. Such a shaft, when loaded, will be bent to the circular shape shown exaggerated at Fig. 254 (a). If, now, one end of the shaft is held in a chuck, whilst

Tool Pressure

Ends simply supported.

Pressure

End built-in

Equivalent Type of Beam and Shape of Deflection

(a) *Bar Supported on Centres*   (b) *Bar Held in Chuck and Supported by Centre*

FIG. 254.—Deflection of Work supported in the Lathe.

the other is supported by a centre, the chuck end of the shaft is kept horizontal by the restraining effect of the jaws, and is unable to take up an angular direction. Such a shaft will bend to the shape shown exaggerated at Fig. 254 (b), and whilst there is still some deflection, its amount will be less than that for the case where the ends are simply supported by centres. For heavy roughing cuts, therefore, we can add to the stiffness of the work by holding one end in the chuck whilst the other end is supported by the back centre.

Thus, for a job of the type shown at Fig. 255, the most efficient way of working would be as follows :

(i) Centre one end, hold the other end in chuck with tailstock centre to support. Rough to within $\frac{1}{16}$ in. of finished sizes.

Fig. 255.—Pin to be Turned.

(ii) Reverse in chuck, centre the other end and again rough out.
(iii) Finish turning to size on both centres.

The Face-plate

The face-plate is used for holding work which cannot be held conveniently in a chuck, for doing operations not suited to the chuck and for finishing work which has been partly turned in the chuck. An example of a job which is more conveniently held on the face-plate than in the chuck is given in Example 3.

EXAMPLE 3. *To bore the hole shown in the plate casting shown at Fig. 256 (a).*

Since the component is a casting, the hole will be cored out about $1\frac{1}{2}$ in. diameter. Before it comes to the lathe for boring the plate should be shaped up on its two sides, and on the step at the bottom. After this the hole must be marked out on the step side of the casting.

Fig. 256.—Boring on Face-plate.

(i) Clamp the work to the face-plate, packing it up on parallel strips if the face-plate hole is not large enough to clear the boring tool when it passes through. Set the bore approximately central, and screw the face-plate on to the nose of the lathe. Clamp a piece of steel or lead to the face-plate opposite to the work, so that the face-plate is approximately in balance.

(ii) Pull the lathe round and tap the work until the marking out is true. Set the scribing block on the bed or carriage and use the scriber point to test the truth of the marking out. Pull up the clamping bolts tight.

(iii) Clean up the hole with a boring tool (or preferably a boring bar). Check the 2-in. dimension by measuring from the step to the edge of the hole, and adding half the hole diameter to the measurement observed. If not correct, adjust, take another trial cut and check again. Check also that hole is central, by calipering between each edge, and the edge of the plate.

(iv) When the hole is correctly positioned, finish bore it to the plug gauge (Fig. 256 (b)).

The next example illustrates the use of the face-plate to complete the machining of a component which, for its first setting, has been held in the chuck.

FIG. 257.—Operations for Turning round Plate.

EXAMPLE 4. To turn the casting shown at Fig. 257 (a) which has to be machined on the faces shown "—"—"

In work of this type it is important that the faces of the machined casting shall be parallel, and that the spigots on each side of the plate shall be exactly true with one another, and with the 1½-in. central hole (i.e. all of them on the same axis).

1st Setting

(i) Hold in 4-jaw chuck on the $7\frac{1}{4}$-in. boss. Set true on the diameters, and on the un-machined top face of the base. Set lathe at about 25–30 R.P.M.

(ii) Rough face, leaving $\frac{1}{32}-\frac{1}{16}$ in. on base thickness. Rough turn spigot recess to $6\frac{15}{16}$ in. diameter, $\frac{9}{32}$ in. deep. Rough bore central hole to $1\frac{15}{32}$ in. diameter.

(iii) Square out recess to $6\frac{31}{32}$ in. diameter (Fig. 257 (*b*)).

(iv) Finish face base to thickness.

(v) With same tool as in (iii) finish bore recess. Traverse the carriage by hand. Measure its diameter with a vernier, allowing for the double jaw thickness (Fig. 159 (*b*)). Face the bottom of the recess with the same tool.

(vi) Finish bore the $1\frac{1}{2}$ in. central hole to the standard plug gauge (lathe speed may be increased for this boring). Remove all sharp edges.

2nd Setting

(i) Fit the face-plate, screw a ring of cast iron or steel to it and set approximately true. The ring should be 8–9 in. diameter and $\frac{1}{2}-\frac{3}{4}$ in. thick with tapped holes for screws. If a number of such rings is available, a suitable one may be selected for any job such as this.

(ii) Turn a spigot on the ring to fit the recess just turned in the job, and face up true. The spigot should be about $\frac{3}{16}$ in. high so that the work seats on its bottom face (Fig. 257 (*c*)).

(iii) Clamp the job to the face-plate, locating it on the ring.

(iv) Rough face front, and rough turn 5·000 in. spigot to $5\frac{1}{16}$ in.

(v) With side tool, finish face to 2 in. thick, turn spigot to $5\frac{1}{32}$ in. diameter and square out corner, finish lower face to make spigot $\frac{1}{4}$ in. high.

(vi) Finish turn spigot to 4·999/5·000 in. diameter with a knife tool. Measure with a vernier (Fig. 257 (*d*)).

(vii) Remove all sharp edges with file and scraper.

The component shown at Fig. 258 (*a*) is essentially a face-plate job, as it could not be set up in the chuck with sufficient accuracy to bore the hole parallel with the base.

Example 5. *To bore the hole and face the bosses on the component shown at Fig. 258* (a).

The bracket is a casting, and the hole will be cored about $1\frac{3}{8}$ in. diameter. The base should be machined before the bracket comes to the lathe for boring.

1st Setting

(1) Screw the face-plate to the lathe, and bolt an angle plate to it. Set the angle plate 3 in. from the centre of the lathe, by clamping a mandril between the centres, and adjusting the angle plate until the distance between the mandril and the angle plate is 3 in., less half the mandril diameter (Fig. 258 (*b*)).

(ii) Clamp the bracket to the angle plate and set the edge of its base flush with the edge of the angle plate. This will bring the bored hole square with the length of the bracket. Sideways adjustment may be effected by threading a mandril through the cored hole, holding it between the centres, and setting the bracket until the clearance between the mandril and the hole is the same at each side. Tighten up all clamps, and balance the face-plate with a lump of lead bolted opposite to the angle plate.

(iii) Rough face the outer boss and rough bore the hole (Fig. 258 (*c*)).

(iv) Finish bore the hole to the $1\frac{3}{8}$-in. plug gauge and finish face. Scrape sharp edge from corner of hole.

(a) Bracket to be Bored

Balance Weights

Test Bar

3" less Rad. of Test Bar

Angle Plate

(b) Setting Angle Plate

(c) Bracket Set on Angle Plate

Bore

Face

(d) Setting with Strip for Facing Boss

Parallel Strip

FIG. 258.—Boring and Facing Boss of Bracket.

2nd Setting

(i) Turn the bracket round, and with the help of a parallel strip set the machined face of the boss parallel with the face-plate. Clamp up tight (Fig. 258 (d)).

(ii) Rough and finish face the other side of the boss. Remove sharp edges from hole.

Taper Turning. Many lathe jobs require that the turned surface shall be conical instead of cylindrical in shape, and the production of such a surface is called taper turning. We saw in Fig. 226 (a) that when the tool is fed parallel to the spindle a cylinder is turned. If,

Axis of Revolution of Work

Half Angle of Taper

Straight Line Movement of Tool

FIG. 259.—Taper Turning.

however, the tool is still kept in a horizontal plane through the work axis, and moved at an angle with this axis, a conical surface will be produced (Fig. 259). The same effect will be obtained if the tool moves in its original direction and the *work axis* is altered to be at an angle with the line of the tool motion.

There are various methods of turning taper surfaces, the chief of which being as follows :

(i) *Compound Slide Method.* Guiding the *tool* at a suitable angle by feeding it with the compound slide set at the correct angle. This method may be used for external turning, or boring, but the length

FIG. 260.—Taper Turning with Compound Slide.

of surface that may be turned is limited to the travel of the compound slide. Another factor which limits this method to short jobs is that the slide may only be fed by hand, which tends to cause fatigue to the operator, and irregularity in the surface being turned. A diagram showing this method of taper turning is shown at Fig. 260.

(ii) *Forming Tool.* A short external taper may be turned with a flat tool set at the correct angle as shown at Fig. 261. This method is only practicable for short work, as if a long surface is being turned there is a tendency for the work to vibrate and chatter, resulting in a rough finish. The edge of the tool must be exactly straight if the work is to be accurate. We have already used this method for turning small chamfers on the corners of examples under discussion.

FIG. 261.—Turning a Taper with a Straight Tool.

(iii) *Setting over the Tailstock.* This method is limited to the production of slow external tapers on work held between centres. The tool is fed in its normal direction parallel to the bed, whilst the *work* is caused to rotate on an axis inclined at an angle. This is achieved by setting over the tailstock centre, so that instead of the line of the centres being parallel to the bed, it is inclined at a small angle. Then, when the tool moves along the bed, it will cut a taper on the work,

(a) *Taper Turning by Setting-over Tailstock*

(b) *Diagram for Example (c)*

Fig. 262.—Taper Turning with Tailstock Set-over.

the angle of which will be *twice* the inclination of the centre lines (Fig. 262). We have already discussed, and illustrated, the method by which the tailstock is set over (p. 244 and Fig. 233 (*b*)); the amount of set-over is determined as follows:

When a taper has to be turned, its proportions will be given in one of three ways:

(*a*) As 1 in so much, e.g. 1 in 10 on the diameter.
(*b*) As so much taper per foot of length, e.g. $\frac{1}{2}$ in. per foot on the diameter.
(*c*) The total angle of the taper will be given in the same way as the angle of a wedge.

(*a*) The total taper on the work will be found by dividing its length by the length in which unit taper occurs, and the tailstock set-over is *one half* this amount.

For example: To find the tailstock set-over to turn a taper of 1 in 20 on a job $9\frac{1}{4}$ in. long.

Taper on diameter $= 1$ in 20.
Taper on a length of $9\frac{1}{4}$ in. $= 9\frac{1}{4} \div 20 = 0.4625$ in.

Tailstock set-over $= \dfrac{0.4625}{2} = 0.231$ in., i.e. about $\frac{15}{64}$ in.

(*b*) If the total taper per foot of length is given, the taper on any other length is in proportion and the set-over is one half of this.

For example : The tailstock set-over to turn a taper of $\frac{3}{4}$ in. per foot on a job $14\frac{1}{2}$ in. long.

$$\text{Total taper in } 14\frac{1}{2} \text{ in. length} = \frac{14\frac{1}{2}}{12} \times \frac{3}{4} = \frac{29}{\underset{8}{24}} \times \frac{3}{4} = \frac{29}{32} \text{ in.}$$

$$\text{Tailstock set-over} = \frac{1}{2} \text{ of } \frac{29}{32} = \frac{29}{64} \text{ in.}$$

(*c*) When the taper is given as an included angle, the tailstock centre must be set so that the line joining it to the headstock is inclined at one half this angle.

In Fig. 262 (*b*) let L = length of work ; x = tailstock set-over and α = angle of taper.

Then the angle ABC will be $\frac{1}{2}\alpha$, and $\dfrac{AC}{AB} = \sin \frac{1}{2}\alpha$, i.e. $AC = AB \sin \frac{1}{2}\alpha$.

For example : To find the tailstock set-over to turn a taper of 6° on a job 12 in. long.

In this case AB = 12 in., and $\frac{1}{2}\alpha = 3°$

AC = set-over = 12 × sin 3° = 12 × 0·0523 = 0·628, i.e. about $\frac{5}{8}$ in.

When the tailstock has been set over as near as possible to the calculated amount, the turning is performed in the usual way, until the small end of the taper will enter the gauge (see later), after which the tailstock must be adjusted to correct any error present, and a second trial cut taken.

Although the line joining the centres is inclined at an angle, their directions are not along this line but still parallel with the bed. This causes their disposition relative to the centre hole in the work to be as shown at Fig. 263, and leads to some distortion in the holes, par-

ticularly when the taper is large. Another point in connexion with this method is that the set-over depends on the length of the job, so that if the same taper has to be turned on a number of pieces whose lengths vary slightly, then there will be some variation in the tapers unless the tailstock is adjusted to suit.

FIG. 263.—Effect of setting over Tailstock Centre.

The safest way, if possible, is to ensure that both length of work and depth of centre hole are kept the same on all bars. Still bearing this point in mind, the reader should visualise the effect on the turned taper, when the tailstock end of the work is badly out of square, and has not been faced up.

(iv) *Long Taper Holes.* When a taper hole is relatively small and long, it is not practicable to bore it with a tool, and it is formed with a taper reamer. We have already discussed the drilling of small taper pin-holes with a taper reamer, and the reamer for larger holes is very similar. Generally, for larger work, the hole is first roughed out with a roughing reamer, the teeth of which are designed to remove metal quickly, as at its best, taper reaming is a slow job. Diagrams of rough-

Roughing

Finishing

FIG. 264.—Taper Reamers.

ing and finishing reamers are shown at Fig. 264, where it will be seen
that the teeth of the rougher are notched to help cutting and break
up the chips. When reaming a taper hole it should first be drilled
as true as possible to a diameter slightly smaller than the small end
of the taper.

The Testing and Measurement of Tapers

The most satisfactory method of testing a taper which has to fit
a similar taper, is either to turn the one to fit the other, or to work
to taper plug and ring gauges of proved accuracy. When tapers have
to be produced which do not fit other tapers, or in cases where some
latitude is allowable, it is possible either to measure the taper angle
with a protractor, or to find the taper by measuring at two diameters
a certain distance apart, with calipers or micrometer.

Diagrams showing taper plug and ring gauges are shown at Fig. 265,
and when they are used they must gauge not only the taper, but also
the diameter of it at some point. On the plug gauge this is often
arranged for by marking a line round the gauge at the large diameter
of the taper, and the plug must be let into the hole being gauged
until this line is flush with its large end face. The ring gauges are
often made with their large end diameter equal to a stated dimension,
and when using this gauge, its end must stand at a certain distance
down the taper, from its largest dimension. Instructions for this are

often given on the working drawings, but
if they are not, it is a fairly simple matter
to work it out; for example, Fig. 266 (a)
shows the drawing of a taper, together with
particulars of the gauge which is to be
used for it. The difference between the
drawing dimension and the large end of
the gauge is $0.9375 - 0.875 = 0.0625$ in.
(i.e. $\frac{1}{16}$ in.).

FIG. 265.—Taper Gauges.

[Brown & Sharpe.

Since the taper is $\frac{1}{2}$ in. per foot of length, a difference of $\frac{1}{16}$ in. on the diameter will correspond to a length difference along the taper of

$$12 \text{ in.} \times \frac{\frac{1}{16}}{\frac{1}{2}} = 12 \times \frac{2}{16} = 1\frac{1}{2} \text{ in.}$$

(a) Particulars of Taper   *Gauge to be Used*

(b) Gauge in Finished Position

FIG. 266.—Gauging a Taper.

Hence when the taper is finished the end of the gauge must stand $1\frac{1}{2}$ in. from the shoulder on the work (Fig. 266 (b)).

Use of Taper Gauges

When a taper is being turned or bored, the gauge should be tried as soon as about an inch length of engagement can be obtained. Put a longitudinal chalk mark on the male portion (i.e. plug gauge, or bar to be tried), fit the work and gauge together and rotate them once or twice. When they are taken apart the chalk will be seen to have been rubbed away more at one end if the fit is not correct, and the setting must be adjusted until the chalk mark is rubbed equally all along its length. After re-adjustment of the setting, be careful not to remove too much when taking trial cuts because, as we have seen from the above example, $\frac{1}{16}$ in. taken off the diameter of a $\frac{1}{2}$ in. per ft. taper, allows the gauge to move a further $1\frac{1}{2}$ in. along the work, and at this rate the taper may be down to size before it has been corrected.

Morse tapers are commonly used in the workshop and particulars of these are given in the Appendix.

Tapers are turned on the more expensively equipped lathes with the aid of a *taper turning attachment*, and when we come to a further discussion of the lathe we hope to give particulars of this method.

Screw-cutting in the Lathe

To many persons connected with the lathe—including some teachers of its technique—the be-all and end-all of lathework is the cutting of a screw. This attitude spreads to those who are learning to use the machine, with the result that many of them wish to cut the most difficult and uncommon screws long before they have mastered the higher aspects of simple turning. Let us warn the reader against such a misapprehension ; screw-cutting does not occupy such an important place in the technique of this versatile machine as many people would have him believe. It is useless to be able to cut the most wonderful screw if one cannot plan and execute one's work so that its axis is in the correct relation to other important surfaces on the same job.

For cutting an accurate screw, it is necessary that the relation between the movement of the saddle, and the turns of the work, should be carefully controlled. This is brought about by means of the *leadscrew*, the long screwed shaft which runs along the front of the bed. This screw is driven by a train of gears from the spindle as shown at

FIG. 267.—Diagrammatic Representation of Screw-cutting.

Fig. 235. Usually the drive is first carried to a spindle called the *stud*, which for all purposes may be assumed to be the spindle itself, as it rotates at the same speed, and in the same direction, unless caused to reverse by the *tumbler* mechanism. From the stud, the drive is conveyed to the leadscrew by a train of gears, and to vary the relationship between the turns of the leadscrew and those of the stud, these gears may be varied. In Fig. 235, gear A on the main spindle is shown driving the stud gear D through B, and since A and D are the same size, the stud revolves at the same speed and in the same direction as A. To reverse the stud for the purpose of reversing the feed or leadscrew, the nut holding the top quadrant is loosened and the quadrant swung so that B comes out of engagement with A and C goes in. (B is in permanent mesh with D.) A now drives D through C and B which, by introducing an additional gear, causes a reversal in the direction of D. To drive the leadscrew or gearbox shaft another gear E is put on the stud and, as shown in the diagram, E then drives F, and G, which is keyed to F, drives H, giving a compound train.   In the arrangement shown a simple train from E to H may be obtained by packing H out level with E and putting a single connecting gear on the lower quadrant.   To provide adjustment for correct meshing, the pin carrying F and G may be moved along the quadrant and the whole assembly swung about the centre of H.

The connexion between the leadscrew and the saddle is effected by a nut, fixed to the inside of the apron, and screwed to suit the leadscrew.   This nut is made in one or two halves and arranged in such a way that, by operating a lever at the front of the apron, the halves may be engaged with the leadscrew (Fig. 236).   When the nut is engaged, the saddle moves along the bed a distance equal to the pitch of the leadscrew for each turn of the screw, and since the tool which is used to cut the thread on the work is for all purposes solid with the carriage, this moves the same distance.   We thus have a rotation of the work, combined with a fixed longitudinal movement of the tool for each turn the work makes and the result is a screw formed on the work as shown diagrammatically at Fig. 267.

Gears for Screw-cutting.   We may now proceed with the determination of screw-cutting ratios.   The speed ratio between the leadscrew and stud is controlled by the gear drive connecting them, and as we have previously seen, this relation depends only on the number of teeth in the gears, with small gears turning more times than large ones.   The types of gear connexions on a lathe are *simple*, and *compound*.   In the simple train shown at Fig. 268 the gear on

Fig. 268.—Simple Gear Train.

the stud drives direct through the *intermediate* gear to the gear on the leadscrew.   The intermediate gear has no effect on the ratio between driver and driven, but merely acts as a connexion between the two, and serves to keep the rotation of driver and driven in the same direction.   A compound train is shown at Fig. 269.   Here the intermediate stud carries two gears which are keyed together so that they rotate as a unit.   The drive now is, (*a*) stud on to driven intermediate, (*b*) driving intermediate on to leadscrew, so that as well as acting as a connexion between stud and leadscrew, the intermediate gears influence the ratio between stud and leadscrew.

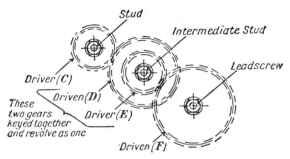

FIG. 269.—Compound Gear Train.

We shall appreciate most readily the determination of the ratio to cut any given screw if we first consider what happens when we cut a screw with a $\frac{1}{1}$ ratio between stud and leadscrew. When the spindle turns once, the leadscrew turns once, the tool moves along one pitch of the leadscrew, and therefore cuts a thread of identical pitch on the work. If the ratio is $\dfrac{\text{Spindle turns}}{\text{Leadscrew turns}} = \dfrac{2}{1}$ the carriage will move 1 pitch of the leadscrew whilst the work turns *twice*, and the thread will have a pitch of *one-half* that of the leadscrew or, it will have *twice* the number of threads per inch.

But $\dfrac{\text{Spindle turns}}{\text{Leadscrew turns}} = \dfrac{2}{1}$ means that we must have $\dfrac{\text{Driver teeth}}{\text{Driven teeth}} = \dfrac{1}{2}$, since a small gear rotates faster than a large one with which it is engaged.

Hence we may say

$$\frac{\text{Driver teeth}}{\text{Driven teeth}} = \frac{\text{Leadscrew turns}}{\text{Spindle turns}} = \frac{\text{Thd. per inch on leadscrew}}{\text{Thd. per inch on work}},$$

or just : $\dfrac{\text{Drivers}}{\text{Driven}} = \dfrac{\text{T.P.I. on leadscrew}}{\text{T.P.I. to be cut}} = \dfrac{\text{Pitch to be cut}}{\text{Pitch of leadscrew}}$

$$\left(\text{Since Pitch} = \frac{1}{\text{No. of thd. per inch}}\right)$$

When the fraction representing $\dfrac{\text{Drivers}}{\text{Driven}}$ has been found, it must be thrown into one containing numbers equal to the numbers of teeth in whatever gears are available to make up the drive. Often lathes are equipped with a set of gears ranging from 20 T. to 120 T. in steps of 5 teeth.

EXAMPLE 6. *Calculate the gears for cutting the following screws on a lathe with a leadscrew of* 4 *T.P.I.* (a) 9 *T.P.I.*, (b) 12 *T.P.I.*, (c) 22 *T.P.I.*, (d) 27 *T.P.I.*

(a) $\dfrac{\text{Drivers}}{\text{Driven}} = \dfrac{\text{T.P.I. leadscrew}}{\text{T.P.I. to be cut}} = \dfrac{4}{9}.$

Multiply top and bottom by $5 = \frac{20}{45}$, i.e. A simple train with 20 T. on the stud driving through an intermediate to 45 T. on the leadscrew.

(b) $\qquad \frac{\text{Drivers}}{\text{Driven}} = \frac{4}{12} = \frac{1}{3} = \frac{20}{60},$

i.e. A simple train with 20 T. on stud driving a 60 T. on the leadscrew.

(c) $\qquad \frac{\text{Drivers}}{\text{Driven}} = \frac{4}{22} = \frac{20}{110}.$

Simple train with 20 T. driving 110 T.

(d) $\qquad \frac{\text{Drivers}}{\text{Driven}} = \frac{4}{27},$

which would give $\frac{20}{135}$ if multiplied top and bottom by 5.

But as a 135 T. gear is beyond the capacity of the usual set supplied with a lathe, we cannot obtain $\frac{20}{135}$ as a simple train. Let us convert it to a compound:

$$\frac{20}{135} = \frac{4 \times 5}{9 \times 15};$$

multiply the first fraction by 5, and the second by 6. This gives

$$\frac{20 \times 30}{45 \times 90}.$$

This is a compound train with 20 T. on the stud driving 45 T. in the intermediate, and 30 T. on the intermediate driving 90 T. on the leadscrew.

When the pitch, instead of the thread, per inc his given, the method is similar.

EXAMPLE 7. *Calculate the gears for cutting the following screws on a lathe with a leadscrew having 6 threads per inch.*

(a) $\frac{3}{32}$ in. pitch.　(b) 0·200 in. pitch.　(c) 5 threads in $\frac{3}{4}$ in. (d) 50 threads per foot.

(a) When the pitch is given we have that

$$\frac{\text{Drivers}}{\text{Driven}} = \frac{\text{Pitch to be cut}}{\text{Pitch of leadscrew}}.$$

Since the leadscrew has 6 T.P.I., its pitch is $\frac{1}{6}$ in.

Hence $\qquad \frac{\text{Drivers}}{\text{Driven}} = \frac{\frac{3}{32}}{\frac{1}{6}} = \frac{3}{32} \times \frac{6}{1} = \frac{18}{32} = \frac{9}{16}.$

Multiplying top and bottom by 5 gives $\frac{45}{80}$ as a simple train.

(b) Here we have $\qquad \frac{\text{Drivers}}{\text{Driven}} = \frac{0·200}{\frac{1}{6}}.$

But since $0·200 = \frac{2}{10}$, this gives us

$$\frac{\frac{2}{10}}{\frac{1}{6}} = \frac{2}{10} \times \frac{6}{1} = \frac{12}{10} = \frac{60}{50},$$

i.e. 60 T. on the stud driving through an intermediate to 50 T. on the leadscrew.

(c) 5 threads in $\frac{3}{4}$ in. gives a pitch of $\frac{3}{4} \div 5 = \frac{3}{4} \times \frac{1}{5} = \frac{3}{20}$ in.

$$\frac{\text{Drivers}}{\text{Driven}} = \frac{\frac{3}{20}}{\frac{1}{6}} = \frac{18}{20} = \frac{9}{10} = \frac{45}{50},$$

i.e. a simple train with 45 T. driving 50 T.

(d) 50 threads per foot, i.e. 50 in 12 in. gives a pitch of $\frac{12}{50}$ in.

Hence
$$\frac{\text{Drivers}}{\text{Driven}} = \frac{\frac{12}{50}}{\frac{1}{6}} = \frac{72}{50} = \frac{36}{25}.$$

This cannot be obtained as a simple train, hence

$$\frac{36}{25} = \frac{6 \times 6}{5 \times 5} = \frac{60}{50} \times \frac{30}{25},$$

i.e. 60 T. on the stud driving 50 T. on the intermediate and 30 T. on the intermediate driving 25 T. on the leadscrew.

Note.—When the reader has made a fraction of the respective thread per inch, or of the pitches, he need not worry in remembering which are drivers and which driven if he realises that to cut a *finer* thread than that on the leadscrew, the leadscrew must turn *slower* than the spindle, and vice versa.

The Lead of a Thread—Multi-start Threads

So far we have only considered the case where a threaded shaft has a single thread running along it as shown at Fig. 270 (*a*). It is possible, however, for a piece of work to have several separate and independent threads running along it, and Fig. 270 (*b*) shows a cylinder

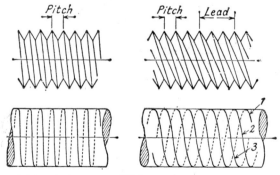

(a) Single Thread.   (b) 3-Start Thread of Similar Pitch
(Starts numbered 1, 2 and 3)

Fig. 270.—Single and 3-Start Threads.

with three threads. Such a screw would not look much different from one having only a single thread, but if one thread is followed round, it will be seen that there are two more fitted in between, and in one complete turn round the bar the thread advances *three times* as far as if it were a single thread. This distance that any one thread advances along the bar whilst it makes one complete turn is called the *lead*. The different threads are called *starts*, and we may have single-start, two-start, three-start, etc., threads. Multiple-start threads are commonly used on fountain-pen caps so that the cap may be screwed up quickly.   In any thread the *pitch* is the distance between two adjoining threads, so that in a three-start thread, since there are three separate threads, the lead will be three times the pitch.   In general, we may say that if there are " n " starts, then **lead** $= n \times$ **pitch**.   A single-start thread has pitch equal to lead.

Now the pitch of the thread determines its dimensions (height, thickness, etc.), and if the reader has followed our discussion regarding the leadscrew-speed ratio for cutting, he will see that it is the *lead* which must be used when calculating the screw-cutting wheels. Hence use the lead when calculating wheels for multi-start threads. (*Note.*—The leadscrew is always single-start.)

EXAMPLE 8.   *Calculate the change wheels for the following threads,*
(a) 16 *thd. per inch 3-start,* (b) $\frac{3}{8}$ *in. pitch 3-start,* (c) 3 *thd. per inch 2-start.*
Leadscrew has 4 thd. per inch.

(*a*) 16 T.P.I. 3-start has a pitch of $\frac{1}{16}$ in., and a lead of $\frac{3}{16}$ in.

$$\therefore \frac{\text{Drivers}}{\text{Driven}} = \frac{\text{lead of thread}}{\text{lead of leadscrew}} = \frac{\frac{3}{16}}{\frac{1}{4}} = \frac{12}{16} = \frac{3}{4},$$

i.e. 30 T. driving 40 T. in a simple train.

(*b*) $\frac{3}{8}$ in. pitch 3-start has a lead of $3 \times \frac{3}{8} = \frac{9}{8}$ in.

$$\therefore \frac{\text{Drivers}}{\text{Driven}} = \frac{\frac{9}{8}}{\frac{1}{4}} = \frac{36}{8} = \frac{9}{2},$$

i.e. 90 T. driving 20 T. in a simple train.

(*c*) 3 T.P.I. 2-start has a pitch of $\frac{1}{3}$ in., and a lead of $\frac{2}{3}$ in.

$$\therefore \frac{\text{Drivers}}{\text{Driven}} = \frac{\frac{2}{3}}{\frac{1}{4}} = \frac{8}{3} = \frac{80}{30},$$

i.e. 80 T. driving 30 T. in a simple train.

Lathes with Screw-cutting Gearbox

On the more expensive lathes it is not necessary to fit up the drive to the leadscrew every time a thread has to be cut, because the ratio

FIG. 271.—Quick Change Gear-box for obtaining Feeds and Threads.

required can be selected with a gearbox. Full instructions are generally given on such lathes and a diagram of such a box is shown at
Fig. 271. The reader will notice that this box enables different feeds
as well as threads to be obtained.

Cutting a Thread

The form of thread which we shall usually require to cut is the
Whitworth, and particulars of this thread are given in the Appendix,
p. 296. Screwing is usually the last operation to be performed on an
otherwise finished piece of work, and when the diameter of the screwed

Cranked Tool for Cut-
ting up to Shoulders
and Chuck Jaws

Fig. 272.—Screw-cutting Tool (for Vee Threads).

portion has been turned down to the top size of the thread and the
change wheels fitted, a screw-cutting tool must be obtained. This is
similar to a parting tool, with its end ground to the vee form of the
thread, and rounded off at the point to suit the radius at the bottom
of the particular thread to be cut (Fig. 272). For obtaining the correct
angle on the tool a *screw-cutting gauge* (Fig. 273 (a)) is necessary, whilst

(a) Screwcutting and Centre Gauge

(b.1)

(b.2)

Internal Tool

(b.3)

(b) Setting the Screwcutting Tool

Fig. 273.

to get the radius at the end, a *pitch gauge* (Fig. 274) is useful. This latter gauge, which incorporates templates of the usual range of threads, is also useful for inspecting the correctness of pitch at the commencement of cutting, and for determining the pitch of unknown threads. For screwing cast iron and brass, the screw-cutting tool should have little or no top rake, whilst for steel, the rake may be about one-half that for an ordinary turning tool.

When the tool has been ground satisfactorily to form it must be set on centre, and with its axis square with the axis of the work. This second setting is performed with the aid of the screw-cutting gauge, as shown at Fig. 273 (*b*). The tool must now be traversed a number of times along the work under the control of the leadscrew and fed in a little deeper each time until the thread has been cut to the correct depth (or slightly less, to leave for finishing with a *chaser*). The procedure adopted for this progressive feeding in of the tool varies amongst different turners, and many feed straight in with the cross-

[*James Chesterman & Co., Ltd.,*

Fig. 274.—Screw Pitch Gauge.

slide. This causes the tool to cut on both faces of its vee form, a condition of cutting which is not always satisfactory. From experience of all methods, we recommend the following as being the one giving the best results both in cutting and in manipulation.

Set the compound slide so that it makes half the thread angle with the axis of the cross-slide (i.e. $27\frac{1}{2}°$ for Whitworth and $30°$ for metric and U.S.S.). This slide should be well adjusted so that its movement has a firm feel about it. Set the cross-slide so that the tool just scrapes the diameter to be screwed, and set the cross-slide stop to prevent the tool moving any further in. If there is no stop, chalk the graduated sleeve so that the cross-slide may be wound to the same place each time. After putting the machine on a slow-speed, engage the nut, and the tool will move along, scraping a thin line for the thread. When it reaches the limit of the thread, withdraw the cross-slide quickly and disengage the nut (the left hand should be kept on the cross-slide handle and the right hand on the lever for the nut). Return the carriage to the starting position, wind in the cross-slide to the stop or chalk mark, and put on a small amount of cut with the compound slide. Engage the nut, and allow this cut to travel along, and withdraw the cross-slide and nut at the end as before. Repeat the process until the thread is almost to its full depth when, to clean it out to form, the last cut or two may be taken by feeding straight

FIG. 275.—Set-up for Cutting Vee Threads.

in with the cross-slide. The final finish should be given to the thread with a chaser, as we will explain later. In Fig. 275, the successive steps of metal removal to form the thread are shown by dotted lines. When used in this way, the top rake of the tool should slope back perpendicular to the left-hand edge of the vee as shown, and the tool will then cut very efficiently. The finish of the thread will be improved by using cutting lubricant.

Chasing the Thread. When the thread has been taken to depth with the screw-cutting tool, obtain an outside chaser of the corresponding pitch, a chaser rest and a *screw ring gauge* (or a good nut of the same size if a ring gauge is not available). Take out the tool, and

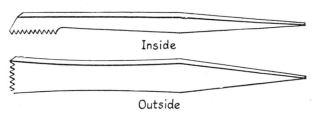

Inside

Outside

Fig. 276.—Internal and External Chasers.

clamp the rest in the toolpost, so that its end lies along the work to form a rest for the chaser, and at such a height that the top of the chaser teeth will be about on the centre. Increase the lathe speed, hold the body of the chaser with the left hand and the handle with the right. Place the end of the chaser on the rest, pick up the thread from the end, and press the chaser teeth into the thread, when it will trim up the thread form, at the same time travelling along. Repeat this a few times and then take out the job to try on the ring gauge. If the gauge will not screw on, repeat the chasing, until the gauge screws on with a nice fit (Figs. 276 and 277).

Chaser Rest

Fig. 277.—Chasing a Thread in the Lathe.

Locating the Tool in the Thread. We have said nothing yet regarding the method to be adopted to ensure that when the tool has been taken along the thread and brought back to its starting position, the nut may be engaged to bring the carriage into such a position that the tool follows the same thread again. If the number of T.P.I. being cut is a multiple of the number on the lead-screw (i.e. 4, 8, 12, 16, 20, etc., for a 4 T.P.I. leadscrew) the nut may be engaged anywhere and the tool will follow the original thread. If, however, this does not apply, the reader will find that if he engages the nut indiscriminately, the tool will probably commence to cut a separate thread alongside the first one and the job will be spoiled. There are several methods for ensuring that the tool shall follow the same thread each time.

(*a*) *Reversing the Machine.* If the lathe is equipped with a means for reversing its spindle, the leadscrew nut may be kept in permanent engagement and the tool returned to its starting position by reversing the machine. The main precaution to be observed if this method is used is to ensure that all the lost motion (called " backlash ") has been taken up before the tool is fed in for each successive cut. This backlash results in a pause in the movement of the saddle at each end, and if the tool is fed on to the work whilst the carriage is stationary, the thread will be spoiled. Always allow the tool to return beyond the end of the screw before reversing and feeding in.

The Hendey Norton lathe has a lever on the apron which reverses the leadscrew without reversing the machine, and this method is about the most convenient of all for bringing the tool back to its starting position.

(b) *Marking the Lathe.* By means of a bed stop for the carriage or a bar placed in front of the tailstock, make some provision to allow the carriage to be returned to the same position each time, with the tool beyond its starting position. Before engaging the nut for the first time, wind the carriage back to this position and stop the lathe. Pull the machine round until the nut will engage, and with it in this position, make one chalk mark at the top of the driving-plate, and another on the leadscrew opposite a corresponding one on some fixed part of the machine. Start up and take the first cut, withdraw the tool, and return the carriage to the stop. The nut must not be engaged for the next cut until the driving-plate chalk-mark is at the top, at the same time that the leadscrew mark is level with its neighbour. With practice, the conditions may be caught whilst the lathe is running slowly, but at first the reader should inch it round with the starting handle until the marks are in their proper positions.

(c) *The Chasing Dial.* The chasing dial is a fitment to the saddle which performs a duty similar to that of marking the lathe as we have just discussed. The dial is shown at Fig. 278, from which it will be seen that the visible indicating face is connected to the leadscrew by means of a wormwheel. A common type used with 4 T.P.I. lead

Saddle

Dial

Leadscrew

16 T.
Wormwheel
meshing with
Leadscrew

Fig. 278.—Diagram showing Chasing Dial.
(*See* also Fig. 236 F.)

screws has a 16 T. wormwheel, and the dial face is divided into 8 parts. The leadscrew nut may be engaged at the instant when any line on the dial is opposite the fixed zero, as well as in the 8 intermediate positions when the zero is between any pair of dial marks (16 positions in all). The rules governing the use of this particular dial for cutting different threads will be followed from the table below.

TABLE 20. OPERATION OF CHASING DIAL

(4 T.P.I. Leadscrew. 16 Teeth in Dial Wormwheel.)

(1) Particulars of Thread to be Cut.	(2) $\dfrac{\text{Column (1)}}{4}$	(3) Lowest Denominator of Col. (2) after Cancelling.	(4) $\dfrac{\text{Column (3)}}{16}$	Remarks.
Any T.P.I. divisible by 4 (e.g. 12)	$\dfrac{12}{4} = \dfrac{3}{1}$	1	$\frac{1}{16}$ rev.	Engage nut anywhere.
Even No. of T.P.I. (e.g. 14)	$\dfrac{14}{4} = \dfrac{7}{2}$	2	$\frac{1}{8}$,,	Engage at any dial division.
Odd No. of T.P.I. (e.g. 11)	$\dfrac{11}{4}$	4	$\frac{1}{4}$,,	Engage at alternate line (2, 4, 6 or 8).
Half threads (e.g. 6½)	$\dfrac{6\frac{1}{2}}{4} = \dfrac{13}{8}$	8	$\frac{1}{2}$,,	Engage every half rev. (2 and 6 or 4 and 8).
Quarter threads e.g. (5¼)	$\dfrac{5\frac{1}{4}}{4} = \dfrac{21}{16}$	16	1 ,,	Engage every complete rev.

For any other set of conditions the divisors in columns (2) and (4) must be modified to suit. For example, with a 6 T.P.I. leadscrew and an 18 T. dial wormwheel, the operation would be as follows:

Odd No. of T.P.I. (e.g. 11)	$\dfrac{11}{6}$	6	$\dfrac{6}{18} = \dfrac{1}{3}$	Engage at every $\frac{1}{3}$ rev.

(The number of teeth in the wormwheel may be found by counting how many turns of the leadscrew are necessary to cause one turn of the dial, with the saddle stationary.)

Cutting Left-hand Threads

Left-hand threads must be cut by reversing the leadscrew so that it rotates opposite to the work, and hence cutting with the tool moving from left to right. This will often involve turning a groove in the work at the end of the thread to provide a space for starting the tool. The groove should be to the depth of the thread, and of a width equal to 1–2 threads.

Cutting Internal Threads

For cutting internal threads with a single point tool, the notes we have given for external work regarding the manipulation of the lathe apply. In general, internal work is more difficult, because the tool is often less rigid, and its progress cannot always be observed. The hole for the thread should first be bored to the core diameter of the thread, this being determined by subtracting twice the depth of the thread from its top diameter (see Appendix, p. 290). When the hole is " blind," a recess should be turned at the bottom as shown at Fig. 279, the depth of this being equal to the thread, and its width

Fig. 279.—Preparation of Hole for Blind Internal Thread.

about 1–2 threads. Care will have to be exercised to avoid running the tool into the metal at the bottom of the hole in such cases, and a very slow speed, together with guiding chalk, marks or stops, must be used as much as possible. For internal work it is helpful if a short recess can be bored at the front end, having a top diameter equal to the outside diameter of the screw (Fig. 279). This serves as an indicator, and when the tool point just scrapes its diameter we know that it has been taken in to the full depth of thread. Often, if there is any length to spare on the work, the material used for the length of this recess can be faced off afterwards.

It is not usual to feed with the compound slide when cutting internal threads, but to feed straight in with the cross-slide, and use the graduated sleeve for putting on a suitable amount of cut each time. The compound slide may be set parallel with the bed, and occasionally a few thousandths of cut put on with it, the object being to clear the sides of the tool.

Finishing the Thread

Internal threads may be chased in the same way as external ones, an internal chaser being shown at Fig. 276. Owing to the greater difficulty of manipulating an inside chaser, some turners prefer to clamp it in the toolpost and feed it with the leadscrew after matching up the threads on the chaser and work. If this is done the chaser should be set so that it is in line, and this may be done by adjusting the tops of its threads to the blade of a small square from the face of the work. When the inside chaser is used by hand the thread should first be tooled to its full depth so that the work of the chaser only consists of putting the radius on the tops of the threads.

If a tap is available of the size being cut, this forms a good way of finishing the thread. Cut the thread to within a few thousandths of its full depth and after fitting a wrench to the tap, start it in the hole. Now bring up the tailstock centre to the centre hole in the end of the tap, and as the tap advances into the work, keep the centre in contact with the tap centre hole by winding the tailstock (Fig. 280).

Fig. 280.—Tapping in the Lathe.

The tapping operation is best performed by pulling the lathe round by the belt with the left hand, whilst the right hand attends to the feel of the wrench, and the screwing up of the tailstock centre. This method of using the back centre to keep a tap in line should always be used when tapping holes in the lathe, and when a hole is tapped from a drilled or bored hole without any previous screwing by a tool it is of great help in obtaining a true thread.

Change Wheels for Metric Threads

Since 1 in. is equivalent to 25·4 mm., to cut a thread of 1 mm. pitch (i.e. 25·4 t.p.i.) would require, on a leadscrew of 1 t.p.i. a

ratio of $\dfrac{\text{drivers}}{\text{driven}} = \dfrac{1}{25\cdot4}$,

$$\text{i.e. } \frac{10}{254} = \frac{5}{127} \qquad \bullet \qquad \bullet \qquad \bullet \qquad \bullet \qquad (1)$$

If instead of 1 mm. pitch we wish the ratio for a pitch of p mm., the above ratio must be multiplied by p. Thus to cut p mm. pitch on a 1 t.p.i. leadscrew requires a ratio of

$$\frac{5p}{127} \qquad \bullet \qquad \bullet \qquad \bullet \qquad \bullet \qquad (2)$$

Finally, a leadscrew with a finer thread than 1 per inch will have to be driven faster in proportion to its no. of t.p.i. If then the leadscrew has n t.p.i. instead of 1 t.p.i., expression (2) will become :

Ratio: $\dfrac{\text{drivers}}{\text{driven}}$ to cut p mm. pitch on a leadscrew of n t.p.i.

$$= \frac{5pn}{127} \qquad . \qquad . \qquad . \qquad . \qquad . \quad (3)$$

And this is the formula for calculating metric ratios. The reader will observe that 127 appears in the expression as a driven wheel, so that to cut metric threads on an English lathe we must have a 127 T. gear as one of the driven gears in the train.

EXAMPLE 9. *Determine the gears for cutting the following threads on a lathe with a 4 t.p.i. leadscrew, using a set of change wheels ranging from 20 T. to 120 T. in steps of 5 T. with an additional 127 T. wheel.*

(a) $1\frac{1}{2}$ mm. p., (b) $2\frac{3}{4}$ mm. p., (c) $4\frac{1}{4}$ mm. p., (d) $3\cdot4$ mm. p.

(a) Here $p = 1\frac{1}{2}$ mm. and $n = 4$.

$$\text{Ratio}: \frac{\text{Drivers}}{\text{Driven}} = \frac{5np}{127} = \frac{5 \times 4 \times 1\frac{1}{2}}{127} = \frac{30}{127}.$$

A simple train with 30 T. on the stud and 127 T. on the leadscrew.

(b) $p = 2\frac{3}{4} = \frac{11}{4}$ and $n = 4$.

$$\text{Ratio}: \frac{\text{Drivers}}{\text{Driven}} = \frac{5 \times \frac{11}{4} \times 4}{127} = \frac{5 \times 11}{127} = \frac{55}{127}.$$

A simple train with 55 T. on the stud driving 127 T. on the leadscrew.

(c) $p = 4\frac{1}{4}$; $n = 4$.

$$\text{Ratio} = \frac{5 \times 4\frac{1}{4} \times 4}{127} = \frac{5 \times \frac{17}{4} \times 4}{127} = \frac{85}{127} \frac{\text{Driver}}{\text{Driven}}.$$

(d) $p = 3\cdot4$ and $n = 4$.

$$\text{Ratio} = \frac{5 \times 3\cdot4 \times 4}{127} = \frac{68}{127}.$$

But since we have no 68 T. gear we must compound it thus:

$$\frac{68}{127} = \frac{4 \times 17}{127}.$$

Multiply top and bottom by 5: $= \dfrac{4 \times 85}{5 \times 127}$

Now multiply by 10: $= \dfrac{40 \times 85}{50 \times 127},$

i.e. a compound train with 40 T. and 85 T. as the drivers, and 50 T. and 127 T. as the driven gears.

EXAMPLE 10. *Calculate ratios for the above threads on a lathe with a 6 t.p.i. leadscrew.*

(a) $p = 1\frac{1}{2}$ and $n = 6$.

$$\frac{\text{Drivers}}{\text{Driven}} = \frac{5 \times 1\frac{1}{2} \times 6}{127} = \frac{45}{127} \text{ (Simple Train).}$$

(b) $p = 2\frac{3}{4}$: $n = 6$.

$$\frac{\text{Drivers}}{\text{Driven}} = \frac{5 \times 2\frac{3}{4} \times 6}{127} = \frac{5 \times \frac{11}{4} \times 6}{127} = \frac{55 \times 6}{127 \times 4}$$

$$= \frac{55 \times 60}{127 \times 40} \text{ (Compound Train).}$$

(c) $p = 4\frac{1}{4}: n = 6$.

$$\frac{\text{Drivers}}{\text{Driven}} = \frac{5 \times 4\frac{1}{4} \times 6}{127} = \frac{5 \times \frac{17}{4} \times 6}{127} = \frac{85 \times 6}{127 \times 4}$$

$$= \frac{85 \times 60}{127 \times 40} \text{ (Compound Train)}.$$

(d) $p = 3 \cdot 4: n = 6$.

$$\frac{\text{Drivers}}{\text{Driven}} = \frac{5 \times 3 \cdot 4 \times 6}{127} = \frac{17 \times 6}{127} = \frac{85 \times 6}{127 \times 5}$$

$$= \frac{85 \times 60}{127 \times 50} \text{ (Compound Train)}.$$

Conclusion

We must now, for the time being, leave the reader to develop his knowledge, hoping that he has benefited at least from some of our discussions, and that we have stimulated him to further thought and enquiry. We encourage him to pursue his course, maintaining at all times, and whatever his knowledge, the simple mind of a student, for upon the simplest of foundations are built the most wonderful works of Nature.

CHAPTER 12

THE SHAPING MACHINE

The main function of the shaping machine is the production of flat surfaces. which are obtained by combining a line tool cut with a perpendicular feed. The arrangement of this is shown at Fig. 281 (*a*) and the result at (*b*), where the tool repeatedly travels along the line

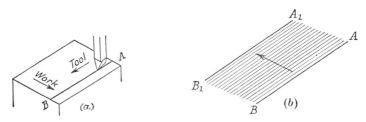

FIG. 281.—Action of Shaping a Flat Surface.

AB whilst the work is fed a small distance each time, in the same plane as the line of tool motion, and perpendicular to it. The tool line eventually reaches a position A_1B_1 and the combination of the two movements results in the flat plane ABB_1A_1 being machined. The machine serves an important purpose in a general machine shop, particularly on account of the quickness with which the work and tool can be set up, and the good standard of accuracy to which a flat surface can be produced.

A diagram of a crank shaper is shown at Fig. 282, the term " crank " being applied because the motion of its ram is derived from a crank pin (see later). The tool receives its straight-line motion from the ram, which is guided by long, straight ways. Underneath the path of the tool is the work-table, which is supported on ways perpendicular to the ram and travels along these slides when a horizontal surface is being machined. The table ways are mounted on vertical slides so that the whole unit may be moved up and down. Vertical surfaces are machined by employing a vertical feed of the tool or work. On machines not provided with any automatic vertical movements hand operation of the tool slide is used for shaping vertical surfaces. It is now becoming general practice, however, to provide for a power vertical feed for the table, and on some of the larger machines the head slide is fed by an arrangement which notches the actuating screw a small amount each time the ram reaches its backward position. Where power feeds are absent the table could, of course, be fed by hand, but this is too laborious and its up and down movements are only employed to suit varying heights of work.

The Shaper Drive

On the machine shown at Fig. 282 the motor is mounted on a

[*The Butler Machine Tool Co. Ltd.*

Fig. 282.—Crank Shaping Machine.

A. Ram
B. Tool slide
C. Handle for clamping ram
D. Screw for adjusting position of ram
E. Screw for locking tool slide unit
F. Speed change lever
G. Starting lever

H. Vertical/horizontal feed selector
I. Feed directional control
J. Lever for adjustment of feed
K. Horizontal table adjustment screw
L. Vertical table adjustment
M. Feed shaft
N. Toolbox
P. End of shaft for adjusting stroke

SPECIFICATION

		in.
Maximum length of stroke		18
Table, top (length × width)		$18 \times 17\frac{1}{4}$
,, horizontal travel on slides		20
,, vertical travel		12
Tool box, vertical adjustment		6
Number and range of speeds obtainable	8.	15–150 cycles/min.
Number and range of feeds	10.	·010–·105 in.
Swivel base, vise, width and depth of jaw		$10 \times 2\frac{1}{4}$
,, ,, vise opens		12
Size of tool steel		$1\frac{1}{4} \times \frac{5}{8}$
Horse power and speed (driving motor)		5×1000

platform at the rear and drives the gearbox intake pulley and clutch by an enclosed vee belt drive. The gearbox provides for eight speeds and delivers the power to a pinion which drives the *stroke wheel* (sometimes called the *bull* wheel). Mounted on the face of the stroke wheel

[*The Butler Machine Tool Co. Ltd.*

FIG. 283.—Link Motion Assembly of 18-inch Crank Shaper.

is the *crank pin,* which is incorporated with a sliding block working in dovetail slideways running across the face of the wheel. The connection to the ram is arranged by means of a link attached to the underside of the ram and pivoted at the bottom of the machine. This link engages with a *driving block* bored to suit the crank pin and having some arrangement whereby it can slide up and down the link. On the machine we have illustrated the link consists of two rods, but in other designs the link consists of a member with a long slot which accommodates the driving block for sliding up and down whilst the stroke wheel rotates. This slotted link form of design, which has dominated the shaping machine for many years, has led to the mechanism being known as the *slotted link* motion. When a link of this form is used it is necessary to employ an additional link for connection to the ram in order to compensate for the distance variation

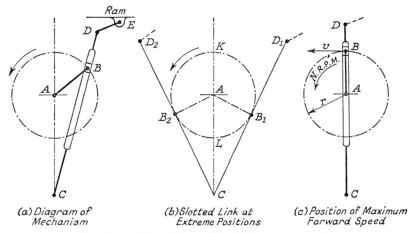

(a) Diagram of
Mechanism

(b) Slotted Link at
Extreme Positions

(c) Position of Maximum
Forward Speed

FIG. 284.—Slotted Link Quick Return Mechanism.
(Lettering corresponds with Fig. 283.)

as the link swings through an arc. This is shown as *DE* on Fig. 284, which also shows the slotted link in diagrammatic form. In the design we have illustrated in Fig. 283, this extra link is unnecessary as the length variation is taken up by the rods sliding in the block where they are anchored at the bottom of the machine. The mechanical details of the link motion are all shown on Fig. 283.

A feature of the shaping machine is that for each productive cutting stroke there is an idle return stroke, and the geometry of the slotted link motion is such that this return stroke occupies a shorter time and so minimises the time wasted. In Fig. 284 (*a*), which shows a skeleton form of the mechanism, the crank pin *B* rotates about the centre of the stroke wheel A and at the same time B slides up and down the link CD. This causes the link to oscillate about C and so drive the ram backwards and forwards. The quick return feature is derived from the configuration of the mechanism and will be understood from Fig. 284 (*b*). When the link is at CD_1, tangential to the pitch circle of B, the ram will be at the extreme backward position of its stroke, and when it is at CD_2 the extreme forward position will have been reached. The forward (cutting) stroke, therefore, takes place whilst the crank rotates through the angle B_1KB_2, whilst rotation through B_2LB_1 returns the ram to its backward position. If AC and AB are known, the $\dfrac{\text{forward}}{\text{return}}$ time ratio can be found, because $\dfrac{AB}{AC} = \cos \widehat{CAB}$, the return angle is twice this and the forward angle is the return angle subtracted from 360°. When these angles have been found, the ratio

$$\frac{\text{cutting time}}{\text{return time}} = \frac{\widehat{B_1KB_2}}{\widehat{B_2LB_1}}$$

and the actual times may be found if the crank speed is known. The length of stroke is altered by varying the radius of the crank pin and its block on the stroke wheel, and the mechanism for doing this is shown at Fig. 285. If the reader lays out the mechanism for various settings of the stroke, he will see that varying the stroke radius AB also causes the angle B_2LB_1 to alter. This causes some variation in the $\dfrac{\text{cutting}}{\text{return}}$ ratio for different settings of the stroke.

Fig. 285.—Details of Mechanism for adjusting Position of Crank Pin Block on Stroke Wheel.

(Details from the Butler Machine Tool Co. Ltd.)

Stroke and Speed

Shaping machine sizes are designated by the maximum stroke of the ram, the most usual ranging from 12 in. to 36 in., with those in the 18 in. to 24 in. group being the best all-round machines for general purpose work. The cutting speed of the tool, starting as it does from rest, rising to a maximum and slowing down to rest again, varies throughout the stroke, but its average speed can be calculated, and if the dimensions of the mechanism are known its maximum speed is not difficult to determine. The average speed, taken over cutting and return strokes, is given by multiplying the stroke in feet by the number of double strokes per minute. To obtain the average speed on the cutting stroke we must know the cutting-return time ratio. Assume a machine working on a 1-ft. stroke and making 30 double strokes per minute, then the overall average speed is 60 ft. per minute. If the ratio $\dfrac{\text{cutting time}}{\text{return time}}$ is $\dfrac{5}{4}$, in 1 minute, $\dfrac{5}{9}$ minute will have been occupied in making 30 cutting strokes, each of 1-foot length. Hence

$$\text{average cutting speed} = 30 \div \frac{5}{9} = 30 \times \frac{9}{5} = 54 \text{ ft. per minute.}$$

The maximum speed occurs when the ram is at the mid point of its stroke, and the mechanism in the position shown at Fig. 284 (c), the slotted link being vertical. In this position B and D are both moving horizontally and their relative speeds will be proportional to their radii from C. Let the speed of B in its circle be v ($v = 2\pi r N$). Then speed of D (and the ram) $= v\dfrac{CD}{CB}$. Ram speeds at other positions may be found by making a layout of the mechanism and drawing a velocity diagram, as discussed in *Senior Workshop Calculations*. Cutting speeds for shaping should be approximately the same as those recommended for turning on similar materials.

The Head and Tool Box (Fig. 286)

The tool box is carried on a vertical slide which is attached to the end of the ram through a circular flange and facing, which can be set in any angular position and is graduated in degrees. The slide is actuated by a screw from the handle on top, a graduated sleeve showing the amount of movement. When the machine is being used for ordinary horizontal machining this slide is clamped in the vertical position and the screw used for putting on the necessary amounts of cut. The slide is also used to traverse the tool up or down for machining vertical surfaces, and by setting the head at some angle for machining angular surfaces. The tool post or clamp is carried in its box on a block, pivoted at the top to allow it to swing forward (sometimes called the " clapper box "). This allows the tool to lift clear of the path of the cut on the return stroke of the ram. An additional feature is that the tool box may be swung a small amount on either side and clamped by a nut. This is for use when shaping vertical or angular surfaces and, by introducing a horizontal element into the swing, allows the tool, on its return stroke, to clear the face being machined (Fig. 287). The larger and more expensive machines are provided with a swivelling

[*The Butler Machine Tool Co. Ltd.*

FIG. 286.—Headslide and Tool Box.

(Shown also is an attachment operated by Bowden cable for raising the clapper box on the return stroke.)

Feed

FIG. 287.—Shaping Vertical Face.

(Tool box swung so that tool will clear face on return stroke.)

table which allows angular surfaces to be shaped by using the horizontal feed of the table. When the tool slide is being used to traverse cuts it should be used at about the middle of its range of travel. If it is high up the movement is easy, but there may not be sufficient length of engagement to ensure accuracy. When the slide is near the bottom it generally becomes stiff and tiresome to operate by hand. The graduated sleeve on this screw should be calibrated and the value of its markings memorised, since they control the amount of cut being put on when shaping horizontal surfaces. The same applies to the horizontal table lead screw which controls the cut being put on when shaping vertical surfaces. If there are no graduated sleeves it is a good plan to make and fit them.

(a) Straight Rougher

(b) Side Tool Cutting Down

(c) Side Tool Cutting Up

Fig. 288.—Rake Directions for Shaping Tools.

Cutting Tools

The general patterns of the tools used for shaping are the same as for turning (see Fig. 126, p. 148), but their shanks should be a little more robust to withstand the shock each time a cutting stroke commences. For this reason a good solid shank tool is preferable to a holder into which tool bits are fitted. Slightly more clearance should be ground on the front (about 10° to 12° total), and the other point to consider is the direction of the side rake. When turning, the tool always travels from right to left, so that all straight turning tools have their side rake sloping from left to right when viewed from the shank end. The usual relative tool-work movement in shaping is from left to right, and this requires a side rake sloping in the opposite direction (see Fig. 288 (a)). When shaping *down* a vertical face with a left-hand side tool the side rake should slope as shown at Fig. 288 (b), but when the bottom has been reached and more cut put on to traverse up again the rake needs to be the opposite way for correct cutting (Fig. 288 (c)). It is thus not always possible to work strictly according to theory, but the reader should observe the rule as much as possible, and for the sake of a good finish arrange that the last cut is taken in the correct direction for utilising the advantage of the rake.

Speeds and Feeds

When turning in the lathe the material passes over the tool at a uniform rate, but in shaping, as we have seen from our discussion with Fig. 284, the tool starts from rest, attains a maximum speed and then slows down to rest again. It then makes a return stroke of the same character, but in a shorter time. This renders the estimation of a precise cutting speed rather difficult, but the following approximate method may be used as a guide for setting the machine.

Divide twice the length of stroke (in feet) into the lowest allowable cutting speed (for turning) for the material concerned (see Table 15, p. 150). This will give the number of double strokes of the ram per minute.

Thus, for shaping mild steel on a 9-inch stroke, and taking a cutting speed of 70 ft. per min. :

Number of machine cycles (double strokes)

$$= \frac{70}{2 \times \frac{3}{4}} = \frac{70}{1\frac{1}{2}} = 47 \text{ double strokes per min.}$$

Feed

The feeding mechanism on many shaping machines consists of a ratchet wheel keyed to the table lead screw, and actuated by a swinging pawl which oscillates under the action of a connecting rod, the end of which is given an eccentric motion from a rotating flange on the side of machine. With such a mechanism the choice of feeds is rather limited, since the greatest movement of the pawl is such as to give up to about four teeth on the ratchet wheel. In general, it will be found that for most jobs one or two teeth of the wheel will prove satisfactory, but the reader should work out for himself the value of the feed given when the ratchet wheel is being indexed by a single tooth. Thus, if the ratchet wheel has, say, 28 teeth and the table lead screw 4 threads per in. :

Feed for 1 tooth $= \frac{1}{28} \times \frac{1}{4} = \frac{1}{112}$ in. = about 0·009 in. per stroke.

It should be remembered that the feed of the tool should occur during the *return* stroke of the ram. On the above arrangement this necessitates arranging the driving end of the connecting rod to one side or other of the driving flange centre, according to whether the table is being traversed to the left or to the right.

Makers are now providing machines with more comprehensive feeding arrangements and the method used on the machine we have shown is explained later.

Holding Work—The Machine Vise

An important method of holding work on the shaper is in the machine vise, and although work can be machined by attaching it to the top or side of the table, the vise is by far the most common method used, except for castings and irregular work. The shaping machine vise is of large, robust construction, designed specially for the machine and attached to the table by a generous, square base. The upper portion is mounted on the base through a graduated turntable, permitting the jaws to be used in line, or perpendicular to the ram, as well as at any other position for angular work. The base is lined up on the machine table by a pair of tenon pieces which fit in a tee slot. Normally the jaw pieces of the shaper vise are not hardened, so that it is possible to clean them up with the tool (Fig. 292 (b)) from time to time when they become bruised or damaged. The sliding jaw is moved through a large, square or acme threaded screw by a long, heavy handle, and it is not necessary to use a hammer on the handle to tighten the vise sufficiently for its work. A good, steady increasing pressure applied with both hands and the weight of the body will usually do all that is required. Blows with a hammer mutilate the handle disgracefully as well as being harmful to the vise and distorting the work being held. It is unfortunate that the layout of the machine makes it necessary, in the cross position of the vise jaws, to have the movable jaw take the thrust of the tool, and although the results seem to suffer little in consequence it is always advisable to take a blow or thrust against solid metal whenever possible.

Although, as we have said, the vise is used a great deal for holding work, the most interesting and rewarding jobs are castings and other work which must be set up on the top or side of the table, and it is work of this character which demonstrates the real capabilities of the shaping machine in the hands of an experienced operator. For this reason, in addition to the vise, the machine should be provided with a good selection of bolts, clamps, stops, setting strips, and the usual collection of bits and pieces associated with setting up jobs on a machine.

The Table Feed

An arrangement for feeding the saddle which provides a more comprehensive range and better control than that employing a ratchet

[*The Butler Machine Tool Co. Ltd.*
FIG. 289.—Cam Feed Box.

wheel on the lead screw is shown at Fig. 289, which is the opened up view of the box carrying the feed lever J in Fig. 282. The eccentric cam A rotates with the stroke wheel (centre O) and actuates the picking lever C by means of the roller B.   A spring-loaded pawl (not visible) is carried on this lever and this engages with the ratchet wheel F. (The half gear G is attached to the picking lever and this keeps B up against the cam by the action of the spring-loaded rack D.)   E is a cam which is keyed to the feed lever J (Fig. 282), and when the box is closed the face of E fits close to the face of A and its edge catches a small length of B projecting from the face of A.   When the feed is set at the full, E is in the position allowing B to be subjected to the full throw of A.   By rotating E, via J, its cam edge will take B partly away from the full effect of A and so regulate the movement of the picking lever.   The intermittent rotation of F is transmitted through bevel gears to the feed shaft M (Fig. 282) and thence into the box on the end of the saddle.   Here more gearing and clutches with control levers (H and I, Fig. 282) allow selection to be made for direction, and for horizontal or vertical movement.

Setting the Machine for Accuracy

The shaping machine, probably more than any other, is given much hack work to do, and in some shops never rises above the position of a means of removing metal and doing rough jobs.   A good shaper, however, in the right hands, is capable of undertaking a wide range of

Fig. 290.—Testing Shaper Table for Parallelism.

accurate work and often in less time than would be occupied by alternative methods.   Accurate results will be encouraged by a few elementary setting precautions carried out before a job is started and we advise the reader never to go far with any important job (on any machine) without assuring himself that the fundamental conditions leading to the desired result are all that they might be.   In addition, he should plan the method and order of his work so as to take advantage of the accuracy built into the machine.   He will then be in the position, not of one who is agreeably surprised if the job comes out right, but to whom it will be a rare experience if the final result is wrong.

For parallel horizontal facing, the tool should move parallel to the table, and when the table is traversed across, its surface should be equidistant from the tool over its width. This can be tested by lowering the tool and using a feeler gauge under its point as shown at Fig. 290. The leg and vertical slides should be clamped up before testing. If the table swivels sideways any cross error can be corrected, but otherwise the only way to effect correction is to take a light cut over the table. Before doing this all table and ram slides should be adjusted

Fig. 291.—Working from Fixed Vise Jaw.

and the table supporting leg locked. The work supporting, upper face of the vise should be parallel with its base, so that if the table is correct work held in the vise will also be parallel. When doing ordinary facing the position of the vise jaws is not particularly important, but to machine a slot or shoulder parallel with an edge clamped against the fixed jaw (Fig. 291 (a)) the tool should travel in line with that jaw. The test for this is shown at Fig. 291 (b). At (c) is shown the test for ensuring that a machined face shall be perpendicular with an edge in contact with the jaw (d). An alternative method for this setting is to work from the vise jaw to the face of the table vertical slides with scribing block or height gauge. If the base graduations on the vise are correct a reasonable setting is possible right away, but these cannot be relied upon for accurate results.

Work bolted directly to the machine table may have an edge set perpendicular to the tool travel by setting with a square from the side-face of the table.

Accuracy in vertical facing, using the ram head slide, may be tested by clamping a square to the table and checking the parallelism of the tool movement with its blade by means of feelers (Fig. 292 (a)). After the travel of the tool has been set correctly it should be used with feelers

Fig. 292.—Accuracy in Vertical Facing.

to check the squareness of the fixed vise jaw with the base, and any error corrected by taking a light cut down with a knife-tool (Fig. 292 (b)).

Angular Setting

In order to try the machined accuracy of shaped angular work the job must often be removed from the machine and should any correction be necessary, the task of setting it up again to its original position may occupy hours of work. This may be avoided by a careful preliminary setting with vernier protractor or sine bar, and Fig. 293 gives some indications as to how this might be done.

Planning and Setting Work

In the design and construction of machine tools their makers go to a great deal of trouble to ensure that very accurate geometrical relationships are maintained between the slides, spindles and faces which control the surfaces they produce, so that when using these machines it behoves us to take advantage of such built-in possibilities for accuracy by using the facilities to best advantage. On the shaping machine the long, accurate slides of the ram ensure that the point of the tool maintains an unvarying straight line, and the accuracy of the

(a) Setting Head Slide with Vernier Protractor   (b) Setting for angular position of vise

Fig. 293.—Angular Setting on Shaping Machine.

other machine surfaces ensures that this line is strictly perpendicular to the vertical and horizontal slides of the table. Thus, as we have seen from Fig. 281, the combination of the tool and table movements results in a flat surface, but this can only happen if other factors which could upset the result are not overlooked. The chief factors which could be detrimental to the plane accuracy of any single surface are (*a*) wear of the edge of the tool as it traverses across a surface, (*b*) a loose head slide or a badly adjusted ram slide allowing the tool path to deviate from a single, constant line, (*c*) movement of the work due to faulty clamping or support. Now for the *geometrical relationship* of two or more surfaces. The line motion of the tool point, when fed downwards from the head slide accurately set (see Fig. 292), sweeps out a plane which is perpendicular to the table and perpendicular to the front faces of the vertical table slides (Fig. 294). If, therefore, two vertical faces of a job are cleaned up *without moving the job* they must be parallel, and they must be perpendicular to a face which had previously been set parallel to the vertical slides. Furthermore, if, *at the same setting*, a third face is machined horizontally, this must be at right-angles to the other two faces (Fig. 294). We will discuss one or two examples showing the application of the above principles.

In Fig. 295, A, B, C and D are the faces to be machined. The horizontal faces must be parallel with the base and both must be *in the same plane*. These faces must be square with the vertical faces, which themselves must be parallel. (The base is machined.)

(1) Check the table and head slide (Figs. 290 and 292).

(2) Set and clamp the job to the table with a stop at the front end (or hold in the vise).

(3) Feeding down and across with side tools, rough out the four faces to within about $\frac{1}{64}$ in. of size.

(4) With rounded parting tool take out the corner undercuts.

(5) Obtain a tool which will cover both horizontal surfaces without

Feed

90° with plane
of vertical slide
faces

Vertical table
slides

Plane swept
cut by
vertical tool
feed

90° with plane of
vertical slide faces
(also parallel with
table tee slots)

Plane 90° with table (if
head set true)

FIG. 294.—Accuracy Relationships of a Surface shaped by Vertical Feeding.

being moved after setting in the toolpost (probably the parting tool used for (4) will do this).

(6) With this tool machine both horizontal faces to within about 0·005 in. of size, then finish one face, *leave the cut setting alone*, stop the machine, wind the table across, start the machine and take the same cut over the other face. Both of these faces should now be in the same plane.

FIG. 295.—To be shaped on Faces A, B, C and D (see text).

(7) With side tools carefully finish the two vertical faces.

(8) Remove the job from the machine.

On the casting shown at Fig. 296 the two vertical faces must be machined parallel and square with the base.   The narrow horizontal

Fig. 296.—Cast Bracket.

facing must be square with the other two, and parallel with the base. The boss faces must be square with the other surfaces.

1st Setting (Fig. 297 (*a*))

(1) Shape the base by clamping to an angle plate or to the side of the machine table or by holding in the vise and packing.

2nd Setting (Fig. 297 (*b*))

(1) Clamp to the machine table against a stop and line up from a tee slot.

(2) By feeding a L.H. side tool from the head, rough down the upper vertical face until there is about $\frac{1}{64} - \frac{1}{32}$ in. left on.

(3) Raise the table and with the same tool rough down the other facing as near as possible to the 2·375-in. dimension.   Rough the horizontal facing using the cross feed.

(4) Lower the table and finish the upper facing to give drawing thickness.

(5) Wind the table over and set the tool to the 2·375-in. dimension using a gauge or a piece of bar ground to size.

(6) Clamp the horizontal slide.   Raise the table and feed down from the head to finish the lower facing.

(7) Finish the horizontal facing with the cross feed.

The three facings now fulfil the requirements above.

3rd Setting (Fig. 297 (*c*))

(1) Clamp across on the table, facings inwards, and set one of the

(a) *First setting. Shape base (clamped to side of table.)*

(b) *Second setting. Clamped to table (clamps and stop not shown)*

(c) *Third setting. Shape boss faces. (corner of bracket broken to show boss)*

FIG. 297.—Shaping Operations on Bracket (see text).

vertical facings parallel with the facings of the machine vertical slides. This is best done by straddling the machine facings with a good parallel strip and working with a height gauge or a setting piece ground parallel on its ends. After setting clamp a stop behind the casting.

(2) Mount a side tool in the box and project it out enough for everything to clear the top of the casting. Set the ram on a short stroke and carefully adjust its position so that the tool stops short of the casting face (pull the machine round by hand for this).

(3) Rough and finish the sides of the boss by feeding down with R. and L. hand side tools.

The sides of the boss will now be square with all the other faces.

In Fig. 298 the vee must be accurately parallel with and on the same centre line as the tenon slot. The sides of the vee must make equal angles with the vertical centre line. (The job is a casting with the vee roughly formed.)

FIG. 298.—Vee Block.

1st Setting (Fig. 299 (a))

(1) Hold in the vise with the base uppermost. Line up with the stroke of the ram. Rough and finish the base surface to within about half a $\frac{1}{64}$ in., allowing for the opposite (top) surface to clean up.

(2) With a parting tool take out the tenon slot to full depth $+ \frac{1}{64}$ in. and with $\frac{1}{64}$ in. each side on the width for opening out. Get this slot as near as possible central with the edges of the base.

(3) Finish the tenon slot to width with knife or pointed side tools.

(4) Skim up the base edges equidistant from the sides of the tenon slot, measure with vernier calipers to get both sides equal (take the minimum amount off the edges and leave a witness if possible).

(5) Finish the surface of the base.

(The tenon slot is now parallel and centrally located with respect to the base edges.)

2nd Setting (Fig. 299 (b))

Hold in vise or clamp base to table of machine. Line up.

FIG. 299.—Shaping Operations on Vec Block.

(Numbers on tools refer to operation numbers in text.)

(1) Rough and finish top surface.

(2) Rough sides of vee leaving about $\frac{1}{32}$ in. on each.

(3) Set a $\frac{5}{16}$-in. parting tool central (from base edges) and take out the slot to depth.

3rd Setting (Fig. 299 (c))

(1) Fit blocks or a strip into a table tee slot for positioning and lining up. Set the head to 45° with a vernier protractor (Fig. 293 (a)). Fit suitable side tool.

(2) Press one edge of base against tee slot location and clamp job down against a stop.

(3) Raise table or move along until the tool just skims the vee surface and traverse the cut across the surface.

(4) *Do not move the table.*   Unclamp, reverse and reclamp the job whilst pressing against the tee slot location.

(5) Using the tool slide, traverse this side of the vee with the same cut as in (3).   It may or may not cut, according to the accuracy with which the vee was roughed out.   If it does not cut, move the table until it does.   Then reverse the job and take the same cut again on the other vee side.

(6) Assuming after a reversal of the job that the same cut has been taken down each face of the vee, we have the vee sides central and parallel with the tenon, and the semi-angles equal.

(7) It now remains to finish the vee to the $2\frac{1}{4}$-in. dimension.   This must be done by taking equal cuts from the faces, using the reversal principle just described and arranging that the last cut down each face is a very light skim of a few thousandths.

By taking advantage of the setting and machining principles discussed above, and by using the base edges as an auxiliary, we can now be quite certain that the stipulated accuracies have been achieved.

An alternative method of maintaining the accuracy of the vee sides would be to locate from a tee-slot strip direct on to the sides of the tenon slot whilst shaping the vee as explained for the 3rd setting above. This would avoid cleaning up the edges of the casting for a location. The practice of cleaning up one or both edges, however, as we have described, often provides a more convenient locating face for subsequent shaping and boring operations to the upper side of a casting.

Examples of Shaper Work

EXAMPLE 1.   *To shape up the block shown at Fig. 300 (a), all faces to be parallel and square.*

(1) Obtain a pair of parallel strips of such a height that when the work is rested on them a portion of its thickness will project above the top of the vise jaws.   Rest the block on the strips and press it down whilst tightening the vise.   Set the machine to a stroke about 2 in. longer than the work and move the ram longitudinally so that the tool overruns the job by about 1 in. at each end.   Check the thickness to see that there is sufficient on for machining and if so put on sufficient cut to get below the scale.   Engage the traverse and let the cut travel across.   When the first cut is complete put on a small finishing cut with a finer feed if necessary and take this across (Fig. 300 (b)).

(2) Turn the work on its edge with a parallel under if necessary, hold in the vise with the machined face against the fixed jaw and clean up one edge square with the face just machined.   Obtaining squareness will depend on the squareness of the solid vise jaw and upon the degree of contact between the two surfaces.   For example, if the block is not parallel, the pressure of the moving jaw on the other face may cant the work and result in the machined surface only contacting the fixed jaw in one place.   This may be avoided by applying the pressure through a small packing block which localises the effect and minimises the tendency (Fig. 300 (c)).

(3) Hold the work on the flat again, as at Fig. 300 (b), with the finished face resting on the parallels and the machined edge in contact with the solid jaw of the vise.   After tightening up the vise knock the

Fig. 300.—Shaping Operations on Rectangular Block.

work down on to the parallels with a lead, or rawhide hammer, until the strips are tight at each end. If the unmachined edge in contact with the loose jaw is not square there may be difficulty in getting contact with the strips due to the lifting tendency. In the author's experience this used to be overcome by using what was known as a " pull down " strip. This is a strip of steel, bevelled on one edge and placed between the work and the jaw in a slightly tilted position so that when tightened it exercised a downward force on the part being held.

Take a cut over the face and check for parallelism with a micrometer. If the strips are tight this should be in order. Machine the face down to size, allowing that the final cut shall be light with a fine feed.

(4) Hold the job by its flat faces, knock the machined edge down on to a parallel strip or to the vise bottom and finish the other edge to size. Check for squareness and parallelism.

(5) Rotate the vise to the other position with its jaws perpendicular to the tool travel. Hold the work on parallels with one end protruding a small amount from the end. Rough and finish the end using the vertical head travel for the feed (e). Check for squareness both ways and correct if necessary.

(6) Reverse the work and finish the other end to length.

(7) With a file remove all sharp edges and corners. During the progress of the job the tool should be taken out if necessary and its edge touched up on a grindstone. This should be done particularly before taking a finishing cut.

EXAMPLE 2.   *To machine up the casting shown at Fig.* 301 (*a*).   (*To be machined where shown* "*f*".)

1st Setting

(1) Hold the job in the vise, clamping if possible on the edge of the 1 in. × $\frac{3}{8}$ in. step and the far side of the raised facing, the step being at the fixed jaw.   If the vise jaws are not deep enough to accommodate the raised facing hold on the sides of this and pack or jack under the unsupported portions of the base.   Set the rough edge of the base approximately level, check the underside for being level and set the edge adjacent to the 1 in. × $\frac{3}{8}$ in. step parallel with the tool travel.

(2) Check to ensure that there is sufficient metal on for machining and take a cut over the face (put on a cut deep enough to get under the scale).   Take additional cuts if necessary to bring the base thickness to about $\frac{29}{32}$ in. (Fig. 301 (*b*)).

(3) Put in a parting tool about $\frac{3}{8}$ in. wide and set it central with the end bolt facings, also checking that it is central with the base. Take it down to cut the tenon slot making the depth $\frac{1}{4}$ in. plus the amount allowed on the base for the finishing cut (*c*).   Open out the slot to about $\frac{15}{32}$ in. wide.

(4) Finish the sides of the slot with a knife tool until its width is correct when gauged with a plug or slip gauge (*d*).

(5) Take a finishing cut over the base.

(6) With a side tool skim up one of the edges (*e*).

(There may not be metal allowed on for this, but the amount taken off will not affect the job and the face created, being parallel with the tenon slot, will be useful for subsequent setting.   A witness should be left if possible.)

2nd Setting

(1) Clamp the job to the table of the machine and set the machined edge parallel with the tool travel.   This can be done from the tool itself, from a tee slot or from the edge of the table.

(2) Machine the 1 in. × $\frac{3}{8}$ in. step.   Use a side tool and get out the corner with a sharp side tool or a knife tool (Fig. 301 (*f*)).   Check step for parallelism with machined edge.

(3) Set the head to 25° with the horizontal and machine the sloping top of the facing.   Check with a vernier protractor (*g*).

(4) Swing round, re-clamp and face up bolt facings.

3rd Setting

The slot in the facing must be perpendicular with the base tenon slot.   Its bottom should be reasonably parallel with the face in which it is cut.

(1) Clamp the job to an angle plate and set the machined edge of base square with table.   Bolt angle plate to machine table, setting the sloping face parallel with the tool travel.

(2) Swing the machine head over 90° and machine out the slot in the same manner as 1st setting (3) and (4), only working from the side instead of the top (*h*).

Fig. 301.—Operations in Shaping Casting.

Broad Cut Finishing

An attractive method of finishing the larger surfaces of castings such as we have just discussed is to employ a broad parting tool and a coarse feed. The tool should be $\frac{3}{8}$ in. to $\frac{1}{2}$ in. wide, its edge ground dead straight and oilstoned to a keen edge (see Fig. 126 (e), p. 148). It must be set rigidly in the tool post with the minimum of overhang, and its edge must be parallel with the face being machined. In operation, a one- or two-thousandth cut is put on and the tool traversed across with a coarse feed which is best worked by hand, taking about one complete turn of the table feed-screw for each stroke of the ram. The result is a striped finish, which is more attractive than the usual feed marks. The method can only be used on cast iron and the tool must be kept very keen with an oilstone. Success is helped by lifting the tool clear by hand on the return stroke and by filing a very small chamfer on the leading edge of the face to remove hard scale which might cause the tool to jump. Do not allow any oil or moisture to get on to a surface which is to be so finished.

EXAMPLE 3. *To shape up the casting shown at Fig.* 302 (a).

This is an example of a job which offers several possibilities for holding and setting up, and when such cases arise in the experience of the reader he must use his own judgement as to which method to employ, bearing in mind time, ease and rigidity of setting, tendency of each method towards accurate results and so on.

One method in this case would be as follows :

(1) Clamp the bracket on its side to an angle plate or to the side of the machine table, with the base uppermost. Set the base as near as possible horizontal. Rough and finish the base (Fig. 302 (b)).

(2) Secure the base to an angle plate with the other surfaces to be machined uppermost. Place jacks or packing under the far end and clamp down on to these, holding on the extreme $\frac{1}{4}$ in. length of the bracket. Set the upper surface horizontal, machine edge of base, $1\frac{1}{2}$ in. slot and its lower land (see later) (Fig. 302 (c)).

(3) Move clamps to hold at bottom of machined slot. Machine portion previously covered by clamps.

A second method, which permits all the machining to be done at one setting, is to hold the bracket partly in the vise and partly by clamps. To do this it might be necessary to move the vise nearer to the edge of the table, and perhaps pack it up higher. Before commencing, the vertical head slide should be tested for its squareness with the table (see Fig. 292 (a)).

(1) Hold the bracket partly in the vise, pack under the edge of the base and clamp down. Set the base approximately square with the table, and the upper surface approximately horizontal (Fig. 302 (d)).

(2) Rough shape surface and edge of base to within about $\frac{1}{32}$ in. of size. Use side tool and vertical feed for base surface. Before machining check that the 4·750-in. and 1·500-in. dimensions may be obtained (Fig. 302 (e)).

(3) Rough the two facings adjoining the slot, making them $1\frac{1}{2}$ in. above the previously rough machined edge of the base. Rough out the slot to $\frac{1}{2}$ in. deep, $1\frac{7}{16}$ in. wide with its bottom side about $4\frac{1}{16}$ in.

(a) Bracket to be Shaped

(b) Clamped to Side of Table for Shaping Base

(c) Set-up for Machining where Shaded

(d) Held in Vise, Packed and Clamped

Fig. 302.—Settings for Shaping Bracket.

from the base (4·750 − 0·750 + $\frac{1}{32}$ in. to finish on two surfaces). Use side tools to go down the sides and match up the surface in the centre (f).

(4) Finish surface and edge of base.

(5) Finish the two facings adjoining the slot. Check for the 1·500-in. dimension with a parallel strip across facings, and a vernier between the strip and the base edge.

(6) With a knife tool finish the side of the slot nearest the base, making it 4·000 in. from the base. Check over parallel strip pressed on base, and edge being machined, with vernier (4·000 in. + thickness of parallel).

(7) Finish width of slot to 1·500 in. (vernier or plug gauge).

(8) Finish slot to depth with parting tool. Check with depth gauge.

Safety on the Shaping Machine

We have already made some reference to safety in Chapter 5, and if by any chance the reader skipped that part of our discussion we hope he will turn back and consider it as seriously as any other part of his work. The shaper is not really any more dangerous than other machines, but as some people will get into trouble in the most innocent situations it may be worth while to issue a few words of advice. We are also encouraged in this where the shaper is concerned because it is often considered, like the drilling machine, to be a kind of general purpose workshop hack which anyone can use for odd jobs without much supervision or advice. Most of the other machine tools have their chief source of danger in members which rotate, and the reader must have heard of lurid examples of hair being torn out by an unguarded drilling spindle or someone being wound up by the carrier of a lathe. We hope he has neither seen nor experienced either, but have no doubt that he has heard accounts which have lost nothing in the telling! The only rotating hazard on the shaper is the squared shaft which projects from the side of the machine for setting the stroke, and this can be dangerous if after setting a stroke we forget to remove the handle from it before starting up. It is also a good precaution not to lean anywhere near this, as the rotating squared end could wind up in loose clothing. The ram is the only other real source of danger, and accidents can occur both by forgetfulness and by knowingly taking chances. On the latter aspect, the writer was once working a machine on a fairly long stroke and thought there was time to micrometer the thickness of the job at its end. Unfortunately the micrometer stuck a little and would not come away in time . . .! On modern, motorised, gear-driven machines the danger from an obstruction to the ram is greater than it was on the earlier belt-driven types, since a belt would often save a serious situation by slipping off. A train of gearing from a high-speed motor, however, is not so obliging. The ram, therefore, should always be considered as a source of danger, and this should never be forgotten, neither should a known risk be entertained. After setting or resetting a job, make sure that neither the tool nor any portion of the ram will foul anything on the table before starting the machine. Better still, pull the machine round by hand to make sure. There is sometimes a temptation to change the stroke or the setting of the ram while the machine is running. This is taking a known risk and should be avoided. Special care is necessary when a fine setting to the forward end of the stroke is necessary for shaping up to an obstruction, and the machine should be pulled round several times before it is started up.

Many mishaps occur through work being insecurely clamped and supported against the force of the cut and it should be remembered that a considerable shock force is exerted by the tool at the beginning of each stroke. Stops should always be used when jobs are clamped direct to the table and clamping should be arranged to come on to solid metal. Faulty clamping and setting up, as well as being dangerous, lead to inaccurate results due to work either moving or distorting. Even if a job is well clamped it may be pushed off the table, or the tool broken, by winding in to a large cut that was not checked or has jumped on due to a loose head slide.

The collection of the cutting chips on a shaping machine is a problem that has never been solved, and when dealing with hard steel particularly it is advisable not to stand at the front of the machine. Also, sweep the floor often if you value the leather on your shoe soles. Finally, since accidents can happen under the best regulated practice, cultivate the ability to stop the machine quickly and always avoid standing in the line of the ram.

Conclusion

We must now, for the time being, leave the reader to develop his knowledge, hoping that he has benefited at least from some of our discussions, and that we have stimulated him to further thought and enquiry. We encourage him to pursue his course, maintaining at all times, and whatever his knowledge, the simple mind of a student, for upon the simplest of foundations are built the most wonderful works of Nature.

Appendix 1

Conversion Table

FRACTION, DECIMAL, METRIC

Fractional in.	Decimals of an in.	mm.	Fractional in.	Decimals of an in.	mm.
1/64	0·0156	0·397	41/64	0·6406	16·272
1/32	0·0313	0·794	21/32	0·6563	16·669
3/64	0·0469	1·191	43/64	0·6719	17·066
1/16	0·0625	1·588	11/16	0·6875	17·463
5/64	0·0781	1·984	45/64	0·7031	17·859
3/32	0·0938	2·381	23/32	0·7188	18·256
7/64	0·1094	2·778	47/64	0·7344	18·653
1/8	0·1250	3·175	3/4	0·750	19·050
9/64	0·1406	3·572	49/64	0·7656	19·447
5/32	0·1563	3·969	25/32	0·7813	19·844
11/64	0·1719	4·366	51/64	0·7969	20·241
3/16	0·1875	4·763	13/16	0·8125	20·638
13/64	0·2031	5·159	53/64	0·8281	21·034
7/32	0·2188	5·556	27/32	0·8438	21·431
15/64	0·2344	5·953	55/64	0·8594	21·828
1/4	0·250	6·350	7/8	0·8750	22·225
17/64	0·2656	6·747	57/64	0·8906	22·622
9/32	0·2813	7·144	29/32	0·9063	23·019
19/64	0·2969	7·541	59/64	0·9219	23·416
5/16	0·3125	7·937	15/16	0·9375	23·813
21/64	0·3281	8·333	61/64	0·9531	24·209
11/32	0·3438	8·731	31/32	0·9688	24·606
23/64	0·3594	9·128	63/64	0·9844	25·003
3/8	0·3750	9·525	1	1·000	25·400
25/64	0·3906	9·921	1 1/64	1·0156	25·797
13/32	0·4063	10·319	1 1/32	1·0313	26·194
27/64	0·4219	10·716	1 3/64	1·0469	26·591
7/16	0·4375	11·113	1 1/16	1·0625	26·988
29/64	0·4531	11·509	1 5/64	1·0781	27·384
15/32	0·4688	11·906	1 3/32	1·0938	27·781
31/64	0·4844	12·303	1 7/64	1·1094	28·178
1/2	0·500	12·700	1 1/8	1·1250	28·575
33/64	0·5156	13·097	1 9/64	1·1406	28·972
17/32	0·5313	13·494	1 5/32	1·1563	29·369
35/64	0·5468	13·891	1 11/64	1·1719	29·766
9/16	0·5625	14·288	1 3/16	1·1875	30·163
37/64	0·5781	14·684	1 13/64	1·2031	30·559
19/32	0·5938	15·081	1 7/32	1·2188	30·956
39/64	0·6094	15·478	1 15/64	1·2344	31·353
5/8	0·6250	15·875	1 1/4	1·250	31·750

mm.	in.	mm.	in.	mm.	in.	mm.	in.	mm.	in.	mm.	in.
1	0·039	5	0·197	9	0·354	25	0·984	50	1·969	80	3·150
2	0·079	6	0·236	10	0·394	30	1·181	60	2·362	90	3·543
3	0·118	7	0·276	15	0·591	40	1·575	70	2·756	100	3·937
4	0·157	8	0·315	20	0·787						

Whitworth Bolts and Nuts

$$d = 0.64p. \qquad r = 0.137p.$$

(Whitworth Thread Form)

Bolt Diam. (In.).	Thread per Inch.	Pitch of Thread (In.).	Thread Core Diam. (In.).	Tapping Size.	Hexagon across Flats (In.).	Hexagon Corners (approx.) (In.).	Nut Thickness.	Bolt Head Thickness (In.).
$\frac{1}{4}$	20	0·050	0·186	5 mm.	0·445	0·51	0·20	0·19
$\frac{5}{16}$	18	0·0556	0·241	$\frac{1}{4}$ in.	0·525	0·61	0·25	0·22
$\frac{3}{8}$	16	0·0625	0·295	$\frac{5}{16}$,,	0·600	0·69	0·312	0·27
$\frac{7}{16}$	14	0·0714	0·346	$\frac{23}{64}$,,	0·710	0·82	0·375	0·33
$\frac{1}{2}$	12	0·083	0·393	$\frac{13}{32}$,,	0·820	0·95	0·437	0·38
$\frac{9}{16}$	12	0·083	0·456	$\frac{15}{32}$,,	0·920	1·06	0·50	0·44
$\frac{5}{8}$	11	0·091	0·509	$\frac{17}{32}$,,	1·01	1·17	0·562	0·49
$\frac{3}{4}$	10	0·100	0·622	$\frac{41}{64}$,,	1·20	1·39	0·687	0·60
$\frac{7}{8}$	9	0·111	0·733	$\frac{3}{4}$,,	1·30	1·50	0·75	0·66
1	8	0·125	0·840	$\frac{55}{64}$,,	1·48	1·71	0·875	0·77
$1\frac{1}{8}$	7	0·143	0·942	24·5 mm.	1·67	1·93	1·00	0·88
$1\frac{1}{4}$	7	0·143	1·067	$1\frac{3}{32}$ in.	1·86	2·15	1·125	0·98
$1\frac{1}{2}$	6	0·167	1·287	$1\frac{5}{16}$,,	2·22	2·56	1·375	1·20
$1\frac{3}{4}$	5	0·200	1·494	$1\frac{33}{64}$,,	2·58	2·98	1·625	1·42
2	$4\frac{1}{2}$	0·222	1·715	$1\frac{3}{4}$,,	2·76	3·19	1·75	1·53

APPENDIX 3

British Standard Fine

(B.S.F.) Bolts and Nuts

Whitworth Thread Form.

Bolt or Screw Diameter. In.	Threads per Inch.	Thread Core Diameter. In.	Tapping Size. In.	Hexagon across Flats. In.	Hexagon across Corners. In.	Bolt Head Thickness. In.	Nut Thickness. In.
$\frac{1}{4}$	26	0·201	No. 5	0·445	0·51	0·19	0·20
$\frac{5}{16}$	22	0·254	G	0·525	0·61	0·22	$\frac{1}{4}$
$\frac{3}{8}$	20	0·311	O	0·600	0·69	0·27	$\frac{5}{16}$
$\frac{7}{16}$	18	0·366	$\frac{3}{8}$	0·710	0·82	0·33	$\frac{3}{8}$
$\frac{1}{2}$	16	0·420	$\frac{27}{64}$	0·820	0·95	0·38	$\frac{7}{16}$
$\frac{9}{16}$	16	0·483	$12\frac{1}{2}$ mm.	0·920	1·06	0·44	$\frac{1}{2}$
$\frac{5}{8}$	14	0·534	$\frac{35}{64}$	1·01	1·17	0·49	$\frac{9}{16}$
$\frac{3}{4}$	12	0·643	$\frac{21}{32}$	1·20	1·39	0·60	$\frac{11}{16}$
$\frac{7}{8}$	11	0·759	$\frac{25}{32}$	1·30	1·50	0·66	$\frac{3}{4}$
1	10	0·872	$\frac{57}{64}$	1·48	1·71	0·77	$\frac{7}{8}$
$1\frac{1}{4}$	9	1·108	$1\frac{1}{8}$	1·86	2·15	0·98	$1\frac{1}{8}$
$1\frac{1}{2}$	8	1·340	$34\frac{1}{2}$ mm.	2·22	2·56	1·20	$1\frac{3}{8}$
$1\frac{3}{4}$	7	1·567	$1\frac{19}{32}$	2·58	2·98	1·42	$1\frac{5}{8}$
2	7	1·817	$1\frac{27}{32}$	2·76	3·19	1·53	$1\frac{3}{4}$

Note. The tapping sizes given above for Whitworth and B.S.F. threads are based on the formula $T = D - 1·1328p$, and give a thread about 88·5% of full form (see page 234).

U.S.S. Standard and Metric Threads

$$d = 0 \cdot 65p. \qquad \text{Flat on Thread} = \frac{p}{8}.$$

Thread Form.

Bolt Diameter and Nut Thickness.	U.S.S. Standard.				Metric.		
	Threads per Inch.	Core Diameter.	Hexagon across Flats.	Bolt Head Thickness.	Bolt Diameter.	Pitch.	Core Diameter.
		In.	Max. In.	In.	Mm.	Mm.	Mm.
$\frac{1}{4}$	20	0·185	$\frac{7}{16}$	$\frac{3}{16}$	3	0·5	2·35
$\frac{5}{16}$	18	0·240	$\frac{9}{16}$	$\frac{15}{64}$	4	0·7	3·09
$\frac{3}{8}$	16	0·294	$\frac{5}{8}$	$\frac{9}{32}$	5	0·8	3·96
$\frac{7}{16}$	14	0·345	$\frac{3}{4}$	$\frac{21}{64}$	6	1	4·7
$\frac{1}{2}$	13	0·400	$\frac{13}{16}$	$\frac{3}{8}$	8	1·25	6·38
$\frac{5}{8}$	11	0·507	$\frac{15}{16}$	$\frac{15}{32}$	10	1·5	8·05
$\frac{3}{4}$	10	0·620	$1\frac{1}{8}$	$\frac{9}{16}$	12	1·75	9·73
1	8	0·838	$1\frac{1}{2}$	$\frac{3}{4}$	14	2	11·4
$1\frac{1}{4}$	7	1·064	$1\frac{7}{8}$	$\frac{15}{16}$	16	2	13·4
$1\frac{1}{2}$	6	1·284	$2\frac{1}{4}$	$1\frac{1}{8}$	18	2·5	14·75
$1\frac{3}{4}$	5	1·490	$2\frac{5}{8}$	$1\frac{5}{16}$	20	2·5	16·75
2	$4\frac{1}{2}$	1·711	3	$1\frac{1}{2}$	22	2·5	18·75
					24	3	20·1

APPENDIX 5

The Unified Thread

Unified Form.

Bolt Diameter (in.).	Unified Coarse.				Unified Fine.			
	Designation.	Thread per in.	Bolt Root Dia. (in.).	Nut Core Dia. (in.).	Designation.	Thread per in.	Bolt Root Dia. (in.).	Nut Core Dia. (in.).
¼ (0·250)	¼–20. UNC	20	0·1887	0·1959	¼–28. UNF	28	0·2062	0·2113
⁵⁄₁₆ (0·3125)	⁵⁄₁₆–18. UNC	18	0·2443	0·2524	⁵⁄₁₆–24. UNF	24	0·2614	0·2674
⅜ (0·375)	⅜–16. UNC	16	0·2983	0·3073	⅜–24. UNF	24	0·3239	0·3299
⁷⁄₁₆ (0·4375)	⁷⁄₁₆–14. UNC	14	0·3499	0·3602	⁷⁄₁₆–20. UNF	20	0·3762	0·3834
½ (0·50)	½–13. UNC	13	0·4056	0·4167	½–20. UNF	20	0·4387	0·4459
⁹⁄₁₆ (0·5625)	⁹⁄₁₆–12. UNC	12	0·4603	0·4723	⁹⁄₁₆–18. UNF	18	0·4943	0·5024
⅝ (0·625)	⅝–11. UNC	11	0·5135	0·5266	⅝–18. UNF	18	0·5568	0·5649
¾ (0·750)	¾–10. UNC	10	0·6273	0·6417	¾–16. UNF	16	0·6733	0·6823
⅞ (0·875)	⅞–9. UNC	9	0·7387	0·7547	⅞–14. UNF	14	0·7874	0·7977
1 (1·00)	1–8. UNC	8	0·8466	0·8647	1–12. UNF	12	0·8978	0·9098
1⅛ (1·125)	1⅛–7. UNC	7	0·9497	0·9704	1⅛–12. UNF	12	1·0228	1·0348
1¼ (1·250)	1¼–7. UNC	7	1·0747	1·0954	1¼–12. UNF	12	1·1478	1·1598
1⅜ (1·375)	1⅜–6. UNC	6	1·1705	1·1946	1⅜–12. UNF	12	1·2728	1·2848
1½ (1·50)	1½–6. UNC	5	1·2955	1·3196	1½–12. UNF	12	1·3978	1·4098
1¾ (1·750)	1¾–5. UNC	5	1·5046	1·5335				
2 (2·00) Thence by steps of ¼ in. to 4 in.	2 4½. UNC	4½	1·7274	1·7594				

(The clearing of the root of the nut by a radius as shown causes this diameter to be increased by 0·072p.)

APPENDIX 6

British Association (B.A.) Threads

$$d = 0 \cdot 6p. \qquad r = \frac{2p}{11}.$$

B.A. No.	0	1	2	3	4	5
Diameter (mm.) . .	6	5·3	4·7	4·1	3·6	3·2
Pitch (mm.) . . .	1	0·9	0·81	0·73	0·66	0·59
Core Diameter (mm.)	4·8	4·22	3·73	3·22	2·81	2·49
Core Diameter (in.) .	0·189	0·166	0·147	0·127	0·111	0·098

B.A. No.	6	7	8	9	10	11
Diameter (mm.) . .	2·8	2·5	2·2	1·9	1·7	1·5
Pitch (mm.) . . .	0·53	0·48	0·43	0·39	0·35	0·31
Core Diameter (mm.)	2·16	1·92	1·68	1·43	1·28	1·13
Core Diameter (in.) .	0·085	0·076	0·066	0·056	0·05	0·044

B.A. No.	12	13	14	15	16	17
Diameter (mm.) . .	1·3	1·2	1·0	0·9	0·79	0·7
Pitch (mm.) . . .	0·28	0·25	0·23	0·21	0·19	0·17
Core Diameter (mm.)	0·96	0·90	0·72	0·65	0·56	0·50
Core Diameter (in.) .	0·038	0·035	0·028	0·025	0·022	0·020

B.A. No.	18	19	20	21	22	23
Diameter (mm.) . .	0·62	0·54	0·48	0·42	0·37	0·29
Pitch (mm.) . . .	0·15	0·14	0·12	0·11	0·098	0·09
Core Diameter (mm.)	0·44	0·37	0·34	0·29	0·25	0·22
Core Diameter (in.).	0·017	0·015	0·013	0·012	0·011	0·009

Appendix 7

British Standard Pipe Threads (B.S.P.)

(Thread Form—Whitworth)

Thread on End of Pipe.

Size = Bore of Pipe.	A	B	C	D	E	F Standard.	F Max.	F Min.	G
In.	In.	In.	In.	In.	In.	In.	In.	In.	In.
⅛	1⅜	0·383	0·0230	0·337	⅜	⁵⁄₃₂ (0·1563)	0·18	0·13	28
¼	1½	0·518	0·0335	0·451	⁷⁄₁₆	³⁄₁₆ (0·1875)	0·22	0·16	19
⅜	1¹⁄₁₆	0·656	0·0335	0·589	½	¼ (0·2500)	0·29	0·21	19
½	⅞	0·825	0·0455	0·734	⅝	¼ (0·2500)	0·29	0·21	14
¾	1¹⁄₁₆	1·041	0·0455	0·950	¾	⅜ (0·3750)	0·44	0·31	14
1	1¹¹⁄₁₆	1·309	0·0580	1·193	⅞	⅜ (0·3750)	0·44	0·31	11
1¼	1¹¹⁄₁₆	1·650	0·0580	1·534	1	½ (0·5000)	0·58	0·42	11
1½	1²⁹⁄₃₂	1·882	0·0580	1·766	1	½ (0·5000)	0·58	0·42	11
2	2⅜	2·347	0·0580	2·231	1⅛	⅝ (0·6250)	0·73	0·52	11
2½	3	2·960	0·0580	2·844	1¼	1¹⁄₁₆ (0·6875)	0·80	0·57	11
3	3½	3·460	0·0580	3·844	1⅜	1¹³⁄₁₆ (0·8125)	0·95	0·68	11
3½	4	3·950	0·0580	3·834	1½	⅞ (0·8750)	1·02	0·73	11
4	4½	4·450	0·0580	4·334	1⅝	1 (1·0000)	1·17	0·83	11
4½	5	4·950	0·0580	4·834	1⅝	1 (1·0000)	1·17	0·83	11
5	5½	5·450	0·0580	5·334	1¾	1⅛ (1·1250)	1·31	0·94	11
6	6½	6·450	0·0580	6·334	2	1⅜ (1·3750)	1·60	1·15	11
7	7½	7·450	0·0640	7·322	2⅛	1⅜ (1·3750)	1·60	1·15	10
8	8½	8·450	0·0640	8·322	2¼	1½ (1·5000)	1·75	1·25	10
9	9½	9·450	0·0640	9·322	2¼	1½ (1·5000)	1·75	1·25	10
10	10½	10·450	0·0640	10·322	2¾	1⅝ (1·6250)	1·90	1·35	10
11	11½	11·450	0·0800	11·290	2½	1⅝ (1·6250)	1·90	1·35	8
12	12½	12·450	0·0800	12·290	2½	1⅝ (1·6250)	1·90	1·35	8

APPENDIX 8

Wire Gauges

No.	English Imperial Legal Standard.	American B. and S.	Birmingham wire gauge.	No.	English Imperial Legal Standard.	American B. and S.	Birmingham wire gauge.
	In.	In.	In.		In.	In.	In.
7/0	0·500	—	—	23	0·024	0·0226	0·025
6/0	0·464	—	—	24	0·022	0·0201	0·022
5/0	0·432	—	—	25	0·020	0·0179	0·020
0000	0·400	0·460	0·454	26	0·018	0·0159	0·018
000	0·372	0·4096	0·425	27	0·016	0·0142	0·016
00	0·348	0·3648	0·380	28	0·0148	0·0126	0·014
0	0·324	0·3249	0·340	29	0·0136	0·0113	0·013
1	0·300	0·2898	0·300	30	0·0124	0·0100	0·012
2	0·276	0·2576	0·284	31	0·0116	0·0089	0·010
3	0·252	0·2294	0·259	32	0·0108	0·0080	0·009
4	0·232	0·2043	0·238	33	0·0100	0·0071	0·008
5	0·212	0·1819	0·220	34	0·0092	0·0063	0·007
6	0·192	0·1620	0·203	35	0·0084	0·0056	0·005
7	0·176	0·1443	0·180	36	0·0076	0·0050	0·004
8	0·160	0·1285	0·165	37	0·0068	0·0045	—
9	0·144	0·1144	0·148	38	0·0060	0·0040	—
10	0·128	0·1019	0·134	39	0·0052	0·0035	—
11	0·116	0·0907	0·120	40	0·0048	0·0031	—
12	0·104	0·0808	0·109	41	0·0044	—	—
13	0·092	0·0720	0·095	42	0·0040	—	—
14	0·080	0·0641	0·083	43	0·0036	—	—
15	0·072	0·0571	0·072	44	0·0032	—	—
16	0·064	0·0508	0·065	45	0·0028	—	—
17	0·056	0·0453	0·058	46	0·0024	—	—
18	0·048	0·0403	0·049	47	0·0020	—	—
19	0·040	0·0359	0·042	48	0·0016	—	—
20	0·036	0·0320	0·035	49	0·0012	—	—
21	0·032	0·0285	0·032	50	0·0010	—	—
22	0·028	0·0253	0·028		—	—	—

Appendix 9
Number and Letter Drill Sizes
Number Drills

Number.	Diameter.	Fraction.	Metric.	Number.	Diameter.	Fraction.	Metric.
	In.	In.	Mm.		In.	In.	Mm.
80	0·01850			48	0·07600		
79	0·01450				0·07810	$\frac{5}{64}$	
	0·01560	$\frac{1}{64}$		47	0·07850		
78	0·01600				0·07874	. . .	2
77	0·01800			46	0·08100		
76	0·01969			45	0·08200		
	0·02000	. . .	$\frac{1}{2}$	44	0·08600		
75	0·02100			43	0·08900		
74	0·02260			42	0·09350		
73	0·02400				0·09375	$\frac{3}{32}$	
72	0·02500			41	0·09600		
71	0·02600			40	0·09800		
70	0·02800				0·09843	. . .	$2\frac{1}{2}$
69	0·02930			39	0·09950		
	0·02953	. . .	$\frac{3}{4}$	38	0·10150		
68	0·03100			37	0·10400		
67	0·03120			36	0·10650		
	0·03200	$\frac{1}{32}$			0·10930	$\frac{7}{64}$	
66	0·03300			35	0·11000		
65	0·03500			34	0·11100		
64	0·03600			33	0·11300		
63	0·03700			32	0·11600		
62	0·03800				0·11811	. . .	3
61	0·03900			31	0·12000		
	0·03937	. . .	1		0·12500	$\frac{1}{8}$	
60	0·04000			30	0·12850		
59	0·04100			29	0·13600		
58	0·04200				0·13780	. . .	$3\frac{1}{2}$
57	0·04300			28	0·14059		
56	0·04650				0·14060	$\frac{9}{64}$	
	0·04680	$\frac{3}{64}$		27	0·14400		
55	0·05200			26	0·14700		
54	0·05500			25	0·14950		
	0·05906	. . .	$1\frac{1}{2}$	24	0·15200		
53	0·05950			23	0·15400		
	0·06250	$\frac{1}{16}$			0·15625	$\frac{5}{32}$	
52	0·06350			22	0·15700		
51	0·06700				0·15748	. . .	4
50	0·07000			21	0·15900		
49	0·07300						

Number.	Diameter.	Fraction.	Metric.	Number.	Diameter.	Fraction.	Metric.
	In.	In.	Mm.		In.	In.	Mm.
20	0·16100			10	0·19350		
19	0·16600			9	0·19600		
18	0·16950				0·19685	. . .	5
	0·17187	$\frac{11}{64}$		8	0·19900		
17	0·17300			7	0·20100		
16	0·17700				0·20312	$\frac{13}{64}$	
	0·17717	. . .	4½	6	0·20400		
15	0·18000			5	0·20550		
14	0·18200			4	0·20900		
13	0·18500			3	0·21300		
	0·18750	$\frac{3}{16}$			0·21654	. . .	5½
					0·21875	$\frac{7}{32}$	
12	0·18900			2	0·22100		
11	0·19100			1	0·22800		

LETTER DRILLS

Letter.	Diameter.	Fraction.	Metric.	Letter.	Diameter.	Fraction.	Metric.
	In.	In.	Mm.		In.	In.	Mm.
A	0·23400				0·31496	. . .	8
	0·23437	$\frac{15}{64}$		O	0·31600		
	0·23622	. . .	6	P	0·32300		
B	0·23800				0·32810	$\frac{21}{64}$	
C	0·24200			Q	0·33200		
D	0·24600				0·33465	. . .	8½
E	0·25000	$\frac{1}{4}$		R	0·33900		
	0·25591	. . .	6½		0·34370	$\frac{11}{32}$	
F	0·25700			S	0·34800		
G	0·26100				0·35433	. . .	9
	0·26560	$\frac{17}{64}$		T	0·35800		
H	0·26600				0·35930	$\frac{23}{64}$	
I	0·27200			U	0·36800		
	0·27559	. . .	7		0·37402	. . .	9½
J	0·27700				0·37500	$\frac{3}{8}$	
K	0·28100			V	0·37700		
	0·28120	$\frac{9}{32}$		W	0·38600		
L	0·29000				0·39060	$\frac{25}{64}$	
M	0·29500				0·39370	. . .	10
	0·29528	. . .	7½	X	0·39700		
	0·29680	$\frac{19}{64}$		Y	0·40400		
N	0·30200				0·40620	$\frac{13}{32}$	
	0·31250	$\frac{5}{16}$		Z	0·41800		

Morse Tapers

Number of Taper.	Diam. of Plug at Small End, Inches.	Diam. at End of Socket, Inches.	Shank — Whole Length of Shank, Inches	Shank — Shank Depth, Inches.	Shank — Depth of Hole, Inches.	Shank — Standard Plug Depth, Inches.	Tongue — Thickness of Tongue, Inches.	Tongue — Length of Tongue, Inches.	Tongue — Rad. of Mill for Tongue, Inches.	Tongue — Diameter of Tongue, Inches.	Tongue — Radius of Tongue, Inches.	Keyway — Width of Keyway, Inches.	Keyway — Length of Keyway, Inches.	Keyway — End of Socket to Keyway, Inches.	Taper per Foot.	Taper per Inch.
	D	A	B	S	H	P	t	T	R	d	a	W	L	K		
0	·252	·3561	2 11/32	2 7/32	2 1/32	2	3/32	1/4	3/32	·235	·04	·160	9/16	1 15/16	·62460	·05205
1	·369	·475	2 9/16	2 7/16	2 3/16	2 1/8	13/64	3/8	3/16	·343	·05	·213	3/4	2 1/16	·59858	·04988
2	·572	·700	3 1/8	2 15/16	2 5/8	2 9/16	1/4	7/16	1/4	·459	·06	·260	7/8	2 1/4	·59941	·04995
3	·778	·938	3 7/8	3 11/16	3 1/4	3 3/16	5/16	9/16	9/32	23/32	·08	·322	1 1/8	3 1/16	·60235	·05019
4	1·020	1·231	4 7/8	4 5/8	4 1/2	4 1/16	15/32	5/8	5/16	1 1/16	·10	·478	1 1/4	3 7/8	·62326	·05193
5	1·475	1·748	6 1/8	5 7/8	5 1/4	5 3/16	5/8	3/4	3/8	1 13/32	·12	·635	1 1/2	4 15/16	·63151	·05262
6	2·116	2·494	8 5/16	8 1/4	7 7/8	7 1/4	3/4	1 1/2	1/2	2	·15	·760	1 3/4	7	·62565	·05213
7	2·750	3·270	11 5/8	11 1/4	10 3/8	10	1 1/4	1 5/8	3/4	2 5/8	·18	1·135	2 5/8	9 1/2	·62400	·05200

INDEX